What's it all About?

What's it all About?

The ALFIE CONN Story

JEFF HOLMES

pitch

First published by Pitch Publishing, 2024
Reprinted 2024
3

Pitch Publishing
9 Donnington Park,
85 Birdham Road,
Chichester, West Sussex,
PO20 7AJ
www.pitchpublishing.co.uk
info@pitchpublishing.co.uk

A CIP catalogue record is available for this book from the British Library.

ISBN 978 1 80150 904 6

MIX
Paper | Supporting responsible forestry
FSC® C013604

Printed and bound in the UK on FSC® certified paper in line with our continuing commitment to ethical business practices, sustainability and the environment.

Typesetting and origination by Pitch Publishing
Printed and bound by CPI Group (UK) Ltd, Croydon, CR0 4YY

Contents

I would like to dedicate this book to my wife, Sue

My children, Samantha and Steven, and their partners, John and Lorna

And my grandchildren, Emily, Laughlan and Iona

Acknowledgements

Samantha Rooney and Steven Conn, Willie Clark, Ian Adam, Stephen Millar, Neil Hobson, George Hutchison, Rick Russell and Darren Cooney.

To Willie Johnston for the Foreword.

To Jeff Holmes for his diligent research, painstaking interviews and wonderful coffee at Costa.

And also to the fantastic team at Pitch Publishing.

Foreword

ALFIE WAS only a laddie when he joined Rangers, but I was privileged to watch him grow into a terrific young man. He listened, worked hard and before too long got his just rewards. His parents moved to Kinghorn, in Fife, just a few miles downstream from Kirkcaldy, so we socialised a lot and I really got to know him well. I'd watched his dad, Alf senior, play for both Hearts and Raith Rovers, and I knew that if the kid turned out to be anything like the old man, then Rangers were getting a cracker.

I was four or five years older than Alfie so with us both being adopted Fifers, I kind of took him under my wing. You could see him developing both as a person and a player in training and when he was 18 I knew that he was going to be a good one. He was getting physically stronger, taller and cheekier. This wee, thin boy had taken a stretch at just the right time, and whether that was down to the work he was putting in, or Jock Wallace's training, he was certainly improving every day.

When he started at Rangers he was quite a shy laddie – and then he got to know me and Willie Henderson! We educated him in the school of life, and I'm still not sure if that was a good thing. But he was a good lad, and he has never changed. I would do anything for Alfie, although that might not have been the case when we came up against each other for the one and only time on a football pitch. I was with West Brom and he was playing for Spurs, and we were two down. Their right-back was sticking to me like glue and Alfie was urging him on, 'Tighter, tighter, don't give him an inch or he'll destroy us.' The poor guy couldn't have got any tighter, but eventually he tired, I got some space, made three goals and we won 4-2. After the game, Alfie came up to me, patted me on the back and said, 'Awle roit, Willie, good gyme …' He was speaking like a Cockney and had only been in London six months! I'd had enough of an issue understanding Brummie, and now he was speaking like this.

When we were at Rangers he was a great team-mate, and always wanted the ball, a bit like me, Baxter or Henderson. He demanded it because he genuinely believed he could make something happen. But he didn't just demand it when we were winning, it was all the time. He wasn't a player who hid when the chips were down – he was the type of team-mate you wanted. He could've been having an absolute stinker but he would still be shouting for the ball. Anyway, it's very difficult to hide on a park like Ibrox as the supporters notice every little thing.

Barcelona only brought us closer together, if that was possible. We weren't sure who would get the last place in the starting 11, after Colin 'Bomber' Jackson had been ruled out through injury. I thought it might be Andy Penman, but it was a toss-up, and

I wasn't at all surprised when it went to Alfie. He was young and fit, and so Willie Waddell went with him – and he didn't let anyone down. The space he covered that night in the Camp Nou was frightening. He did the unglamorous work and did it ever so well, and was one of the unsung heroes of that cup win.

After his stint in England he signed for Celtic. I remember reading it in a newspaper and I nearly fell off my seat. Our paths hadn't crossed for a year or two so I was out of the loop with his career at Spurs. I actually had to read the newspaper story twice, and my first thought was, 'You're a brave lad, Alfie.' It certainly didn't make any difference to our friendship, why would it? Alfie had long admired Jock Stein, that wasn't a secret. Football can be a short career for many and if Alfie and his wife wanted to come back up to Scotland, his options were severely limited, so when big Jock came in for him he probably didn't take too long to think about it. He had a strong mentality and I know he needed that mental strength in the coming years, and probably ever since.

Jock Stein gave me my first Scotland cap and I loved working under him. Everyone I knew respected him. He was a lovely man and a great manager, and it's little wonder that Alfie wanted to play under him at club level.

I recall a few of us going up to Aberdeen one night for a function. It was long after Alfie had left Celtic. There was myself, Alfie, Alex 'Doddie' MacDonald and Graham Fyfe. I had the bright idea of stopping off at a pub in Perth – as the owner was a mate of mine – for a small refreshment. We walked in and the pub was busy. A group of lads in the corner noticed us and started coming over for autographs, which we were happy to sign. Then one of them noticed Alfie and made a few comments, which we had come to expect. But then a few of them joined in and before we knew it the 'banter' had long crossed the line and was a disgrace. We walked out of the pub and the owner was furious. And I'll tell you this, if Colin Stein and I were with Alfie at Ibrox and the same thing happened we would walk straight out of Ibrox with him. Some of the behaviour that he's had to put up with over the years is inexcusable and completely out of order.

If the team that won in Barcelona had stayed together we would undoubtedly have become a far better team, grown together and won more honours, but it's a short career and I had always wanted to play in England as I believe it made you a better player. Alfie and Steiny were no different.

We make choices in life that others might not agree with, but the truth is we make them for ourselves and our families. It's really not for others to get involved and judge. They make their own decisions and have to live by them. Alfie made a decision that was not just about his career, but which also affected his life. He had to work. That should be no one's business bar his. I would imagine the people criticising him don't know him as a person, because he is one of the warmest, kindest people I've had the good fortune to know, and I value his friendship far more than anything to do with football.

Willie Johnston
Rangers FC

1

A Chip off the Old Bloke

MY EARLIEST recollection of kicking a ball was at Tynecastle when I was around three or four years old. Dad had taken me to his 'work' with him as the gruelling pre-season training got under way. I had little concept of anything in those days. I had no idea Dad was a footballer, and no idea that Tynecastle was a football stadium. I believed he had taken me to a park in Edinburgh and that all his mates had decided to come with us. Guys I would later become acquainted with, including Willie Bauld and Jimmy Wardhaugh. I used to love going to the park as a kid and it was even better when someone produced a football – which the Hearts trainer did that day. He passed the ball to me and I passed it back. I had a great time, but despite it being the height of summer my mum had obviously been taking little chance that her wee boy would catch a cold, so I was dressed in a big, long coat and matching scarf. Imagine how difficult it was to show off your silky skills swathed from head to toe in something that wouldn't have looked out of place in a harsh Russian winter!

One of the few memories I have of that day is standing there on the grass and looking around at the sheer vastness of it all. 'So this is where you work, Dad?' I probably thought to myself. His place of work had the wow factor and despite being just a toddler, my interest was aroused.

When I was a wee bit older, perhaps six or seven, I started to appreciate what he did for a living. By then he had moved on from Hearts and was playing for Raith Rovers – and I equated football with a ride on an old steam train. If I was off school, Dad would sometimes take me to training with him. I'm sure it was because I was either nagging him incessantly or hanging on to his coat-tail as he was leaving the house. By this time I was well aware of where he worked and I thought it was pretty cool that he wasn't stuck in an office all day.

I loved going to see him play for Rovers on a Saturday afternoon. I was playing for the school team and understood the game a bit better – but the highlight of my day was definitely travelling to Stark's Park. In those days there weren't any bridges for cars, so you had to make your way to North Queensferry, get a ferry across to South Queensferry, and then get a train to Kirkcaldy. I just loved the journey across the Forth Bridge on the old steam train.

There was something magical about the sounds and smells of train travel back then, and I enjoyed sticking my head out of the window as we crossed the bridge, looking the way the train was travelling and watching the puffs of smoke coming from up front.

When we pulled into Kirkcaldy station we would walk the mile or so to the ground, and that 20-minute walk was always full of anticipation. Dad had to be there earlier than the others, but when we arrived at Stark's Park there were always supporters milling around and it would take him quite a while to get into the ground. I was always very proud of him being a footballer as it seemed everyone looked up to him. He had obviously dropped down a level but the adulation was still evident.

Whether or not seeing him go about his business had any bearing on me becoming a footballer I'm not sure; after all, it's the dream of most young lads to pull on a pair of boots for a living one day, or if that isn't an option then most lads follow in the footsteps of their dad regardless. Maybe where I benefitted was in having an old man who had seen and done it all before. He did guide me on my way but he was also mindful to let me carve my own path.

When I did eventually become a footballer, I spoke to more than a few people who had seen Dad play and they were never anything less than complimentary about the way he played the game or how he carried himself in life. He may have been one third of a very famous footballing trio, but just like Jimmy Wardhaugh and Willie Bauld he was also very much his own man.

Dad worked down the pit in his youth as Prestonpans was a true mining community when he was growing up. Most of his family worked down the mines too. There were about four or five pits in the area and it would have been a horrendous job, but it was all most folk knew.

When he signed for Hearts he would do a shift down the pit and then go and train with the team. But the day he was able to give up mining would've been a great day for him. There was also a prominent paper mill at Inveresk, which was a big employer at that time. I think my dad would've been advised to keep his job in the pit by his parents in case the football didn't work out. But, boy, did his chosen career work out. Hearts had endured a barren spell for decades before the Terrible Trio clicked into gear, and once fully up to speed, Conn, Bauld and Wardhaugh helped the team win the League Cup in 1954, the Scottish Cup in '56 and two years later the biggest domestic prize of them all, the league title.

My dad was the first of the trio to join up at Tynecastle and would go on to score an impressive 223 goals in 410 games, and all from the inside-right position. Of that magnificent goal haul, 166 were scored in competitive fixtures, making him Hearts' sixth-top goalscorer of all time. Remarkable. Bauld scored 277 times, while Wardhaugh bagged 271. Is it any wonder these guys were nicknamed the Terrible Trio and that there were more than a few knobbly knees around when Conn, Bauld and Wardhaugh were due in town?

Dad joined Hearts from Inveresk Juveniles – a team from Musselburgh – in 1944, when he was just 17, having joined them from Prestonpans YMCA, but it was a couple of years before he established himself in the first team, and that was the same season his two mates also made it into the first team. The first time they played together was in 1948 and Hearts stuck six past East Fife with Dad scoring twice and Willie Bauld getting a hat-trick. Dad was just 22 and it was said that his movement and passing was vital to the success of the front three. He always maintained that Willie Bauld was the brains of the outfit, but he was being modest. I think all three became equally as important to each other and by the time they had played a few games together their understanding was already veering towards telepathy.

Around a month after Dad had played his one and only game for his country, he suffered a nasty ankle injury, which would dog him for the remainder of his career. He managed only 15 games in the following two seasons, and nine of those came in the 1957/58 campaign when Hearts won the league, and the team scored an incredible 132 goals, which is still a British record to this day. Dad played in five league games (due to yet another ankle knock), but scored four goals, which proved he hadn't lost his striking instincts.

It was inevitable though that Conn, Bauld and Wardhaugh would eventually go their own ways, and for Dad that meant a trip into the (almost) unknown as he was approached by a South African club called Johannesburg Ramblers. They had first seen Dad play during Hearts' 1954 tour of South Africa – and no wonder they wanted to sign him. He played in nine of the ten tour matches and scored 11 goals. The Conn family started to excitedly prepare for a new life in South Africa's largest city. Dad had also been offered a job and a house, so it was a good deal for us all. About a week before we were due to leave Prestonpans my parents held a house sale, not to sell the actual house but all the contents. They reasoned that emigrating to the other side of the world would necessitate a clean slate, and so everything was up for grabs. It also makes me think they weren't planning on coming back for quite some time. Apparently house sales were perfectly normal back then, but an alien concept to me. You would be sitting in the house doing your homework, the doorbell would ring and two complete strangers would walk in, have a look around and say, 'OK, how much for your kitchen table?' Dad would name the price, they would hand over the cash and off they'd go with your table and yours truly would be left to finish his homework on the chilly linoleum floor.

It got to the stage that after a couple of days we were sitting on orange boxes eating our dinner as everything had been sold!

And then there was a snag, although not immediately. The owner of the Ramblers wanted Dad to go over to Johannesburg and sign the contract, but he refused, asking them to send the contract over so that he could run it past his lawyer. So, while he was waiting on this contract arriving he organised a going-away party in our barren household. All the Hearts players were there. I was about five or six years old and at one point I was sitting on the staircase alone with my thoughts when this voice drifted into my mind. It was the great Dave Mackay and he sat down beside me. He might have been a hard man on the park but he was such a gentle person and he asked if I was looking forward to my new life in South Africa. I told him I didn't know an awful lot about South Africa and he told me it was on the other side of the world, which made it sound like this great adventure. When we'd finished chatting, he stood up, ruffled my hair and handed me a ten bob note, before saying, 'That'll get you some sweets for the journey over.' 'Thank you, Mr Mackay,' I beamed. He smiled and joined the rest of the grown-ups in the living room.

Now, ten shillings in 1960 was a small fortune. As I pondered being one of the richest kids in Prestonpans, I couldn't take my eyes off this crumpled brown piece of paper. This was a game changer. At first I hadn't been wildly keen on the idea of South Africa, as I had some good pals at school and around our local area, but this conversation with one of Scotland's greatest ever players had got me thinking – and with ten bob in my pocket I was ready to take on the world. I hid the money somewhere safe in my room – not from my parents or siblings, but from outside influences. Well, you never know, right? Off I went to school the next morning and told my mates that I was moving not just to South Africa, but to the other side of the world, like Mr Mackay had said. Of course, what I didn't know about our impending journey, I made up. I had my audience eating out the palm of my hand and might even have mentioned that I was now rich enough to self-finance the trip. I skipped home from school but when I walked through the front door the living room was like a morgue. It didn't help that the entire house was bare, but immediately I realised something big was wrong. Kids weren't normally party to adult conversations in those days but we were included in this one. Dad asked me to sit down while my mum was staring at the floor. He came right out with it. 'We're not going to South Africa.' And that was that. After this bombshell announcement I was in pieces. I hadn't wanted to leave my friends in the first place but the idea had kind of grown on me, and all I could think to ask was, 'Do I still get to keep the ten bob?' Part of me thought I'd need to hand it over to help finance the hunt for replacement furniture!

I later recall Dad telling my mum that the deal had fallen through because the owners of the South African club had been adamant that he go over to Johannesburg and sign the contract. He was never going to do that without some sort of insurance policy in place, so we were staying put – in the same house in Prestonpans, just with no furniture. Mum wasn't happy but had no alternative but to accept it. I'm sure they must've spent the next week or so shopping to replace all the items they'd sold in our cut-price house sale.

By the following week, South Africa was no big deal. I was over it. It's what we do as kids and how we process and handle events in the early days of our life.

Dad had stopped playing for Raith Rovers but decided he wanted to stay in the game, and he was soon appointed player-manager of Gala Fairydean Rovers. We didn't have to move house because he would travel down twice a week for training and again on the Saturday for a game. It was just over 30 miles from our house to Galashiels but the A7 wasn't the best of roads so it could be a lengthy journey. He would pick a couple of players up in Newtongrange and head down to Netherdale. He did well down there. The Rovers finished runners-up in the East of Scotland League to Berwick Rangers 'A' in his first season, and won the King Cup. Dad finished as the league's top scorer with 21 goals in 25 games, including two hat-tricks.

He then hung up his boots to concentrate on management but wasn't always allowed to do his job free of interference. In those days, the board had a big say in how the whole club was run, and also added their tuppence worth in many of the football-related decisions, but Dad wasn't too chuffed with that arrangement. He was more than capable of making these decisions himself, and he eventually had it out with the committee. He told them, 'Look, you brought me down here to manage the team. Let me do my job or sack me!' On the park, the season was going great guns, but all came to a head in the midweek before the title decider on the Saturday. He had travelled down for training as usual and was invited into a meeting with the board. They asked him the team for Saturday's big game, and he named his one-to-11. They said, 'But we think so and so should be playing.' He reminded them that he was the manager and that as long as he had that title, HE would pick the team – no one else. He told them that in his opinion, the guy he had in at that position was better than the player being suggested by the board. It ended in an almighty argument and Dad quit. He was a strong-willed and very principled man, but knew he had the experience and drive to back it up. It was a shame, because he was building something special at Netherdale. In his second season, deciding to concentrate solely on management had been a great decision. He led the club to an unprecedented four trophies. He resigned deliberately on the eve of the match which clinched the league title, as the championship had already been won comfortably. His team scored a staggering 138 league goals that season and had been hailed far and wide for the attractive brand of football they were playing. Who knows what he could've gone on to achieve at Gala had there been harmony between board and manager?

He was also strong-willed during his playing career, and on one occasion, at Tynecastle, he was in the dressing room just moments before an important game against Rangers. The manager, Tommy Walker, approached Dad and said, 'Alf, just one job for you today. All you have to do is mark Sammy Baird out of the game. Nothing else.'

Dad was stripped and ready to go, but replied, 'Are you kidding?'

'No,' Walker insisted, 'just keep him quiet.'

Dad immediately peeled off his strip and started putting his clothes back on.

'What are you doing?' asked Walker.

'If that's what you're asking me to do, I'll decline. Get someone else to do it. If I'm on my game Sammy Baird will be marking me!'

Mr Walker thought for a moment and said, 'You know what – you're right!'

And Dad put his strip back on!

He wasn't long out of work when he was offered the manager's job at Raith Rovers, and he accepted. He had been in charge of Gala for two years and the board at Stark's Park had clearly noticed something special about him, but he only stayed a year and that was the end of his involvement with football.

It was work that led to my parents moving to Kirkcaldy in the first place. When Dad was at Hearts a rep from a company called Harris Brushes had visited the stadium to see Willie Bauld. He offered Willie a job endorsing and selling paintbrushes. My dad had been chatting to Willie when the rep approached them, but Willie hadn't been interested. Never one to miss an opportunity, Dad asked what the job entailed, and the rep was more than happy to chat to another member of the Terrible Trio. The players were coming to the end of their careers and in those days they needed a job when they finished playing. When Dad said he would consider it, the rep was delighted. He talked it over with my mum, informed the rep that he would take the job and was a salesman initially. He was an intelligent man, and quickly worked his way up the ladder, only too aware that football wasn't going to provide for the family long after he had hung up the boots. It was the season before he left Tynecastle and getting a job had been on his mind for quite some time.

He then moved to the Derby-based paint firm, Joseph Mason, and headed up their operations in Kirkcaldy for a while. He was good at what he did and had a tremendous work ethic.

When it came to my football development Dad was never pushy, but very hands-on and keen to help me improve. I loved that he was normally already home when I got in from school and I couldn't wait to get out the back garden. I wanted to play football non-stop. I was hopelessly obsessed. He would teach me how to trap the ball and how to move it and I enjoyed that. We had a big wall in our backyard, and he would hand me a tennis ball, and I would kick that wee ball against the wall, control it, move it on to my other foot and do it all over again. And I would ask, 'Why a tennis ball?' And he would say, 'If you can control a tennis ball then a bigger one shouldn't be a problem.' Wisdom. It definitely helped me a lot.

He didn't ever speak about the rough and tumble side of things as that wasn't his style, but he was still a tremendous worker. Along with Bauld and Wardhaugh, it was like a sixth sense these guys had. Every time my old man got the ball, he knew exactly where the other two would be, and vice versa. The Hearts Terrible Trio. He didn't even have to look. My dad was inside-right, Wardhaugh inside-left and Bauld was centre. They were revered by supporters at the time but even as the years passed I would always meet someone that had been a big fan. Away from the football, Dad was also the best of friends with Willie and Jimmy, and they were often round our house.

They remained pals for many years and would play golf together regularly at Ratho Park.

They reckon that at one time Dad had the most powerful shot in the country – the original Cannonball Kid. I saw shades of that in the back garden, although I'm sure he 'took the edge off it' so as not to hurt me. I didn't have a particularly powerful shot, but apparently the majority of his goals came from outside the box. A lot of that was down to him practising for hours with a tennis ball, and he passed that on to me. Dad was stocky and muscular, and he had fantastic technique. Goalkeepers simply didn't save a Conn (senior) piledriver.

At the start I liked playing as an inside-forward, getting upfield and both making and scoring goals. I was a number eight. People often say they loved my style of socks at the ankles and the long hair, but my playing style changed down at Tottenham. I was more or less given a free role, and I played wider, but with the freedom to go wherever I wanted.

I probably suffered more than my fair share of injuries throughout my career and I know that Dad also had a couple of really nasty ones. A couple of ankle injuries he sustained in the latter part of his career meant he was never the same again. He still had the guile and the craft but the body wasn't as mobile and flexible. Personally I don't remember too much about those but I do recall the broken jaw he suffered in a feisty Edinburgh derby match with Hibs. I was five, and after the game, we all went up to see him in hospital and he looked awful. In order for the doctors to wire up his jaw, he had to have two teeth extracted so that they could get fluids in. They had a special cup and they poured it into his mouth through the gaps in his teeth. He couldn't talk, and therefore he couldn't give me a row for anything, so I was probably quite happy!

When he signed for Raith Rovers it wasn't a case of him desperately trying to prolong his career. He still had value to the team, otherwise he wouldn't have signed. He was as honest as the day was long and knew exactly when it was time to hang up the boots.

When he died in 2009 it had a profound effect on me. He was the first member of my family to pass away and it hit me hard. He was 82 and had had a mixture of a hard life and a good life. I was very close to my parents up until my career took off and then I was away living the good life at the likes of Rangers and Tottenham. I was always away from home, even though I technically still lived with them until my mid-to-late teens. I'll never forget the time I was told that Dad was really ill. He was in hospital in Dunfermline and thankfully I made it up in time to see him before he passed. I was completely overcome by grief and didn't really know what to say to Mum, as she had just lost her soul mate. I was very close to Mum when I was growing up, and her passing in January of 2024 also hit me hard.

When I officially 'moved out' of my parents' home, it was to get married to Sue, but I still made a point of getting home to Kirkcaldy when I could and would sit for a couple of hours telling them all my news – well, the news I wanted them to know! I mean, who tells their parents everything? Over the years I've had a lot of people tell me that I was born in Kirkcaldy – because they saw it on the internet! I can assure you I'm a Prestonpans laddie born and bred.

But you know what, even though my visits back home were only a couple of times a month, I always knew that Mum and Dad had my back. That's not something a parent tells you, but more of a feeling, and something that is either there or it isn't. That was a great comfort to me.

When I would eventually move to Celtic I know they also got a bit of stick, and that they felt that too, which made me sad, but on a visit home they both said to me, 'You're a big boy and you've made your bed, so lie in it.' That was their attitude, but equally they were supportive. It was my decision, and while Mum didn't have any interest in football, Dad had obviously filled her in regarding the implications of such a move. Mum never watched me play, but Dad made a point of coming to watch me every time I made my debut for a new club. He didn't make the European Cup Winners' Cup Final but was at both the League Cup Final in 1970, and the Scottish Cup Final three years later.

It'll be no surprise to anyone that out of both my parents, my dad had the bigger influence on me. He had been there and done it and knew that he could help shape my career in some ways. He knew what was in store for me and could foresee the pitfalls. And even though he had always been an Edinburgh man, he knew exactly what would happen when I joined Celtic. He didn't try to talk me out of it but he wasn't daft. He knew of the backlash that would've befallen him had he moved to Hibs at some point in his career. He was a guiding light throughout my life, without ever being pushy. When I was 15 or 16, and all my pals would be going out on a Friday and Saturday night, down to youth clubs etc., I would be stuck in the house – and that was tough. But that came from my old man. He would say, 'If you want to be a success, you need to make sacrifices – and it starts now.'

I would always counter with, 'For goodness sake, Dad, it's Saturday night and all my pals are going out,' and he would say, 'It's completely up to you Alf, but if you want to go out you won't make it in football.'

And I did make that sacrifice but it was tough at first, especially as we would meet up the next day and they would all be talking about what they'd got up to the night before and I felt completely out of things. Looking back, he was 100 per cent right, because I know that if I hadn't made those sacrifices, I definitely wouldn't have made it to the standard I did. That required a fair bit of dedication.

It's changed days now. It's the case for many that if they screw the nut and sign a two-year contract they're made for life. Kids are getting too much money now and it definitely affects them. At Dundee United Jim McLean would give a decent wage but good bonuses, and then there was a hunger and desire to achieve great things so that the bonuses would come your way. I'll always maintain that a minimum wage and an attractive bonus is the perfect incentive. Nowadays, some of the younger players are getting £200,000 a year before they kick a ball. Where's the motivation to go on and achieve something really great in the game? Unless you're naturally a super-motivated individual, then it ain't going to happen.

I like to think I grew up with two parents who tried to teach me and my siblings right from wrong. They were both fantastic role models, and that was mirrored in the number of people who always stopped to talk to them. It was probably more my dad, as he spent an awful lot of time in our front garden – but he wasn't sunbathing or lounging around. I remember when we moved into our first house in Prestonpans he spent days digging up the front garden. All these people would be asking him what he was doing, and he would reply, simply, 'potatoes'. When they asked, 'In the front garden?' he would say, 'Of course, it enriches the soil and gives you better grass.' I still don't know if he was telling the truth, but I think he did it to save a couple of bob. He was a resourceful man that never forgot himself. He was a huge star of Scottish football in his day, but he remained grounded, approachable and made time for anyone who wanted a quick word about Hearts, football in general or current affairs.

He was self-taught, read books and learned by error. He planted all these seeds and when the time was right we had our own crop of Maris Pipers, if they were around back in the day. He would grow all his own vegetables. When we moved into our next house his impressive vegetable patch took up half the garden. The other half was for football, of course. We had the most amazing carrots, turnips, cabbages and, of course, our

Prestonpans-wide famous potatoes. I was a happy kid. Before we got our house with a garden we had lived in a couple of flats. The first was up above a petrol station, and we paid rent like everybody else. I must admit, it was a nice feeling when we got our first council house with a garden. It was just the extra space it gave us, and the garden allowed Dad and I to go out and play football.

I also had lots of pals growing up and we would be out getting up to no good; not really bad stuff, but just general mischief. Football was king, though, and the boy with the ball was always guaranteed a game, and we would play wherever we could – on a vacant patch of grass, preferably, or on the street if that was all we had. Like everything else, I lost touch with all my pals when I moved away from Prestonpans.

When I was a kid I was a delivery boy for a local butcher. It was a Saturday morning gig and would give me an extra couple of bob. My pal's dad owned the shop and a few years ago he appeared at my door one day and said, 'John Gilmour!' We had known one another from school and had a great catch-up. Moments like that transport you back to the days when you were just starting out in life, and it's nice to wallow in nostalgia occasionally, but probably best that as far as the future is concerned, you don't know what's round the corner.

2

Kicking Rugger into Touch

THE ROUND ball or a misshapen one, that was my choice. But despite attending a largely rugby-playing high school – and being half decent at stand-off or centre – I was football mad. There was never a time when I found myself at a crossroads, or conflicted while choosing between both sports. There was no decision to make.

Before going to Preston Lodge Secondary School I attended Prestonpans Public School, which was for ages five to 12, and they had a school football team, so that was where my first steps in the game were taken, and probably the time in my life when I had the most fun. When you start high school, and juvenile teams are looking at you, then junior and senior clubs, that's when it starts getting quite serious. My thing was playing football, that's what I did, and I always believed that if I took care of playing the best I could, then the rest would take care of itself. We can call it fate, destiny or whatever, but sometimes you have to make things happen for yourself and I probably didn't push myself enough in life. It wasn't my thing. I've never really suffered from a lack of confidence, but I didn't, as some people say, have sharp elbows.

Still, I didn't do too badly. Being born and raised in Prestonpans meant that by the time I started primary school I knew most of my fellow pupils. In those days you didn't play for the school team until the latter years of primary so the team more or less picked itself. We played in the playground every day so the teacher in charge of the team knew exactly who he wanted to represent the school by the time we were old enough.

When I reached primary five and six, I was well aware that Prestonpans was a rugby town, and that when I went to high school I would have to play rugby, but that didn't bother me – probably because as kids we didn't ever look too far ahead. While I was playing football for my primary school team the teacher would invariably list me as either a forward or as an inside player. I had no preference, even though most kids craved the number nine jersey when they were young.

I remember we were drawn against a team from Haddington in a local cup competition and the first game was to take place in Haddington, around ten miles away. This was a big adventure for us kids, and while I realised it wasn't quite as far away as South Africa, it was still a fair jaunt. We were all buzzing at the thought of representing our school against a rival town and just before the game we got a pep talk from the manager, 'This is going to be a tough game; they're a decent side so I want you all switched on from the start.'

We were ten or 11 years old and we were fearless. We had a great team spirit even at that age and we went out there and had a ball. Our goal wasn't to try and keep it tight for the second leg, but to win the game, which we did – 18-0, and I scored eight. I was an inside-forward that morning. I don't think anyone scored more, but I only ever counted my goals. That game was the talk of the school on the Monday morning and we all enjoyed the adulation of our fellow pupils. By the end of the week we were looking forward to the second leg on the Saturday. 'How many do you think we'll score this weekend?' 'Do you think we'll get a hundred?' Well, we'll never know because the school team from Haddington didn't show up at Prestonpans Public on the Saturday morning and we were left deflated. Loads of our pals had also come along to witness part two of the massacre. We had a kick-about and then the manager told us we would be awarded a 3-0 victory. We couldn't believe it and said that it was so unfair as we would definitely have scored more than three goals. I'd like to think I learned a valuable lesson that day. Our players were focussed only on one thing – and that was scoring as many goals as possible, which is the name of the game, and we would enjoy ourselves in the process, but we never once thought about the lack of enjoyment that would bring for our opponents. We were only kids, and that was the way kids operated. The teacher had a word with us about it and it's something that never left me.

By that time I had started going to watch Rangers whenever I could. The first thing that attracted me to the team was the colours. I loved the red, white and blue. My local supporters' bus was named after the great Jimmy Millar, and Jimmy travelled on the bus to Ibrox quite often. My first trip on it wasn't for a match, but for a tour of the stadium. Jimmy was also there and he was chatting to me on the journey through to Glasgow, and he said to me, 'I think you'll be blown away by Ibrox, Alfie.' He was friends with my dad and they had played against one another. I had been expressing an interest in Rangers for quite a while and as my dad also knew the guy who ran the local club, he got me a seat on the bus. I'll never forget the moment we pulled up across the road from the main door at Ibrox and I just sat there, open-mouthed, staring at this incredible building. Jimmy chuckled when he saw my reaction. The moment I walked through the front door I was completely blown away, and felt like I had just entered a different world. The marble staircase, the wood panelling, it's such a magnificent sight. And then you walk up the tunnel and out on to the park, and you can't see the far side due to the camber in the pitch. And you looked up at the vast terraces in this iconic stadium which comfortably accommodated 80,000 people. I remember thinking that it was like a stairway to heaven, that's how vast it was. It seemed to go on for ever.

Jimmy knew I was showing a bit of potential as a young player and his advice to me was that if both Rangers and Queen's Park showed an interest in me, I should sign for the latter, and promised me that if I was good enough, Rangers would eventually sign me. He told me I would have more of a chance of getting regular football at Queen's Park. But Queen's Park didn't come in for me – although Leeds United did.

I think the first time I saw Rangers play was at Easter Road. Something tells me it was around the start of 1965, and it wasn't long after Jim Baxter had broken his leg in Vienna. I remember walking down Easter Road with two of my friends and one of them said, 'Baxter's playing today, I can't wait to see him.'

I said, 'He isn't playing, he's got a broken leg.' But Baxter played that day. And someone near me in the crowd had a gun, a starter pistol. It's incredible the things that stick in your mind.

It was soon time to leave primary school, and I suppose I had enjoyed my time there as much as the next boy, but when I left to go to Preston Lodge reality kicked in quickly as I realised that if I wanted to continue playing football I would have to travel – as there were no teams in my town for my age group. I would have to go to Musselburgh, which was a few miles up the road.

My Saturdays were now preordained. It was rugby in the morning for the school, which to my surprise I enjoyed, but not nearly as much as football. I played stand-off, as they supposedly control the game, although I would sometimes be utilised at centre, which meant I helped get the ball out to our wingers. I enjoyed playing rugby and I must've been pretty good as I was chosen to take part in trials for the south of Scotland team. I didn't get any further but given the south of Scotland was almost exclusively rugby country I could be proud of getting that far. The competition would've been keen, but one thing I never shirked in my life was a challenge.

It was probably a blessing in disguise because I preferred football. After playing for the school rugby side in the morning it would be a quick dash through to Musselburgh to join up with my football team. It was a bit bizarre playing with an egg-shaped ball in the morning and then a round one, but in some ways it helped as it was far easier to control the round one.

We've briefly covered the sporting side of school, but how was I academically? Truth is I wasn't great. I went to school because I had to, no other reason. I didn't enjoy it too much. I remember one year being given my report card to take home to get signed by my parents and my dad refusing to have anything to do with it. He refused point blank. I mean, algebra? It was like a Chinese menu. I got one out of 50, and that was for spelling my name correctly. My mother ended up signing it, because obviously it had to go back to school and she was good at keeping the peace. Don't think for a moment Mum was a pushover – she was far from that. She was a strong enough character, but she also knew the value of a happy house, and she kept a good one. At teatime there was one meal made and if you didn't eat it, then tough. That same meal would be put back down in front of you in the evening and the rest was up to you.

The contents of my report card didn't get me into any trouble with Dad but he was a man of principle and didn't feel he could put his name to something substandard. In my mind I just wanted to play football, so I didn't take school seriously.

I know it was wrong but it was what seemed important to me at the time. Later on, I realised why my dad had wanted me to persevere with my studies, but by then it was too late.

If primary school football gave me a decent grounding in the game, and allowed me to enjoy it, then the moment I signed for Edina was the start of something special. One of the favourite periods of my early days playing football was the time I had with Edina, a juvenile team from the east end of Edinburgh. They were a good side with an excellent reputation and they were soon on my radar. In those days boys weren't pushy and didn't 'offer' themselves to clubs the way some do today. We were a bit more reserved. If you were playing well enough they would seek you out. Very few players were missed as the jungle drums were very effective. Probably a forerunner of social media.

We played at Inverleith Park, which is still being used for football to this day, although it has changed somewhat from my days. Back then it seemed as though there were about 50 or 60 pitches – and the one we regularly played on had a slope worse than Easter Road! It was great when you were shooting downhill in the first half, but you knew that when we changed ends it would be a slog.

Our big rivals were Edina Hibs, and when we locked horns it was Rangers v Celtic. There was no quarter asked and the tackles would be flying in, but I thrived in that type of environment. Alex Cropley, who played for Hibs, Arsenal and Aston Villa, was an adversary in those games and even then his quality was clear for all to see, although the best of our generation never made it. That was Jackie Murphy – every club in Britain wanted him, but he was knocked down and killed by a police car.

I think my dad knew the manager at Edina and got me in, and I would travel through to Leith for training and games. With few prospects of playing football in rugby-mad Prestonpans it was the best option at that stage of my career. I was only with Edina a year but the highlight was definitely playing in the 1966 Scottish Juvenile Cup Final at Stenhousemuir's Ochilview Park. It was an under-16 competition, even though I was just 14. Our opponents were Sauchie, and they were a fine team. That competition was a tough one to progress in, so we didn't really think they would be anything other than an excellent side.

It was a massive occasion, and being the youngest player on the park probably meant I should've been terrified, but I wasn't. It was a huge thrill and I wasn't immune from pre-match nerves but once out on the pitch, any butterflies had gone and I was able to settle into the game pretty quickly. My family and friends were in the stand cheering us on and it was a tough game, but playing from midfield I managed to score the winning goal and you can imagine how I felt.

And that wasn't the biggest thrill of my day. That was still to come. After the game, as we stepped up to receive our winners' medals, I couldn't believe who was stood there in front of me. None other than the Rangers star John Greig. Suddenly, taking part in the final AND scoring the winner paled into insignificance. It was before I moved to Ibrox and, like most other youngsters of that era, I was overawed by Greigy. That completed my day. For me to win my first medal AND get to meet John Greig was all a bit much in one afternoon. I needed a lie down – with my medal still round my neck, of course. Probably the only player who wasn't overawed at meeting John Greig was our right-back, Mervyn James, who was John's nephew.

Not long after winning the Scottish Juvenile Cup I was on the move to a juvenile club nearer home. Musselburgh Windsor had apparently been keeping tabs on me and when they asked me to sign I was happy to do so. I had really enjoyed my season at Edina but the Windsor played at Pinkie Park, and everyone locally knew that the playing surface there was among the best in the region. The park was just across from the world-famous Musselburgh racecourse, and not too far from my house. Jim Jeffries and his former Hearts assistant, Billy Brown, had both played for the Windsor, as well as many other well-known football luminaries. They were a well-run club and after gaining my first Scotland cap I received a congratulatory telegram from them, which showed a real touch of class.

I was at the Windsor for two years and just loved playing football with guys I classed as my mates, and we were winning more often than not, so it was a lot of fun. The two years flew by and it seemed like no time at all when I started making waves among the bigger clubs. One of the first senior clubs to show an interest was Hearts. Of course, they were almost local and had scouts watching us regularly. There was a tentative enquiry about me joining up at Tynecastle, but it was pretty much a no-no from me right away, for two reasons. The first was that I had always set my heart on joining Rangers, but had been told many times – mostly by my parents – that we don't always get what we want in life, which was sage advice. I was also an inside-forward, like my dad, and I didn't want folk comparing me with him. He was a Hearts legend and so the bar had been set extremely high. Comparisons could've been made more readily had I joined Dad's old team.

Leeds United had a scout who covered my area and he had approached me about going down to Elland Road during the school holidays. They would organise these official club camps and run the rule over boys from all over Great Britain and we would all try to impress. A bit like *Pop Idol* for wannabe footballers.

I had been down to Yorkshire two or three times and I loved it there. In those days Leeds seemed like a world away but their scout, Andy Ley, was great at keeping in touch with my dad and I, and he always said he would let me know if the club were interested in signing me. It got to the point where Andy was really keen for me to go to Leeds, and so he called the manager Don Revie and said, 'You'll need to come up to Scotland and watch this boy for yourself.' So, I was playing a match in Leith, at Seafield, out Portobello way, and I had a decent game. Don Revie was standing at the side of the pitch which, for a start, seemed surreal. We all knew who he was because *Match of the Day* was one of the country's best-loved programmes and all us boys had our noses pressed against the TV screen every Saturday night. There was I, giving it my best shot on this mud-splattered pitch at Seafield and trying to impress this giant of a man.

After the game, Mr Revie spoke to my dad and arranged for him and my mum to accompany me down to Elland Road. Could this really be happening? We were picked up at the train station in Leeds and driven to Don Revie's house. It wasn't a bad-sized house and I just stood outside for a wee while taking it all in. We chatted for around 20 minutes before he said that he had to go to his kid's school sports day, so we all ended up going to that as well, which was quite bizarre.

Later that night, mum and I were in the hotel room while dad went to have a meeting with Mr Revie. He was away a couple of hours and when he got back he said, 'OK, all sorted. You're signing for Leeds.' I was just gobsmacked. The way Dad said it all sounded so blasé, but of course he had been sorting out contracts all his life, as in those days players signed a new contract every season. But I still couldn't believe it. Me, 15 years old, and about to join one of the biggest clubs in Great Britain. I had no idea of the finer details of the contract, but quite frankly, I didn't care.

I had no problem getting up bright and breezy the next morning and Mum quipped that I would have to sign for a new club every day, if that was how easy I got out of bed. We had breakfast and then caught the train back to Prestonpans, and I used the four-hour journey to contemplate being (almost) a professional footballer. As much as I could, anyway, because when you're 15 there are more important things than a contract.

As the train pulled in, we gathered our things together and I skipped out of the train station. We began the short walk to our house, which wasn't far, but as we turned into our street we noticed a wee bit of a commotion outside our house. Quite a few of my pals were standing around staring at this car. It was a nice car, a bit too posh for our street, perhaps, and so it looked out of place. As we got closer, both car doors opened and out got a very familiar gentleman. A man who was without doubt one of Scotland's most famous at that time, the Rangers manager, Scot Symon. I was completely gobsmacked (part two). He was with a man who I would soon learn was Ian McLaren, a Rangers director who owned a business in the Kinning Park area of Glasgow. But the minute I saw Mr Symon my heart sank. I knew exactly who he was, and I looked at my dad, and all he said was, 'You want to go, don't you?'

I said, 'But I've just signed for Leeds.'

All the time we were getting closer to the manager of Glasgow Rangers and I was looking at my dad, and mentally saying to him, 'Would you phone Mr Revie and see what you can do?' That was probably the first time I realised that two people could communicate without saying a word. My dad knew exactly what I 'wasn't' saying, and he later called Don Revie and they had a short, but very cordial chat, and the upshot was that Mr Revie ripped up my contract. That is something

I have always appreciated and I respected that man more than he would ever know. Mr Revie actually told my dad that if anything changed in the future he was to give him a call and he would get me back down to Elland Road. How was that for class?

As we neared the house, Mr Symon approached Dad and said, 'Hi Alfie, great to see you again.' They knew each other! Of course, they had probably played against one another and crossed swords when Mr Symon had become manager of East Fife. Mr Symon and Mr McLaren were invited into our humble abode and they spoke about my future with my dad, while I sat and listened (children should be seen and not heard!). I'm not sure if the fact I was a signed Leeds player was mentioned, but Dad and his magic wand were on the case. Mum brought through a tray with a pot of tea and four cups. Thankfully, Mr Symon and Mr McLaren didn't have to sit on orange boxes as my parents had replenished our missing furniture. The adults seemed to have a fruitful conversation and only occasionally did the two gentlemen from Rangers look over at me and smile. I smiled back, of course.

A few days later, Dad was invited through to Ibrox to meet Scot Symon and they discussed terms and a signing-on fee, etc. He was away most of the day but when he came back he said, 'Congratulations, son, you're now a Rangers player, and you start training on the first day of pre-season.'

What a roller coaster of emotions it had been over the previous week or so, and if I had been feeling overjoyed at signing for Leeds, try multiplying that by a few hundred. As a diehard Rangers fan, I'll never forget how I felt when Dad uttered those words.

The chief scout at Rangers at the time was a man called Bob Macaulay. He looked after the Edinburgh youth scene for the club, and he was normally on the ball. When the big day arrived I was to meet Mr Macaulay at the Maybury Roundabout in Edinburgh, and he would drive me through to Ibrox from there. This was on the Monday morning and when we got through to Ibrox I couldn't believe it, as all the shutters were down. Ibrox was closed! It was the Glasgow Fair holiday, and so it was back to Edinburgh without having trapped a ball or ran round the track. I didn't know what to think.

The Tuesday morning was like Groundhog Day, as we did it all again. The first person we met when we walked through the door was Sandy Jardine, who was a forward at that time. Bob asked Sandy to take me up to the manager's office, and so I took my first meaningful steps up the famous marble staircase. On the way upstairs Sandy gave me my first lesson in Rangers etiquette, and it was a valuable one. He said, 'When you go into the manager's office you call him either Sir or Boss. It's up to you, but that's what he likes to be called.' When we reached the top of the stairs there was a small red light outside the door. 'That means you don't go in until it turns to green,' Sandy told me, so I waited patiently for it to change to green, and when it did Sandy patted me on the back and said, 'Good luck, Alfie.'

I walked into the office and Scot Symon was sat behind this magnificent oak desk. He looked every inch a Rangers manager while the office itself simply oozed tradition. Mr Symon looked up at me and said, 'Welcome to Rangers, son.' He had a warm face which immediately put me at ease. Everything beforehand, the marble staircase, the red light, this opulent office, all had me a bit on edge. I was a wonderfully confident individual but this was on another level to anything I had experienced before. At 16 you think you know it all. You believe you're worldly, and then you walk into an office like this and soon realise you're just a bairn in a man's world. It takes your breath away and it's why the warmth of the manager was so welcome. It gave me the breathing space to try and take everything in. I was completely overwhelmed, but soon got myself together. Scot Symon himself had been 27 when he signed for Rangers, but I had just left school. It was terrifying and wonderful at the same time. I think the only words I uttered at first were, 'Thank you,' sir,' when he welcomed me to the club.

In those days, there were quite a few managers who had this incredible aura surrounding them, and Scot Symon was one of them. Others included Bill Nicholson, Don Revie, Jock Stein and Bill Shankly. The minute any of these guys walked into a room you knew they were a figure of authority: individuals who demanded respect. Of course, they had all earned that respect over many years but they wore it like an opulent overcoat. Quite often they didn't even have to say anything: you simply knew they were in charge.

I sat at the other side of the desk from the manager and tried to take in all he was telling me. He told me what would be expected of me over the coming weeks and months and that it would be up to me whether or not I progressed from the third team into the first team. The pathway was there and he would accept nothing other than hard work and commitment as I set about reaching my goal. He told me he had signed me because he wanted me to play for the first team eventually, and that everyone at Rangers would help me to achieve that. There were also some warm words of advice on how I should live, and what it meant to be a Ranger. 'We all have a tradition to uphold,' and that should always be foremost in my mind. When he told me I could go, and to report to the away dressing room downstairs, I skipped out of that room. I think I said, 'Thank you, sir,' again. We hadn't really exchanged many words when he had visited my house with Mr McLaren. My dad had taken care of things that day, so on this fine morning I had walked into Mr Symon's office cloaked in an air of apprehension. I was meeting Scot Symon for a face-to-face meeting and my dad wasn't there to protect me. I needn't have worried as Mr Symon was a gentleman and I appreciated the manner in which he had conducted my first informal chat as a Rangers player. I didn't work under Mr Symon that long but long enough to know that he was a good person, a man of his word and he certainly earned my full respect.

I signed initially on an S Form, or at least I think I did. What wasn't in doubt is I was paid £10 a week. The reason I question my S Form is because it was almost common practice back then for a player to sign a form, but for it never to see the light of day or be registered. You thought you were a signed player but you weren't and if you didn't make the grade the club could just let you go. Pretty awful when you think about it, but it happened everywhere.

Rangers also covered our travel expenses, thank goodness, because in those days it was just under £1 for a week's train fare to Glasgow; 19s 11d, to be exact, which was a lot of money for a young apprentice. At the time, the Rangers players from Fife included Willie 'Bud' Johnston, Andy Penman, Willie Mathieson, Billy McFie, Davie Cairns and Billy Laing, while the Edinburgh contingent included Sandy and John Greig. I was still living in Prestonpans and would get the bus or train into Edinburgh Waverley and meet all the guys there and we would get the train through to Queen Street station. We would then walk through to Buchanan Street and get the subway over to Ibrox. No big fancy cars then. It would take me hours to get to Ibrox. I'd leave the house at the back of seven just to be at Ibrox for ten. You had to be in and stripped and over to the Albion training ground for 10am on the dot. Most of the training took place at the Albion, with some running work at the Ibrox track. And after that, we had our chores to complete. On a Monday morning after a home game we would attack the messy terraces, armed with brushes and shovels and a load of metal bins and would give the place a good clean. We would fill dozens of boxes and bags with empty beer cans and then empty them into the bins. And if we were lucky we might find a couple of bob.

Other tasks included making sure the first-team players had clean boots for a game. The players would have a pair for training (which also had to be cleaned) and a pair of training rubbers/moulded boots, but their match boots had to be pristine. The main pair of boots had metal screw-in studs. You had one pair of each. We didn't have a specific player that we looked after but just cleaned boots as they came into the boot room, which was next door to the home dressing room. Next door to that was a small gym that the ball boys used to get changed on a matchday. We never got a bung off the players for cleaning the boots but if they weren't done right we would soon know all about it. On one occasion one of the senior players approached me with his boots in his hand. 'These boots haven't been cleaned properly,' he barked. I looked at them and there honestly wasn't a mark on them – and I told him so. 'You'll need to clean them again,' he ordered. 'Not a chance,' I said, just as manager Davie White appeared. He said, 'What's going on here?'

I said to him, 'Look gaffer, the boots are clean, but he's saying they're not.' Davie White took a good look at them and said, 'They look fine to me. Just hang them up, the boots are clean, and go and do a bit of training.' The next day I was called into the manager's office and I thought I might be in for an ear-bashing after the carry on the day before, but the gaffer said to me, 'Alfie, don't worry about yesterday. You won't be on the ground staff much longer, but keep that under your hat.' I looked at him for a second before a smile broke out on my face and I said, 'Thanks, gaffer.' I had no idea how it came about, or whether or not it was anything to do with the complaint by the senior player, but I would soon be training all day rather than cleaning boots. This was progression and I knew it.

When I joined Rangers at first, there were several players I looked up to. Among them was Sandy Jardine, Willie Johnston and Willie Henderson. Sandy was a midfielder when I arrived at the club, and was even moved up to centre-forward for a spell. One of the first games I saw him play was against Celtic at the end of the 1966/67 season at Ibrox and he scored a fantastic goal. There were around 80,000 inside Ibrox and when he scored it almost brought the house down. We drew 2-2 that day and even though Celtic had won the league the supporters still backed the team in large numbers. Sandy made his competitive debut after the Berwick debacle of 1967 (when Rangers lost to tiny Berwick Rangers in the Scottish Cup) and simply never looked back. He was too good to leave out of the team. He started at right-half, with the regular number four, John Greig, being moved to left-half to accommodate him. The following season he was in and out of the team and the campaign after that, 1968/69, he started off at centre-forward, a position he shared with Colin Stein. He wasn't a prolific scorer at centre but it wasn't until season 1970/71 that he found his true home at right-back, taking over from Kai Johansen.

Sandy and I were very close even though he was a few years ahead of me at Rangers. I had just left school but had settled in quickly at Ibrox, and was one of the boys. It didn't matter that you were on the ground staff, or in the reserves, you were a Rangers player and you were treated well. You had the established reserve players and just before each season there would be an influx of S Forms, or ground staff boys, who would supplement the guys already in the reserves – and every one of us had the same aim – to get into the first team. Each of us wanted to get transferred into the home dressing room, that was the goal, and if the first-team players saw us as a threat then they certainly never showed it.

In those days it wasn't unusual for a young player to be farmed out to a smaller club in order to gain some first-team experience. It was also seen as a good way to toughen up a youngster. I was quite fortunate that I was never farmed out to a junior team, because at the time we had a third team, which was taken by the Rangers great Jock 'Tiger' Shaw and the groundsman, Davie Marshall. I treated Tiger just like any other coach, and even though I knew he had been a former player, I didn't realise exactly how much of an Ibrox legend he was. Tiger was in with the bricks at the club as he had been a Rangers player for 15 years and then coach with the thirds and reserves before going on to work with the ground staff. He was great to play under and was very fair, but if you deserved a bit of a dressing down then he wasn't shy at giving it. I knew only too well that it was a long road to the first team, so the first man I had to impress was Tiger, as he was ultimately the man who could get you a step up to the reserves, and eventually the first team if you were good enough. I knew it wasn't going to happen overnight and I was in it for the long haul. Rangers were my team and there was nowhere else I wanted to be, and I was prepared to work my socks off to get to the top. But I suppose the reality was that my rise was still classed as meteoric. I wasn't long there when Scot Symon was replaced by Davie White, who gave me my first team debut at the age of just 16, so I was making big strides.

We had to wear a collar and tie every day, even if you were just coming in for training. So we would travel through on trains, buses and subways with a collar and tie on, and the only time you were allowed into the stadium minus these garments was a Sunday morning if you were in for treatment. You could go in casual, as there was no one about to see you.

There was an occasion when one of the younger players turned up for training in casual gear, and was immediately sent home to Edinburgh to get his collar and tie on – and by the time he got back training had finished. It was a harsh lesson for the lad, but also a warning shot to the rest of us. And it wasn't even acceptable to put your tie on just before you walked in the front door at Ibrox as you were representing Rangers from the moment you left your house in the morning until you got home. I didn't have an awful lot of dealings with Scot Symon but he was always my first port of call if there was a problem, and everyone answered to the manager.

Playing for the reserves was a good step up from the thirds as we were then playing in the Scottish Reserve League. Joe

Mason helped out with the reserves and we would play our home games at Ibrox. There was more chance of the first-team boss seeing you playing for the second string, although there was a highly effective internal chain of command and nobody slipped through the net. You knew that if you were good enough your chance would come. Being a Rangers player was beyond my wildest dreams, and when you turned up for work every day, and walked through the front door of such a marvellous stadium, you were instantly reminded of just how privileged you were.

3

Irish Eyes are Smiling

DAVIE WHITE was now the man I had to impress and that was fine by me. Any dealings I'd had with him were always handled with respect and fairness, and that was all I wanted. There was a large group of us aiming for the same prize, and while I was a team player in every sense of the word, I was also a hungry young individual who wanted to climb the ladder as high as I could.

I knew the gaffer had been keeping an eye on me in the reserves, but I had just fought my way back to fitness after missing seven or eight games due to a nasty thigh strain. You will see a pattern emerging. We had been playing Hibs reserves at Easter Road on the Saturday and after the game Tiger Shaw took me aside and told me I wouldn't be joining the Scotland youth squad at Largs to prepare for our forthcoming European Championship tie against Norway. I think Tiger saw the disappointment on my face. I hadn't only been desperate to get back from injury to play for the reserves but had been aiming to be fit for the tie against the Norwegians. He spotted the gloom and said, 'No, but you'll be joining the first-team party for the midweek European game in Ireland.'

You can imagine I had a damned good Saturday night. It was a totally unexpected call-up, but a welcome one. Suddenly, a frustrating period had just gotten a whole lot better. There had apparently been a tug-of-war for my services but I was glad that Rangers won the battle. Someone at the SFA had spoken to Davie White and asked if I was going along just for the ride, or if there was a good chance I would be taking part. The gaffer was adamant I would play some part in the match and that was that. But anytime I was asked to represent my country – at any age group – I was always proud and privileged to do so and looked upon it as a great honour.

When I saw my name on the squad sheet that was pinned up in the dressing room my heart swelled with pride. So, first team, here I come!

The few days between the game at Easter Road and the European tie in Dundalk passed in a blur. As we arrived at the airport for the short flight across the Irish Sea, I felt every inch the Rangers player, albeit one who was yet to kick a ball for the first team. But this 16-year-old kid was about to make his first-team debut for Rangers – AND in a European game, no less.

The trip to Ireland was both exciting and nerve-wracking. We had lunch at Glasgow Airport and I was sitting next to John Greig. I wasn't long out of school and it was as though I had won a competition to accompany the Rangers team abroad and the skipper was my chaperone for the day. It wasn't that long since Greigy had presented my Scottish Juvenile Cup medal, and I'd stared at him like he was a Martian. I tried not to put him off his lunch and between just smiling, I said the odd word. On the other side I had Willie Mathieson, our regular left-back, giving me culinary advice. It was strange, to say the least.

And as we're climbing the steps to board the plane I've got Davie Smith chatting to me about anything and everything. Probably trying to ensure I wasn't too nervous as this was the first time I'd been on an aeroplane. Thing is, I was fine but for those of you who don't remember Davie playing football, he was one of the greatest left-sided players I had the good fortune to play with. Chances are he was more nervous than me about being on an aeroplane, but I still appreciated what he was trying to do.

And then the drama started as soon as we boarded our flight; a dozen little pow-wows going on. We knew that John Greig was suspended for the game but learned that he shouldn't have played in the first leg at Ibrox, and that there could be serious repercussions. Ronnie McKinnon had been ruled out with a dodgy knee, while Örjan Persson had only a 50/50 chance of making it due to a cold and a sore throat, which had only come to light at the airport. Davie White planned to bring in Andy Penman (and move Willie Johnston to the left wing) if Persson didn't make it. So there were a few permutations running through the gaffer's mind as we crossed the water. It was an easy journey for the travelling party, but it was still a trip into the great unknown for me, and as the plane sat above the puffy clouds, speculation as to who would play was the main topic of conversation, for a while at least.

Meanwhile, unknown to us, the offices at our destination were a hive of activity. We had thumped Dundalk 6-1 in the first leg at Ibrox and they were as good as out of the tournament. There was no way on this earth they were clawing back such a deficit, but they had found out that Greigy shouldn't have played in the first game, which up until a few minutes earlier had been news to me and the rest of the lads. At a club the size of Rangers you didn't expect administrative errors like that to occur. But while we had been told that our captain would be suspended from the second leg, it was fleetingly mentioned that whatever we did over in Ireland might not be enough to get us through to the next round. That was a big shock. The phone line between Ireland and UEFA was no doubt red hot as the Irish club tried to convince the governing body that they had been wronged – and that Greigy had made all the difference in the first game. Davie White explained to us that the club's case was watertight and that he had been liaising with Peter Joris, the Inter-Cities Fairs Cup secretary, every step of the way. Greigy had been sent off along with Trivić, of Vojvodina, in the second leg of our first-round tie in Yugoslavia, and therefore should have been suspended for the next scheduled tie in the competition. Straightforward, you might think, but as the referee's report was late in arriving at UEFA's headquarters (it didn't get there until the DAY of the first leg against Dundalk at Ibrox), Greigy was suspended by UEFA for the second leg.

I could understand Dundalk's frustration – to a certain extent – because the ref's report was five WEEKS late in reaching its destination. Now, I know it was 1968, but carrier pigeons had been phased out a long time ago.

It was a relief to know that this administrative cock-up clearly had nothing to do with Rangers and the gaffer was in the clear as he had kept in touch with Mr Joris throughout the process. And he had a whole pile of telegrams to prove he had been thorough in his dealings with the governing body. God knows why the referee's report was so late, and no one could quite understand why Greigy had been allowed to play at Ibrox, but if UEFA had given him the all-clear because the match report from Yugoslavia hadn't yet made it through the system then the club was right to play him. And anyway, we all believed Dundalk were clutching at straws in trying to claim the tie. Would we have done the same thing had the boot been on the other foot? I doubt it, but it was strange preparing for a game properly knowing that our efforts could perhaps still amount to nothing. We were also told that the SFA were 100 per cent behind us and that we should go out there and forget the whole issue.

But here's the irony: I wasn't over in Vojvodina for the tie in which Greigy had received the first red card of his career, but the boys all said it was the biggest travesty they had ever seen. Their players had been swinging arms and boots the whole game, and the incident which saw both players sent off had occurred as Greigy stood back with his arms in the air, refusing to get involved with the hot-headed Yugoslav. Quite why the referee sent him off was anyone's guess.

Once a good bit into our journey, the mood among the players relaxed and we started talking about things other than UEFA. No matter who had erred it had all conspired to me being named as a substitute along with Alex Willoughby. That was the bottom line, and this wee laddie from humble Prestonpans was in line to make his debut for the famous Glasgow Rangers. The gaffer had already told me he wasn't taking me along just for the ride, and that his intention was to give me part of the second half. That was sweet music to my ears, and if everything went according to plan I would become one of the youngest players ever to play in the Fairs Cup.

I was a typical 16-year-old lad. Confident, but not cocky; but of sufficient character to rub along with the more experienced pros, and they were in good supply in this Rangers team. During the flight, there were a few thoughts running around in my head, but the overriding one was of the following night's game. I tried to drink in as much as possible and lap up being with the first team. At the time we had a very competitive reserve-team setup and many first-team players had turned out for the reserves as they tried to get back to full fitness after being out injured, or they'd lost their place, so despite being the age I was, I had actually played alongside a good number of these guys. That said, it was still a big step up and I knew my place.

The whole build-up was fantastic. On the morning of the game we were told not to worry about being eliminated from the competition over Greigy's suspension and to just concentrate on getting a result. A crowd of 10,000 had packed into Oriel Park and the noise before kick-off was incredible. I was part of the team but had the safety net of being on the bench so I was really looking forward to it. After a brief team talk we jogged out for a quick warm-up before Alex Willoughby and I made our way back to the dugout. This was it. Hopefully the beginning of something magical for me at a club I had supported since I was a young lad.

Colin Stein hadn't long signed from Hibs but what an impact he had made. He couldn't stop scoring. He was one of the best I ever played with and that night in Dundalk he was on fire. He'd made his Rangers debut at the start of the month, at Arbroath, and scored a hat-trick. A week later he hit another treble as Rangers demolished his old club 6-1. Dundalk away was only his third game for us and he scored twice that night. To be honest, he should've had a third but his shot hit the post late on with the keeper beaten. I know, because I was close to him when it happened! And that means, yes, I did make my Rangers debut that night – and a prouder 16-year-old you would've struggled to find. I was 5ft 7in when I walked into Oriel Park – and a foot taller when leaving after the game.

I replaced Alex Ferguson just after our second goal and, let's be honest, at 8-1 on aggregate the tie was over. Willie Johnston moved up front and I slotted into midfield, and as soon as I got on and got my first touch any nerves disappeared.

We won the game 3-0 and the home crowd gave us a great ovation, although they reserved a special cheer for Colin Stein, and he deserved every bit of it. Around that time, we were being linked with the Linfield striker, Brian Hamilton. I'm sure the fee quoted was around £15,000. No disrespect to Brian but I think in Steiny we chose the right man. Charlton were also said to be interested in Alex Ferguson and maybe Brian Hamilton was being lined up as Fergie's replacement, but we did OK out of the deal for Colin, even though he cost a hell of a lot more than £15,000.

Being with the first team in Dublin was such a magical experience, and I was proud as punch. I was doubly proud because the manager had deemed me good enough to fight the Scotland youth boss for my inclusion.

To be fair, we won at a canter. We had been warned beforehand not to be flying into any unnecessary challenges but to play it sensible and come back with limbs intact. They were clearly a decent enough team as they had knocked out Dutch side Utrecht in the first round. On the journey back to Glasgow, I was sitting next to Örjan Persson (who was passed fit to play) and he asked how I'd found the whole experience of playing in Europe. I told him I'd enjoyed it far more than I had initially thought, as I'd expected the nerves to get the better of me. He started laughing and said, 'Did you notice the lad who was marking me? His name was Tim O'Reilly.'

I said I didn't.

Örjan said, 'I couldn't move an inch on the park as it was like he was glued to me. He was taking his man-marking instructions to the extreme. I eventually asked the lad that if I was to move over to the other wing, would he follow me, and he said he would.'

So Örjan moved over to the other wing and, sure enough, the lad was right at his back. After half-time, when the teams were coming back out on to the field, Örjan slipped him a sweet and said, 'Here you go, you're doing a great job!'

But late in the game, with the boy clearly tiring, Örjan managed to get over to the other side of the park without being tailed, but immediately shouted over, 'Hey, Tim, I'm over here!' And O'Reilly ran straight across to shadow his man.

It was hilarious, and from that day on I got on so well with our talented Swedish winger. I loved the craic in the first team, and all the lads were up for a bit of a laugh. Training and travelling can be quite mundane so the best possible tonic is to have a bit of fun, and we certainly did that at Ibrox.

We arrived back in Glasgow around lunchtime on the Thursday and went our separate ways. I headed home to Prestonpans every inch the Rangers player. We were back in at Ibrox the following morning, to prepare for the Scottish League match against St Mirren at Love Street – well, some players were. Davie White asked to see me in his office and up the marble staircase I went. The green light was on outside the door, so I knocked lightly and was invited in. He asked how I'd enjoyed the experience of being with the first team, and especially making my debut. I could still feel the electric current running through my body and told him it was the greatest feeling I'd ever had.

What he told me next wasn't a surprise, but it was still disappointing. I was back with the reserves and would be playing at Ibrox against St Mirren's second string the following day. It was back to reality, and the away dressing room, and the following midweek I lined up for an under-21 challenge match at Kilbowie Park against a useful Clydebank side. I was an adaptable player and person so there was no Billy Big Time behaviour and I just got on with the task in front of me. I was on the bench but when I got on at half-time I was up against a guy called Jimmy Caskie, whose dad had apparently been a well-known Ranger back in the 1940s. The son was definitely handy and scored a couple that night. It ended three apiece and I managed one of ours, a cute shot from outside the box just a few minutes after getting on. I always enjoyed playing at Kilbowie. There were only a couple of hundred there and it was about as far removed from a European night as you could get, but the one thing that remained with me virtually throughout my career was my love of football. That's why losing so much of it to injury was, at times, like a dagger through the heart.

When you're 16, you just want to play. Working closely with all the big names at Rangers was magnificent but there comes a time when these guys are just your team-mates and it's time to ditch the starry eyes and knuckle down and work hard.

At Rangers the setup was simple, but very effective and clear. There was a big group of players and three teams. How you performed, and to a certain extent your age, determined what team you were in. The first team spoke for itself. The reserve team would be a mixture of solid guys knocking on the door of the top team, first-team players returning from injury and needing game time, and my group, young lads who had played in the third team and who were ready to make the leap into the reserves. My first destination was category three. The natural destination for a kid just out of school.

It was 1968 and the Rangers third team played in a competition called the Combined League. It had been going for a couple of years and included clubs like Glasgow Transport, who played at Helenvale Park, over in Parkhead, Glasgow University and Jordanhill College, as well as a couple of teams affiliated to the senior clubs. There were nine teams in the league and the games were always very competitive.

We played our home games on the grass pitch at the Albion training ground and that was when we knew we were properly representing Rangers. We would change in the away dressing room at Ibrox and walk across the street to the Albion, and there would be supporters milling around looking for autographs.

I was only 16 but in the Combined League there was no quarter asked and the tackles would be flying in during games. Coming through the juvenile ranks meant we weren't a protected species and the only difference in the Combined League was the age of the guys we were playing against. They were proper 'men' and they didn't give special dispensation to us kids. You had to learn to think quicker than them and avoid any potential pitfalls, such as high tackles or anything off the ball. Looking back, it was the perfect grounding for kids coming through the ranks. From the moment you start playing organised football all you want to do is improve, play proper competitive games and that was what the Combined League offered. I played for the third team for about four months, and in that time I learned so much. One afternoon, after a training session on the Albion, I was taken aside by Tiger Shaw and told I was being moved up to the reserves. I was elated. This was what I had been working towards and to know that all the graft had paid off was just fantastic.

I was still in the same dressing room at Ibrox, but I now knew that talk of a pathway from the third team to the firsts was real and genuine. If I could be promoted to the reserves, what was to stop me knuckling down again and eventually making it to the first team?

Reserve-team football was definitely a step up from the Combined League team: quite a noticeable step, actually, and it took me a little while to adapt, but before too long it was second nature and I was enjoying playing again. One of the big bonuses was the opportunity to play regularly at Ibrox, which meant that if the first team eventually came calling then, once again, it would be second nature. At that time, Ibrox was an imposing arena, with room for more than 80,000, and high up on the list of iconic stadiums.

And after just a few weeks in the reserves I was once again invited into Davie White's office for a chat. I had no idea what it was about, but I was again smiling like a Cheshire Cat afterwards. It was a Tuesday morning and the gaffer told me I would be in the first-team squad for the following day's trip to Pittodrie to face Aberdeen. It was about five months after my first-team debut and while I knew I hadn't been forgotten about, I had enjoyed being with the first team and couldn't wait to get another taste of it.

That night, I had a good chat with my dad, and he was quick with a couple of pointers. My first game had been in Ireland, but this was now the bread and butter: playing in Scotland in front of a large travelling support. This was the time when I had to start earning my keep, and also learning how to handle criticism, if any came my way. I was probably exempt from much of that due to my age but it was an opportunity for me to lay down a marker and I was determined to make the most of it.

We were still in the hunt for the title, albeit we were five points behind Celtic with five games to go, but all we could manage at Pittodrie was a goalless draw. I was on the bench that night, but came on to replace Sandy. It was a real eye-opener for me as the pace was again far quicker than anything I had ever witnessed. I struggled at first to adapt but five minutes in I was up to speed. On the same night, Celtic thumped Falkirk 5-2 at Parkhead to edge another point in front. They then drew their next two games and lost their penultimate league match 4-2 at home to Morton, but we had only managed to take one point from back-to-back games with Dundee so we didn't do ourselves any favours. I replaced Willie Johnston at Dens Park for my first league start, but it was a bittersweet evening as we lost 3-2.

On a personal level it was amazing to be considered good enough to get a league start, and I knew then that I had what it takes to play for Rangers. Celtic would win the league, but I still had a chance to grab a winners' medal in my first season when I was named at number seven, in place of Willie Henderson, for the Glasgow Cup Final against Partick Thistle at Ibrox. The competition was far more valued in those days and it was always first-team players who were involved. We had disposed of Queen's Park and Celtic in the first two rounds and Willie Johnston had scored five times in the two games – including a hat-trick against Celtic. He scored again in the final but the game ended 2-2 and the replay was held over until the following season.

As the campaign drew to a close, so much had happened in such a short space of time. I had signed for the club, played for the third team in the Combined League, stepped up to the reserves, where we regularly played our games at Ibrox, and made four appearances for the first team, the first of these a European tie. It was a lot to take in, but I was determined to use the close-season as a means of getting really fit, so that when I reported back for pre-season training, regardless of whether I was in the first-team squad or reserves, it wouldn't be a lack of fitness which would let me down. That was something I could control.

I spent the summer weeks working hard and lazing about – in equal measure! My pre-season as a Rangers player was, for the most part, enjoyable, but it was hard. I knuckled down and showed the manager – still Davie White at this point – that I was growing physically and ready for the demands of a full Scottish First Division season. As it would transpire, 1969/70 would be another difficult campaign for the club.

My season started on 11 August with the delayed Glasgow Cup Final replay against Partick Thistle at Firhill. It was a well-contested 90 minutes and we won 3-2. I had my first medal as a Ranger, and it was a proud moment. Sadly, it would be my one and only game for the first team in 1969, so it was back to the away dressing room for me. I had good people around me so adapting wasn't a huge issue. I played away happily for the reserves but always had one eye on what was happening with the first team. We had been playing second fiddle to Celtic for a few years by this time and it was six years since we had won the league title. That's a long time for a club the size of ours and understandably the supporters weren't best pleased. The mood in the camp was still good, though, and everyone was hopeful that our fortunes would soon change for the better.

When I wasn't playing for the reserves, I liked to go and watch the first team and it was clear that the fans were still behind the manager. Crowds were high but back-to-back defeats against Ayr United and Celtic early in the season was bad news for the gaffer. In October, we lost to Hibs at home and drew with Motherwell at Fir Park, and suddenly the next month was make or break time for Davie White. We all knew it.

November started well, with consecutive league wins over Dundee, Airdrie and Kilmarnock, but a European defeat in Poland against Górnik Zabrze was a setback. They were a decent side with good players but when the second leg at Ibrox was lost by a similar scoreline of 3-1, it seemed the board had run out of patience, and the manager was sacked. Ironically, it came in the middle of our best spell of form in the league, but the decision had been taken. Who knows, but perhaps the reaction of our supporters after the final whistle of the Górnik game helped the board make the decision. The jeers were as loud as I'd ever heard at Ibrox. There were 70,000 there that night, and it seemed as though every single person was booing. I wasn't involved in that game, or the 3-1 loss in Poland, but I felt it as much as the next player.

According to the press, the club was in crisis. I'm not sure that was strictly accurate, but it was clear that big changes were on the horizon. The great Willie Thornton, who had left Partick Thistle to return to Ibrox as assistant to Davie White, was put in temporary charge while the club sought a replacement. Mr Thornton was only in the hotseat for a fortnight before Willie Waddell was announced as the new manager. It was one of these quirks of fate that football often throws up as Thornton and Waddell had been team-mates in an excellent Rangers side around the time of the Second World War. It was thought by many that Willie Thornton had been one of Rangers' greatest ever players. Certainly, in his short spell as caretaker, we had won both league games.

I was sad to see Davie White go, because he was a really good football manager. And most of the players from that era will perhaps tell you the same thing, but if Davie White had been given a year under Scot Symon then I think he would've been a much better and more successful manager. He had come from Clyde and gone straight into one of the hottest seats in British football. He was a good tactician and had handled the job well, but perhaps lacked a bit of experience. He did really well in his first season and it was only a final-day defeat at home to Aberdeen that saw us lose the league. He was a lovely person with no airs and graces, completely different from the likes of Stein, Shankly, Nicholson, etc. He was a lot quieter, but could shout and bawl when he needed to, although I'm not sure he had the full respect of the players. Probably the younger players, but maybe not the older ones. I think he was perhaps too friendly.

When Willie Waddell was announced as the new boss, I was flitting between the reserves and the first team. I wasn't a first-team regular but I would often be on the fringes and ready for action when called upon. When it came to practice matches between the first team and the reserves I would invariably get stripped for the latter. That was probably the only time the two camps would mix. At all other times the reserves would train separately.

Jock Wallace had arrived from Hearts to work as a coach, while Willie Thornton was assistant to Waddell. The two old-timers back together. When Jock was taking training you didn't see a ball for days, sometimes for the entire midweek, and it was designed to make you hungrier for the ball on a Saturday, but I don't think it worked. The training was intense. We were a fit, fit team under Jock. Some of the sessions were incredible. Every Tuesday without fail we used to do 40 minutes' non-stop running. No walking, it was a jog. We were up and down the terracing, people on our backs and then bunny hops all the way up the old terracing. It was steep and went on for ever. Twelve sets of 220 yards in under 30 seconds each. A full lap under 65 seconds. I used to dread going in on a Tuesday.

There was one occasion we were about 20 minutes into the session and this young boy was really toiling – as we all were – and he stopped to be sick. We were all on the other side, and Jock spotted him, sprinted across to the other side and got him running again, shouting, 'You're a Rangers player now, if you're gonnae be sick then be sick while you're running. Now, move it!' He was unbelievable.

Before Jock arrived, training was taken by Davie Kinnear or Joe Craven, and we thought it was hard going, but it went up a few notches when the big man arrived. Jock would take us regularly to Gullane, but not always the big, infamous hill. He would often take us to the smaller hills, close to Muirfield golf course, in the morning, and then we would go to a local hotel and get something to eat – and then we would hit the big hill in the afternoon. By the end of it your legs had swollen so much you couldn't get your trousers on. You had to sit for a while until your muscles relaxed, but the next day around the track at Ibrox, it was like running on air. It was kind of like mind games. Do the hard work first, and then the second part seems far easier. And after the final hill – no ifs or buts, but the moment you were at the top of the hill for the last time big Jock would shout, 'Right, guys, into the North Sea,' and you would run down and straight into the frozen water. It was a mixed blessing. You knew it would be freezing, but you also knew there were no more sand dunes to run up that day!

I first met Mr Waddell when he was introduced to the players ahead of his first game in charge – against Dundee United in the league at Ibrox. He had an air of authority about him, and seemed like the type of man you didn't mess with. He was 48 years old but had a lifetime of experience as both a player and manager, and journalist, his most recent profession.

But the most important aspect of his arrival at the club was the change in fortunes it brought for me. Three days after his first game, we travelled down to Dumfries to play Queen of the South in a friendly, which would give the new gaffer an opportunity to see one or two of his fringe players in action. I was in the starting 11 with guys like Greigy, Willie Mathieson and Alex 'Doddie' MacDonald. It was my chance to show him what I could do, and I gave it 100 per cent. We won 5-2 and I scored twice. Greigy, wee Doddie and Dennis Setterington also scored. It was great to be back in among the first team and I enjoyed that game at Palmerston as much as any I had played in previously.

As we were nearing the end of the 1969/70 season, I had my first proper interview with a national newspaper, and it taught me a valuable lesson. Don Morrison of the *Sunday Mail* called me up and asked what I thought of the pressure on Willie Waddell. I genuinely wasn't sure what he meant. The gaffer had taken over in the December, and it was now April, and here was someone suggesting that the pressure was mounting on the manager. When the story was printed, the former Ranger Eric Caldow insisted the manager must be given time to prove himself, as success didn't materialise overnight. For my part, I just spoke about how I was adapting to life as a first-team player, as I had been involved in the last seven league games of the season. I didn't say anything remotely controversial, but when I read the story I sat there open-mouthed. And this is why, 'One youngster who could make his mark soon at Ibrox is wing-half Alfie Conn. This 18-year-old could be another John Greig. He has drive and energy, and is the type of player needed in Rangers' bid to emulate Celtic's success. Conn is confident and aggressive, and has quickly adapted to life as a top-team player.'

Wow, the next John Greig! Good thing my head wasn't easily turned by the newspapers, but it was still nice to read that someone thought I was good enough to be mentioned in the same breath as the man who would go on to be voted as the Greatest Ever Ranger, but the bottom line is it was his opinion, and not mine.

It again took me a few matches to adjust to the pace of First Division football, as at first I used to jockey for the ball with the result I got knocked about a bit. I soon learned I had to go for the ball first. But what probably helped me more than anything was the knowledge that I was accepted as a fully fledged member of the first-team squad. It meant that I wasn't afraid to express myself the same as the other established players, and that I could give them a bit of stick just the same as they did if I made mistakes. I was called a cheeky wee bugger on many an occasion.

Something else I had to get used to was the recognition of being a Rangers player, but I think I came to terms with that pretty quickly. It was more of an issue in Glasgow, naturally, than in Edinburgh, but in my hometown of Prestonpans there were also Rangers and Celtic fans, so that helped keep my feet on the ground.

After just a few weeks, I was able to kiss goodbye to the away dressing room. The gaffer had clearly been happy with my performances and my attitude and I made my first league start under Willie Waddell in a win over St Mirren at Love Street. I then started the last six league games of the season. At one point I had been lamenting the removal of Davie White from the manager's office, as he seemed to have a lot of faith in me, but here I was starting all these games under Willie Waddell, and the confidence I took from that was off the scale.

Another personal milestone was reached a week after Valentine's Day when I was named in the starting line-up for my first Old Firm game: a Scottish Cup quarter-final at Celtic Park in front of 75,000 spectators. I'd played in the first two rounds against Hibs and Forfar, the first of these attracting a 70,000-plus crowd to Ibrox. If I thought the pace of my league debut at Aberdeen was fast, then this game was just utter madness. Wee Doddie was sent off as we battled for a place in the semis, and when Jim Craig put through his own goal we thought we had a good chance, but Bobby Lennox equalised before half-time. When Doddie was red-carded in the second half, the stadium erupted and it took a while to calm down our supporters. Celtic scored twice late on to win the tie but I remember going home that night and just trying to gather my thoughts. Even though we'd lost, my overriding emotion afterwards was one of pure elation. I thoroughly enjoyed my Old Firm debut, despite the score.

As the end of my first full season as a top-team player was drawing to a close, Willie Waddell had one more surprise up his sleeve. He decided he would send a group of us through to Edinburgh twice a week for sprint training under a professional coach called Tom Patterson. That was music to my ears. I wasn't big on training but this was something a little different, and it was happening a lot closer to home.

The likes of myself, Sandy Jardine, Willie Henderson and five or six others were chosen to undertake this specialist training. Jock Wallace was put in charge of the sessions which took place every Wednesday and Thursday throughout May. He worked alongside Mr Patterson, a highly respected sprint coach. When we were first told about the initiative, Mr Waddell said he was keen to improve the strength of the squad, both collectively and individually. He wanted us to play at a faster tempo, thus the need for training in spiked shoes! He wanted us not only to play faster but to think faster too, and I completely bought into his philosophy.

I remember telling my dad that the coach had put us on sherry cocktails, and he couldn't believe his ears. Tom told us the cocktails would help build up our stamina. After sprint sessions we would neck this drink, which consisted of whisked egg, milk and sherry. The mixture was used a lot in bodybuilding and was full of protein and iron, while the sherry was good for the digestive system. We had regular races but no one could get near wee Bud, apart from Sandy, but only with the help of a one-and-a-half-yard handicap. I definitely felt better for it and when the close-season arrived, I was actually looking forward to training on my own at the dunes near my home. We started preparing for the new season a bit earlier than normal, but in effect, Willie Waddell had started preparing us for 1970/71 long before the old campaign had finished.

We were due to play a couple of games in West Germany at the end of July, before facing Spurs back on home soil. Celtic had been dominating Scottish football and had won the league again in 1969/70, so there was a determination within the squad to put the brakes on their run of championship wins. Waddell was the consummate professional and was a very driven man who demanded success, but he was up against a Celtic team under Jock Stein, at the peak of their powers, and who just three years earlier had won the European Cup. He had been handed the difficult task of halting their success and restoring Rangers to the top of the league – but he knew he needed time to complete his mission.

The manager would go on to prove that the club was far bigger than any individual by putting in place the building blocks that his successor Jock Wallace would eventually use to overhaul Celtic and Stein. Waddell was more than happy for someone else to take the glory – just so long as the other lot were stopped in their tracks.

A measure of the man was his insistence that he accompany the youth team to a high-profile tournament in Amsterdam to see exactly what he had coming through the ranks. All part of the bigger plan. I was included in the travelling party along with the likes of Kenny Watson, Graham Fyfe and Ian McDonald, who had just recovered from a cartilage operation.

Season 1969/70 had been a good one for me, personally, and there were definite signs that under Waddell and Wallace, the club as a whole was also improving. There was an air of expectation building up, and it was good to be a part of that.

I had broken new ground on several occasions, but particularly enjoyed my first Old Firm match. It was just a wall of noise. You couldn't hear your team-mates, nor Bertie Auld's wisecracks, but I wasn't daunted coming up against Celtic's Lisbon Lions. They might have been great players but at that age I was fearless and it didn't matter who was in front of me. I would later discover that many of the players on opposing sides were actually great friends, and sometimes faked the aggro for the pure theatre of it. Two guys jabbing fingers at each other could have been discussing where to go for a drink afterwards, for all the crowd knew. My boozing buddies would soon include Jimmy Johnstone and Dixie Deans. The banter was terrific, and any player back then who claimed they didn't enjoy the Old Firm game was in the wrong profession.

I won only four of the 16 games I played against Celtic, but two of them brought trophies, plus the win bonus for the League Cup in 1970 was £500. Three years later we received £750 a man for winning the Scottish Cup, thanks to Tom Forsyth's late winner. Has there ever been a better Old Firm game than that?

They were all great, but I've got this fantastic photo from an Old Firm game. The teams are running out of the tunnel and all the Celtic boys have nice short back and sides, and then there's us: Greigy, Doddie and me, all with the massive sideboards. You grew your sidies big to make up for the Rangers rule of not being able to have your hair touching your shirt collar. Honestly, we looked like we were appearing in a cheap remake of *Planet of the Apes*!

Even though I was hobnobbing with guys like Doddie and wee Bud, it didn't ever cross my mind to think I'd finally 'made it'. Even when I broke into the first team, I knew I hadn't made it, and that it wouldn't be the case until I got a proper run of first-team games. When I played against Dundalk in the Fairs Cup, I was just 16. Now, Davie White would have his reasons for playing me in that game, but it didn't spark a lengthy run in the team. That was my only first-team game that year. I played in a couple more before the end of the season, so I knew I hadn't made it at that point. And that was OK. My old man had always said to me, 'It's hard to get to where you want to be, but it's ten times harder to stay there,' and he was spot on. That was drilled into me from the start so I knew only too well what my status was both in the team and in my career. I had no illusions of where I was in the pecking order and that was fine, and all down to a single piece of advice from my dad.

4

Standing up to Authority

WILLIE WADDELL was now firmly entrenched in the hotseat and the new season was upon us. We had all been keen to impress the manager in pre-season training and show that we were worthy of pulling on that famous light blue jersey. I had started the last six league games of the previous season, but it was a new campaign and everything was reset to square one. Nearing the end of July we were looking out our passports for a short pre-season tour of West Germany. We were scheduled to play Hamburg and Kaiserslautern, and I was desperate to feature. Greigy was unavailable for both games and I was privileged to be handed his number four shirt. Before the first game we were picked up at our hotel in this luxurious coach and I was proud as punch walking out of the hotel in my Rangers blazer complete with club crest. We always looked our best when representing the club, and that was one of the things I liked best about being a Ranger.

Tradition was everything at Rangers in those days. Folk would comment on how smart we looked and that helped puff out your chest an extra inch or two. It meant something special to represent Rangers.

I also enjoyed the different style of football the Germans played and despite losing one and drawing the other, the games served a purpose. On our way back from Germany we stopped off in London for a friendly against Tottenham Hotspur, and once again I started. We lost again, but on a personal level, I felt good. I was still only 18, but treated as just another member of the first-team squad, and that felt good. It was an achievement I was proud of, and dad was always the first with a pat on the back: but only when it was merited. My dad's sage advice, 'It's tough to get into the first team at Rangers, but even tougher to stay there,' was ringing in my ears. I was determined not to throw away this great opportunity that Willie Waddell had given me. This Rangers legend had been just 17 when making his debut for the club, so he wasn't afraid to give youth its chance.

Waddell's attention to detail was one of his great strengths. He would often go to spy on teams, especially our European opponents, and come back with a detailed dossier. On one such occasion he had been over to Europe and before the game we were sitting in the dressing room awaiting our instructions, and he looked at me and said, 'Their right-back isn't the quickest, Alf, so every time you get the ball, get it out to wee Bud and let him destroy the defender for pace.' So the game had been going about 15 minutes when I picked up the ball in the middle of the park. I did as I was told and played it out to the wee man and he was off and trotting, leaving the defender for dead. Two minutes later I've got the ball again and immediately I look for Bud. High ball over the top and he's left the full-back trailing in his wake. It was working well. Their keeper kicks the ball out and it lands straight at my feet. Right away, I knocked it out to Bud and he shouts, 'For f**k's sake, Alfie, gimme a break, I'm fu**in' knackered!' I loved Bud, there was never a dull moment with him.

We had six group games in the Sectional League Cup before the league kicked off. Once again, I was an ever-present as we topped our group with five wins and a draw. A couple of tough home and away games against big-hitters Hibs – both of which we won – saw us into a semi-final against Cowdenbeath, and we won comfortably to qualify for the first final of the season.

I was a mere 18-year old 'nipper' when we lined up at Hampden against Celtic in the in the final, but as 103,000 looked on, it was someone a couple of years younger who would make the headlines that day. Sixteen-year-old Derek Johnstone scored the only goal of the game to give us our first trophy since winning the Scottish Cup in 1966.

The day before the big game we had a light training session. Willie Waddell, or 'Deedle' to the players, emphasised it was a no-contact session and so the boys were on their best behaviour. The session lasted no more than an hour and a half and then it was time to relax and mentally prepare for the next day. After getting showered and changed, I was summoned to the manager's office and trekked up the marble staircase to speak to Mr Waddell. The green light was on so I entered the room. Even though just a teenager, I had been around the club for more than two years. The boss looked up at me through his half-rimmed glasses and motioned for me to sit.

'John Greig has failed a fitness test, Alf, so you're playing tomorrow. I'm telling you just now because I want you to go home and get some rest and a good sleep. I need you in tip-top condition tomorrow. Any questions?'

Naturally I felt a bit sorry for Greigy, as he had the flu and that was horrible, but I was allowed to be happy for myself and I reckon the beaming smile assured the gaffer that no questions were necessary. I skipped out of the office and down the stairs. This was it, the chance I had been waiting for. The big time. Playing in front of more than 100,000 at the national stadium. That night I slept like a baby. My mum had to wake me up in the morning or I'd probably still be sleeping!

I had breakfast, showered and got dressed and my dad gave me a lift to the train station. I was nervous, sure, but not unduly worried and, anyway, it's not like I would be the baby of our team that afternoon. That honour was reserved for DJ, Derek Johnstone, the teenage upstart from Dundee, and one of my best mates at the club. We got on very well, but I suppose all the players got on with each other. We had a great team spirit in those days and it made us all the more determined to win the cup. We were fighting for each other, as well as the club and the supporters.

I recall years later doing hospitality at Spurs and one of the questions was, 'Who did you most fear playing against while you were at Tottenham?' The answer was an easy one for me. 'No one.' I concentrated on me. I was super confident and would work out as quickly as possible the weaknesses of my direct opponent, and then try to play on that as much as I could. I wanted opponents to fear ME, not the other way around. And that might even stem back to the story my dad told me about the Hearts manager asking him to mark a Rangers player one day, and my dad refusing, saying that Sammy Baird should be worrying about him. Well I had that in me virtually from the moment I started playing football and it was something I never lost.

I arrived at the stadium in plenty of time and we jumped on the coach to take us to our pre-match lunch. Celtic were in the middle of their nine-in-a-row purple patch but we always believed we could beat them, so we were fairly confident about getting a result.

I had been in the first team from day one of the 1970/71 campaign so even though I was called in as an 11th-hour replacement for Greigy I still felt that I had more than earned my place. And I felt I contributed to our victory. Of course, the plaudits were mainly reserved for Derek, which was absolutely right, but it was a good, solid team performance which won us the cup. Just five minutes before half-time, wee Bud received the ball out wide on the right. He swung over a good-looking cross and somehow Derek managed to squeeze between Billy

McNeill and Jim Craig to steer the ball home with his head. It was an outstanding goal.

Steiny – who was magnificent that day – hit the post in the second half, which, had it gone in, would've made things far more comfortable, but all it did was make the last moments more nervy than they should've been. We were worthy winners, and even Jock Stein said so after the game.

I wasn't surprised that Derek scored the goal he did. His heading ability was second to none. He had the uncanny knack of being able to put the ball exactly where he wanted nine times out of ten. After the game, Derek and I were going wild on the pitch, shouting our heads off and celebrating like two teenagers who had just won a national cup final. I remember wee Bud coming across and saying, 'Enjoy this medal lads, you deserve it, but the next time you're in a cup final you'll be more concerned with what the win bonus is!' Trust wee Bud.

After leaving the dressing room, we walked out of Hampden and piled on to the team bus. Destination: Ibrox. I remember walking into the stadium and grabbing a bottle of beer and winding Derek up by saying, 'You'll be able to do this in a couple of years, DJ.' He was on the Coca-Cola, but I think I had about three bottles of beer and was tipsy. We had a great night and I remember thinking that it would be the start of something special at the club. I thought back to the journalist suggesting that Deedle was under pressure because he hadn't won anything, and saying to myself, 'Just watch him go now!' We knew the defeat would see Celtic double down in their efforts to prove it was a one-off, and so we readied ourselves for the challenge. And it would come.

It was great to be a part of the team that broke the trophy hoodoo, but we were all acutely aware that the big prize had continued to elude the club since season 1963/64. The league championship was the big one, but we agreed that we had taken the first steps to solving that particular problem.

Training the following week was very enjoyable. The lads had a spring in their step and I was in good spirits as we were being put through our paces at the Albion. We always had great banter at training but when one of the older players asked if I had been given a pay rise now that I was a League Cup winner, it made me stop and think. 'I hope you're not still on kids' wages,' he shouted as he ran off. I knew the answer, of course, but let it go and had soon forgotten all about it. After training a few of us jumped the subway into Glasgow city centre and got the train back to Fife. When we were all going our separate ways the issue of wages came back into my head and I thought, 'I must do something about that tomorrow.'

The morning arrived and I travelled through to Ibrox with a new-found sense of purpose. It was the day I would ask for a rise. I didn't mention anything to Mum or Dad but thought I'd deal with it my way. I was probably overthinking it as I climbed the marble staircase. We'd won the League Cup and were definitely en route to more success. That was my safety blanket as I jumped up the last couple of stairs. Willie Waddell was a no-nonsense man and manager. He wasn't our friend; he was there to do a job on behalf of the club, and he did it very well. I'm genuinely not sure if he was feared, because more often than not we dealt with Jock Wallace on the training ground, but as I stood outside the Deedle's office door I was a little apprehensive – definitely not frightened. I was brought up to know my worth, and to fight for what I believed to be right. My dad had instilled that in me, and had no doubt fought many similar battles, so I took my inspiration from him.

The door to the room in front of me was the stuff of many a myth and legend. It was generally accepted that it had proved a graveyard for many players over the years and the fact that you had to press a button to let the manager know you were outside – and wait until the little light above the door changed from red to green – only added to the legend. But this morning, this teenager from East Lothian pressed the button as calmly as possible and awaited the green light. It did seem like a while before it came on, but when it did I walked into the office. It was a grand room, and measured some 12ft by 10ft. The oak panelling theme continued from the walls above the staircase outside and the desk was to your left as you walked in. Mr Waddell was sat behind the desk, his trademark half-rimmed glasses staring down at some paperwork. I quickly wondered how he would've handled this situation when the roles were reversed; when he was a young player and the imposing Bill Struth sat where the new manager was now perched.

Without looking up, he gestured for me to take a seat. I continued to stand. When he looked up, all he said was, 'What is it?'

I stood there, hands clasped tightly behind my back and said, 'I've been part of the first-team squad for a couple of years now, and I'm still on youth-team wages. I'd like to be put on the same as guys like Bud and Steiny.'

He took stock, looked up at me with narrowing eyes and replied, 'Oh, you would, would you?'

It kind of threw me a bit and I mumbled, 'I think it's only fair, gaffer, that if I'm old enough and good enough to play with these guys every week that I should be on the same money.'

As the minutes passed and it looked increasingly like I wasn't getting anywhere, I was starting to get frustrated – and with that I became emboldened. 'I would like a rise Mr Waddell, that's the bottom line.'

He looked straight at me, his glasses at the end of his nose, looking like they were now about to fall off, and he said, 'OK, I'll give you a rise, an extra £2 a week. How's that?'

'How's that?' I was furious and felt insulted. I said, 'That's it? £2? I don't think so. I'll tell you what, I'm off home. You have my phone number. When you come up with a figure that isn't insulting, give me a call and I'll come back in. Until then, cheerio.'

And I walked straight out of his office, down the marble staircase and out the front door. I was finished. If he valued me at all he would phone and ask me back in to continue the 'negotiations', although at that point I wasn't quite sure that would happen. If he called, great, but if not, well, we would cross that bridge when we came to it. For now, the only bridge I was crossing was the Forth Road Bridge as I headed home to Fife.

I walked into the house and my dad took one look at my face and asked, 'What's wrong, Alf?' I told him. He eyed me for a moment and I thought I was in for a lecture about being privileged and throwing it all away, but my mind had jumped the gun. He told me I'd done the right thing and that if Waddell thought anything of me at all then the phone would ring. He did add, 'Probably not for a few days, though, as he'll want to save a bit of face and leave you stewing for a while.'

Aye, if there was a font of knowledge then it was my dad. Sure enough, the phone rang a couple of days later and the Deedle ordered me back into Ibrox for 'talks'. Once again the conversation was short, but sweet. He offered me terms which I didn't find insulting and I signed the contract there and then. I hadn't wanted to leave, I believe the boss hadn't wanted me to leave and perhaps it was just a case of two adult males seeing whose hair was the longest!

Up until the League Cup Final, we had won five of our eight league games, but damaging losses to Celtic and Aberdeen had left us playing catch-up. A poor November virtually put us out of the title race. Successive losses on the road to Ayr United and Hibs were a massive blow. December wasn't much better and as we headed into the new year, the mood around the stadium wasn't great. We were at Brockville on New Year's

Day; losing 3-1 to Falkirk really left us in the doldrums, and the fact I scored meant very little. These were the days when we often played on the first two days of January, and we were hosting Celtic the following day so we had the opportunity to make it up to our supporters almost instantly.

Little did I know when I jumped out of bed on the morning of the Old Firm game just how much the football landscape would change in Glasgow. Rangers and Celtic would be relegated to bit-part players as tragedy on an unimaginable scale engulfed a great city.

It was matchday, and this teenager had already put the disappointment of the previous day behind him. I woke up on the Saturday morning having slept like a log. I got dressed and went through to the kitchen and Mum had my breakfast on the table. 'What are you up to today, son?' she said, with a wink. 'Nothing much,' I replied, 'just a game against Celtic in front of 80-odd thousand, no big deal. Are you up to anything?'

She smiled and started clearing away the breakfast dishes from the first sitting, as Dad was already sat in the living room reading the morning paper. When I finished my boiled egg and toast I joined him on the sofa. He looked up from his paper and asked if I was looking forward to the game. I told him I was and we passed the time with some small talk. He might have been 46 years old, but looked as though he could still do a turn on the park.

After a short time I went through to my room and stuffed a few things into a bag and before I knew it I was in the car with Dad and we were heading for the Park View Hotel, in Kirkcaldy, the rendezvous point for Rangers' Fife contingent. Dad wished me well and off he went. When he was giving me a lift I was always early. I leaned against a pole in the car park, waiting on Willie Mathieson, wee Bud and Andy Penman, and had only been there a few minutes when the others arrived, but by that time I must've received the best wishes of at least a dozen passers-by. The Old Firm was huge in Glasgow, but also spread its tentacles throughout the country and most people probably had a leaning one way or the other.

I might have been a teenager but was already something of an Old Firm veteran. This would be my fifth game against Celtic with the highlight undoubtedly the League Cup Final a few months earlier. So I knew what to expect. I would go on to play many competitive Old Firm games while at Ibrox and I can safely say I loved the occasion surrounding these games.

My daydream was broken only by wee Bud rolling down the window of the car and shouting, 'Right boy wonder, in ye get.' Although born in Ruchill, in Glasgow, Bud had moved to the kingdom when he was just two or three years old and considered himself a true Fifer. We were soon on our way and the banter was top-notch as usual. Whether some of the guys used the banter to calm their nerves, or there were no nerves, I'm not sure, but certainly I never picked up on any nerves on those journeys through to Glasgow.

When we arrived on the south side of the city we parked up and made our way along Edmiston Drive to the main door.

There was the usual queue of young autograph hunters, some older than me, and we stopped for a while to chat and sign pics and programmes. When we walked into the dressing room we were welcomed like long-lost pals even though we'd all seen each other the previous day. Celtic were the dominant force at that time but there were no inferiority complexes at Ibrox, and every time we went out on to the park we thought we could beat them. That afternoon, we knew it would be packed to the rafters; 80,000 inside the ground screaming themselves hoarse for the duration of the match. Six bob for a ground ticket, the equivalent of 30p in modern coinage, and every single brief had been snapped up.

The game itself was probably unremarkable. The usual to-ing and fro-ing, and battling for possession, for the upper hand, and played in a thick, gloomy haze, with a rolling mist meaning it wasn't always possible to see everything that was going on. It was goalless until the 89th minute when Jimmy Johnstone – probably the smallest man on the field – headed home after a Lennox shot cannoned back off the crossbar. It looked like being the only goal of the game and some might say it wouldn't have been a great shock, given the form of both teams, but Old Firm matches have always been different gravy, and we were on cloud nine when Colin Stein forced home a dramatic equaliser.

I'm sure we were happy enough to get a point from the game, given how late Celtic had taken the lead, but we certainly weren't second best on the day, and every time we matched

Celtic or beat them, it was one step closer to a football power shift in the city.

When the final whistle sounded we shook hands with our opponents and, to a man, made for the dressing rooms, desperate for a bath to wash away the afternoon's grime, and there was lots of it. Everyone jumped into the communal bath and that was it. Some of the players relaxed, others were in the mood for a carry on and once we had dried and dressed, the usual suspects said our goodbyes and headed out into the crisp January evening. We were probably in the car and away before 5pm. As was normally the case, we spoke very little about the game on the way home. Willie Mathieson was driving and it was a tedious journey given the poor visibility.

When we pulled into the car park at the Park View the four of us went straight inside for a drink, with Willie on the fresh orange. We were sitting having a pint and a bit of banter when one of the barmen shouted over, 'Alfie, that's the phone for you.' It was my mum, and she sounded really stressed. I was immediately worried and asked if everything was OK. 'Oh Alfie,' she replied, 'I'm so glad you're all right.' I didn't have a clue what she was talking about, but when she mentioned that reports were saying more than 30 supporters had died I went chalk white. I couldn't believe what I was hearing. Had she got it wrong? True, we'd heard the ambulance sirens as we were driving away from the ground, but to be honest that was a common occurrence after an Old Firm game back then. We were thinking it was the fans fighting, which would've been nothing out of the ordinary. I assured Mum I was fine, and that I was heading home in a few minutes. She sounded mighty relieved to hear that.

When I walked back over to the table, the boys were all worried that something was wrong with one of my family, but when I told them what she'd said, they couldn't believe it either. We asked the barman to turn on the TV and there it was, the news coming live from Ibrox. We sat there stunned. Hardly a word was spoken between watching the news and us all going our separate ways. How could such an awful thing have happened?

It was without doubt the worst period of my life. As an 18-year-old attending three and four funerals a day, the emotions were all over the place. It was definitely the right decision by the club, but it took its toll on the players as well. I attended the funerals at Markinch – which wasn't too far from me – and that was the saddest thing ever: just a group of kids who had gone to the game and didn't come home. Such a tragedy. My heart ached for their families. I can only begin to imagine how hard it must've been for the poor people who were left behind. On a personal level, I lost up to a stone in weight in such a short period as I wasn't eating. It was an awful time and simply so difficult to comprehend.

A few of us went back to Markinch to lay a wreath when a memorial bench was being dedicated. Along with the Lord Provost, former Dunfermline manager Jim Leishman, I discovered on that visit that most of the victims in the village had lived very close to one another. Such a tight-knit community and such an overwhelming sense of loss. I can only imagine that a dark cloud still hangs over Markinch, and always will. Those poor boys.

I think our next game – against Dundee United – was postponed for a week, but that was nowhere near long enough. We weren't ready to play a week later, but that decision was taken out of our hands, sadly. Rangers have such a large fanbase from all over the country, so there were few places that weren't touched by the tragedy, and it heartens me to see that our supporters have never forgotten those who perished at Ibrox that dark day, and still hold an annual memorial service every 2 January.

There was disbelief among the players when we were told we would be playing Dundee United just a fortnight after the tragedy. We knew we had to get back on to the pitch at some point, but everything still seemed so raw, and the timing felt off. We drew against United and then won a couple in a row. Our form was erratic and we seemed to take one step forward and two back. What we needed was to go on a long unbeaten run but time was against us and the games we either lost or drew had outnumbered our wins by the end of the campaign.

We finished fourth, behind Celtic, Aberdeen and St Johnstone and, quite frankly, it wasn't good enough. We underachieved big time, which made it easy for our detractors to say that the League Cup success had been a flash in the pan. There had been few highlights in the second part of the season and on that basis alone our league position was probably justified. I had played more than 40 top-team matches and contributed a modest haul of eight goals. I was happy with my game time but unhappy with my contribution in front of goal.

It was my first full season as a member of the first-team squad and even though I was usually quite hard on myself, I knew my football journey was just beginning. That was certainly my mindset when we broke up for the summer and everyone went their separate ways. As was the norm, I kept myself fit and if I wasn't going for a 'walk' on the dunes at Gullane, I was out doing a bit of road running. When we reconvened for pre-season training we received a wonderful present from the manager – the signature of Tommy McLean, a £60,000 capture from Kilmarnock, and a player who joined Rangers after Willie Waddell had travelled out to Copenhagen, where Tommy was part of the Scotland squad, just to make sure he got his man.

The 1971/72 season was now upon us and we looked leaner, hungrier and determined to make our mark. I get that players say that at the start of every season, when optimism is high, but I just had a feeling. The history books now show that this campaign would be remembered as the one in which Rangers secured their only European trophy in 152 years. Isn't that quite something? But the truth is that on a personal level, it was probably my worst season for Rangers. I simply couldn't get going, and I now know that it was probably more mental than anything else. In the lead-up to that unforgettable evening in Barcelona – for a couple of months, in fact – I was in the reserves. On one hand it felt like an eternity, but on the other it really did give me an extended opportunity to sort myself out, because in that time I changed so much about myself and my way of playing.

Being at Rangers was often about so much more than playing football. We were expected to interact with fans at supporters' club events, and that was something most of us enjoyed doing. It's like anything in life, some folk are just more comfortable with certain things than others, but I always enjoyed getting out and about and meeting our supporters.

I remember on one occasion being really made up when I heard that the Dalkeith Rangers Supporters Club was changing its name to the Alfie Conn RSC. It was the first time I'd had a supporters' branch named after me and it was a fantastic feeling. The bus left from the Maybury Roundabout in Edinburgh, a spot which most people know. It was a new club that had started at the beginning of the season and I was proud to put my name to it. One of the members had apparently talked about starting an Alfie Conn Fan Club, but at a committee meeting they suggested naming the club after me, and I was asked to be honorary president, an invitation I accepted gratefully. The club accrued 100 members in its inaugural season and ran a bus to every game. What I particularly liked about the Dalkeith club was that it seemed ahead of its time. Any money they made in that first season went towards holding a Christmas party for the residents of an Edinburgh children's home and each kid got a present.

I was proud to attend their first annual dinner/dance and got up and made a short speech. A few of the players were present that night and everyone seemed to be having a great time until they announced their player of the year – and the club named after me gave it to Sandy Jardine! We had a great laugh about that and Sandy ribbed me the following week in training.

The Rangers fans were wonderful to me, and in my early days I used to receive lots of fan mail – as well as a few marriage proposals! I remember one girl writing to me and saying, 'Alfie, you are my favourite Ranger, but you are a player who doesn't get enough praise for what you do. I dream of you at night and see you as a Scottish George Best, only much more super looking than the guy from Manchester!' I'm not sure if I ever got round to telling George about that one.

Another letter said, 'I'm just daft about you, Alfie. You're the most handsome man I have ever seen – and my bedroom is covered with photos of you. You are really lovely, with your fair, curly hair and big blue eyes. Your fiancee, Susan, must cherish the most beautiful man in the world.' And it got even more embarrassing. Because another letter said, 'I need to know if you're married or engaged? Also, is it true that you have a brother who plays for Hearts?' It was true, Bobby was on the ground staff at Tynecastle. These are the only ones I can reproduce!

There were also the very few occasions when senior management let their hair down and joined the players in some sporting therapy. Willie Waddell and Jock Wallace had made a good footballing partnership at the club, but they were also a pretty good golfing double act. I recall a club tournament at

Barassie, in Ayrshire, one summer, when Jock and the Deedle teamed up to play against the players in a winner-takes-all competition. Other pairings that day included Colin Stein and Willie Johnston, and John Greig and Sandy Jardine, while I teamed up with wee Doddie. Success that afternoon belonged to Jock and Willie, who beat John and Sandy in the final, but it was a brilliant day out. And it wasn't finished there. We were staying overnight in Troon and in the evening the hotel put on bingo for us and asked 'Beer Keg' – John Greig – to call the numbers. We had a great laugh and Graham Fyfe and I won the snowball, and received £6 – between us! These days out were great team-building exercises and brought us all closer together.

At the end of the season we would all be invited to numerous player of the year dances, and a sheet would go up on the dressing-room wall with the times and dates of all the events. We would police it ourselves and ensure they were all covered. That season, the brilliant Davie Smith was walking away with most of the awards, and well deserved they were too. Occasionally, Peter McCloy or John Greig would win one or two, and Davie would pretend he was annoyed with them for raining on his parade. Davie was one of the Fife contingent and so when I was voted tops with the Leven branch, I said to Davie, 'I won't be able to make it that night, would you go on my behalf, you know how it works.' Of course, I was winding him up, but then, straight out of the blue, big Peter told us all that we were invited to his wedding and that it was on the same day as the Leven event. Davie said, 'It's OK, Alfie, I know where your priorities lie!'

In November 1971, wee Bud and I fell foul of the manager when we turned up late for training one Thursday morning – but we had a perfectly good excuse. 'Sorry we're late, Jock, but we were nearly killed!' We had decided that after training on the Wednesday we would drive up to Aberdeen and watch their cup tie against Juventus at Pittodrie. It seemed like a good idea at the time but after the game – which we enjoyed – we were travelling down the road when the car decided it needed a rest. It packed in, right in the middle of the road, and left us vulnerable to the night-time traffic. We had to get out and wait for the breakdown truck to arrive, which took many, many hours. Maybe I'm being a wee bit dramatic when I say we could've been killed, but if we hadn't hammed it up then big Jock would've killed us instead! We were still in the clothes we had been wearing at the game and the fact we looked slightly ruffled made the big man feel sorry for us – I think.

We were always getting requests from outside agencies to make appearances at the opening of this or that. Obviously we couldn't be everywhere, but one invitation which was accepted gleefully each year was the request for Rangers to appear on the BBC's popular *Quizball* show. Two teams of four would attempt to work their way through a myriad of rounds in order to reach the grand final, and it was treated with great respect back in the day. But this season, a couple of us were invited on to a BBC Scotland programme called *The Generation Gap*.

It was recorded at the studios in Queen Margaret Drive and the Rangers 'Present' team was myself, Derek Johnstone and a well-known Rangers comedian. We were up against the great George Young, that colossus of a Rangers and Scotland defender, and his team, and naturally the winners were, well, not us. But it was great fun going into the studio and seeing how everything worked behind the scenes. We were given a guided tour and had a fantastic day.

There was one more duty to perform and it was one which every single player in the squad enjoyed – and that was a night at the annual Rangers Rally. This one was the 23rd and was held at Green's Playhouse, which later became the Apollo concert venue in Glasgow city centre. There was an early disappointment for the 3,000 supporters in attendance when the great comedian Lex McLean was forced to call off on doctor's orders. It was a last-minute decision but the Rev. James Currie, that well known Rangers supporter, stood in for Lex and he was brilliant. He had us all in stitches with some gags that even Lex would have been proud of. Most of the players were there along with the management team and members of the board. The Rangers Rally was always guaranteed to be a great night.

5

Striking Gold in the Camp Nou

POPULAR TELEVISION show *The A-Team* was still some years away when I arrived home from Barcelona, but I still managed a pretty good impersonation of bejewelled main man B.A. Baracus. When my mum returned home from the shops I was sitting on the couch with this huge, shiny medal round my neck. She took one look at me, I smiled and she gave me the biggest hug. It was magical. While I was waiting on her coming in I was just staring into space, reliving the last couple of days. The final whistle sounding; the fans coming on the park; being presented with the cup. I had left my teenage years behind just a few weeks before and the enormity of this little piece of gold hadn't quite sunk in yet. But the feeling was wonderful. I had flown out to Spain the week before just counting my blessings that I was part of a fantastic group of guys. We had come through quite a bit together to reach Barcelona and while we undoubtedly had a talented squad of players, one of the most successful ingredients of that cup run was our togetherness. We had a great camaraderie going on at Ibrox and I'm still convinced that helped pull us through on the occasions when the going got tough, and boy had the going got tough on more than a few occasions.

The French side Rennes were a dour, physical opponent and tough to shake off over the two legs, but we had matched them over the 180 minutes and narrowly came out on top in the first round. The second round paired us with Sporting Lisbon, one of Portugal's best, and a club that came with a decent overall pedigree. The memories of that tie – particularly the second leg – will live with me for ever, as will the four games against Torino and Bayern Munich, even though I didn't play a moment in any of them. But the campaign as a whole was the stuff of dreams, and I was proud to play the part I did.

That season hadn't been the best for the team, as we finished third in the league and exited the Scottish Cup after a semi-final replay defeat to Hibs. In the League Cup we failed to escape from our section due to home and away defeats to Celtic, even though the first group game – technically Celtic's home match – was played at Ibrox. That was a real low point for the players, and an opportunity lost.

So, we qualified for the European Cup Winners' Cup via the back door, but who cares? Celtic had won both the league and Scottish Cup, and we were in the draw thanks to being runners-up in the Scottish Cup Final.

Apart from the League Cup triumph from the season previous, it hadn't been the best time to be a Rangers player or supporter. I know I'll harp on about being convinced that we would eventually get out of the doldrums, and the pleasure of being part of such a fantastic group of players, but the stats didn't lie. We weren't successful and no one felt that more than us. There was a lot of pride within that group of players and it hurt so much to know that we weren't the dominant force in Scotland.

At the start of our European campaign, no one had mapped out the route to Barcelona. It wasn't quite a 'who are we playing next' but more of a boring one-game-at-a-time mantra. The Bayern Munich semi-final was when it began to get very interesting. On one hand, we were a single tie away from a European final, but on the other it was Bayern Munich, one of the best sides on the continent. Still, as I said, we were a confident bunch.

Our league campaign had stuttered to a halt on 1 May, when we beat Ayr United 4-2 at home. That meant we finished third, and the next time many of those fans saw us in action would be in Barcelona. Maybe we deserved it due to a string of unimpressive results, but that night's crowd of 4,000 was hardly a ringing endorsement ahead of a European final.

Still, we had two games to play before the final, and the management team had carefully selected challenge matches at Inverness and St Mirren to act as our final preparations. The first was a testimonial for three long-serving Highland League players. The Rangers team which finished at Grant Street that night was almost the same as the one which started the game in Barcelona. Willie Waddell's plan was formulating in his head. John Greig played the last 13 minutes, replacing Andy

Penman. Derek Parlane also started. Apparently Greigy, who was carrying an ankle injury, had asked the Deedle if he could play the full 90 – a request which was turned down flat, as the ground was considered too firm.

A few nights later, a shadow team took on St Mirren at Love Street in the final preparation match, in the guise of the Paisley Charity Cup. Greigy was again on the bench, but after a second-half cameo, he gave out the news that every Rangers supporter wanted to hear – he would be fit for the final.

Willie Waddell had jetted out to Russia to watch Moscow Dynamo in action against Kairat, and his great friend Willie Thornton was in charge of the team. There were a few of us playing that night who were hoping to take an 11th-hour route into the final line-up, not least myself, Andy Penman, Derek Parlane and Graham Fyfe, but only one would make it eight days later. It was like a sing-off in a live talent show and I know that I was busting a gut to get the nod, while I'm sure the other lads were doing the same.

St Mirren manager Tommy Bryceland later revealed that he had been asked by Mr Thornton to treat the game like a competitive fixture, and I can confirm that he complied as Saints made it tough for us on the night.

At the time, Colin Jackson was having round-the-clock treatment on a leg injury while wee Tommy McLean was struggling with a throat infection. Bomber would ultimately lose his fitness battle which meant there was definitely a team place up for grabs.

A crowd of 8,000 turned out for the game in Paisley and for the great many Rangers fans in attendance, it was another opportunity to wave cheerio to the players embarking on the journey to Spain. I put us ahead in the first half, but Saints scored twice to take a shock lead. Andy Penman had missed a first-half penalty but scored another in stoppage time to draw us level. Wee Bud replaced Steiny at the break and started to create chance after chance. Greigy then replaced Derek Parlane, and moments later I lobbed the keeper to put us 4-2 up. Late on I completed my hat-trick by bulleting home a header from a Penman cross.

After the game Mr Thornton told us we had all given ourselves a chance of being involved in Barcelona, but did go a step further when asked by a newspaper reporter outside Love Street what he thought of my first Rangers hat-trick. He said, 'Alfie might just have shot himself into contention for a place in the final.' Over the next few days I couldn't get those words out of my mind. I played them over and over again in my head – and always in Mr Thornton's laid-back tone!

While we were playing just a few miles along the M8 from Ibrox, it emerged that the gaffer was enduring countless hurdles in his efforts to watch Moscow Dynamo. With his hotel next door to the Kremlin, he was convinced someone was spying on him. There was supposed to be a ticket for the game left at the hotel reception, but it was a voucher, and he was told that it entitled him to queue up to BUY a ticket.

It was a strange feeling for the players back home. Our domestic season was over, which would normally have been the cue for us all to go our separate ways to beaches – or golf courses – the length and breadth of Europe. Sure, we were going to Europe, but not on holiday. We headed our separate ways, home for a few days before meeting up again five days later to head to Barcelona. It was the start of our great adventure: like a mini pre-season, but with a pot of gold at the end of the rainbow. A coach took us to Glasgow Airport and when it was time to board our flight we were joined by a great many well-wishers. They gave us a fantastic send-off and we vowed to do our best to bring home the trophy.

Once again, our management team had done their homework. When we arrived in Barcelona, and the coach took us to our hotel, it was clear why Willie Waddell had chosen the one he had. It was well away from the hustle and bustle of the town centre, a mile or so up a steep hill in the quiet suburb of Castelldefels. Contrast that with Dynamo, who were booked into a hotel right on the beach. The day they arrived it was a public holiday in Barcelona and I reckon half the population of the city was in the perimeter of the Russians' hotel! That's when you realise just how important it is to recce a location in advance. I remember the Russian coach, the great Lev Yashin, bemoaning the drinking, shouting, car horns and loud music from nearby discotheques as his players tried to rest.

We were told that the time leading up to the big game would include a mixture of light training, time for ourselves and rest. Apart from one 'team-bonding' session, we would be monitored at all times. It was at that moment I wished we had been monitored at ALL times. One of the guys had the fantastic idea of going to the go-karts. I must say here and now that I have very little recollection of this event but was told about it by Sandy Jardine a couple of years before he passed away. We were sitting chatting before a function one night and he said to me, 'Remember that time you nearly killed yourself, Alfie – two days before the European Cup Winners' Cup Final in Barcelona?' I looked at him blankly, and he told me that we had all gone to the go-karts where, at one point, I had taken a corner so fast that the kart flipped over several times. He said to me, 'Michael Schumacher couldn't have kept up with you!' The race was stopped at once and there was total shock among the players. Everyone apparently thought I was a goner. An uneasy calm descended over the track. My team-mates jumped out of their karts, some acting as marshals to stop others from ploughing into the back of us, while others became 24-hour medics. I was slowly helped from my vehicle and as I emerged, Sandy was staring at me and he said I just shook my head and gave a big smile. The boys started cheering and immediately knocked the karting on the head. There was a team meeting and everyone agreed not to say anything about it back at the hotel. It was a huge secret – until now. The incredible thing is that I suffered absolutely no ill effects – to my knowledge – and after a good night's sleep, I was right as rain.

The preparations continued, and the next big announcement would be the one we had all been waiting for. Plenty of folk had predicted that the team would be along similar lines to the

11 who had disposed of Bayern in the semis, with John Greig replacing Bomber, and Derek Parlane retaining his place. And that would've been fair comment, but I always hoped I would be involved, especially as I still had those Willie Thornton words ringing in my ears. I had big-game experience and looked upon myself as a big-game player, also mature, something that different Rangers managers had agreed with. I'd played my part in the 1970 League Cup Final, I would have a pivotal role in the 1973 Scottish Cup Final, and would play in 16 Old Firm matches. That season I had played against Rennes and then had an important hand in getting us through against Sporting Lisbon. In fact, I might even look back at that night in Lisbon and see it as my rehearsal for the final. We were 3-2 up after the first leg at Ibrox, and while I didn't get my name on the scoresheet against the Portuguese, I did have a hand in a couple of the goals in our 4-3 defeat. Just 60 seconds after we had gone a goal down, I tore through the Sporting defence to set up Steiny for our equaliser. And just after the break, while trailing 2-1, my flighted free kick allowed wee Doddie to knock the ball into the path of Steiny, who did the rest.

Both Waddell and Wallace knew exactly what I could bring to the table. I was a hungry player, full of aggression, and would not stop fighting for the Rangers cause. It was ingrained in me, which I felt was the quality Rangers were looking for in Barcelona. At least I hoped it was. I liked to think that I would roll my sleeves up and leave it all on the park, just like I had done so many times. I knew that if given the chance, and we won, I would've earned that medal. I also knew that if everything went according to plan, I could look at that medal in the future and say, 'That's what comes from hard work.'

Supporters were beginning to converge on Barcelona from all corners of the globe, but mostly from back home. The Alfie Conn Loyal, from Dalkeith, was also en route, and the members were paying around £40 for three days' full board in the Catalan city. Doesn't sound like a lot now, but back in '72 it was a fortune. Our fans were going all out to see the final and we knew that. We were all Rangers fans and whoever would be in the starting 11 was determined to give it everything they had for the club and our brilliant supporters.

The day before the match I was hanging around outside the hotel while the guys were loading the hampers up with the kit. One of the lads was counting out the shin guards. 'One for each of the players, but three for big Derek!' 'Why is that?' I asked. 'If the big man plays against Moscow Dynamo he will wear six shin guards. Two at the front of each leg and one at the back.' I quizzed DJ about this and he said that ever since Ronnie McKinnon had broken his leg against Sporting Lisbon, this had been his tactic against the continentals. 'I'm taking no chances,' he said. In the games against Torino and Bayern he had doubled up the pads at the front and slipped one down the back of each stocking to protect against kicks from behind. The big man wasn't daft. He said he could still run OK. While this was going on he was still wearing just a single pair in the Scottish games. I recall mentioning this to DJ in front of John

Greig, who quipped, 'He'd need cricket pads if he was playing against me!'

Willie Waddell named the team the day before the game, and I was of the mind that if I wasn't in then I could probably put that down to my general form that season, which had been erratic. A spell in the reserves had no doubt been the best thing to happen to me, but now was the big moment.

Here we go. 'Number eight – Alfie Conn.' That was all I could hear, and I was elated. You really could've knocked me down with a feather, but once the news had sunk in, that was when I started preparing in earnest for the biggest day of my life. I spoke to my dad that night and he told me he had been watching the news and they had reported that Andy Penman would be playing and not me. It was a shame for Andy, but I was delighted.

All 11 starters were desperate to write their names into the history of this great club. 'The first Rangers side to win a European trophy!' The prize doesn't come any greater, or the stakes higher. But we had been given this opportunity to become legends of Rangers, and we were going to give it everything we could. The other side of the coin is the sacrifice the supporters make to be in a venue like the Camp Nou for the biggest date in the club's history. You're busy preparing for the final itself, but you see so many supporters milling around, wearing their sombreros and having a drink, and you wonder just what the back story is. Have they been saving up for ages to get to Barcelona? Have they taken time off their work that they didn't have and been dismissed in the process? Rangers fans are among the most loyal around, and you just knew there had to be many stories of real sacrifice, and that was also a driving factor for us.

That starting 11 had a really good mix of youth and experience, and an abundance of enthusiasm. John Greig, Willie Johnston, Davie Smith and Sandy Jardine had played in our last European final, in Nuremberg, so we had guys who had been over the course, and all four were never shy with a word or two of encouragement.

Willie Waddell eventually got in to see Moscow Dynamo play Kairat in a Russian league match, and his thoroughly prepared dossier was also of great help to us. He was the kind of man who left no stone unturned and we were the recipients of his fantastic groundwork.

When we turned up at the Camp Nou on the night of the game the atmosphere was unbelievable. The number of fans who greeted us as we jumped off the bus on our way into the ground was phenomenal. It was like a home match. We had so many good luck messages ringing in our ears as we walked along a corridor and into the dressing room. Willie Waddell and Jock Wallace appeared to be consumed with going around the players and making sure we were all OK, attempting to occupy our thoughts in the empty moments leading up to kick-off. I was nervous, no doubt about that, but I was also really looking forward to getting out there and getting started. The boss had a little talk with us before we went out for a walk on the pitch.

It was such an imposing stadium, and while Barcelona were a successful enough side at that time, they weren't the perennial winners they would eventually become. For instance, they won La Liga in 1960, but didn't win it again until the mid-1970s. One title in the '70s, one in the '80s, you get my drift.

By the time we got back inside and changed into our strips, there was time for just one more little pep talk, while big Jock went round everyone individually and gave them a hug and a back slap. It was time. We were ready, and the next 90 minutes would determine our European fate.

The match itself passed in a blur; 35,000 inside the ground roaring us on and to find ourselves 3-0 up just minutes into the second half was the stuff of dreams. But when they pulled one back with half an hour still to play, we realised we had to up our game again. Big Peter then made a couple of good saves, and Sandy cleared one off the line. And with 87 on the clock, they grabbed a second. When the Russians got the ball and rushed back to the centre spot, it was squeaky bum time. They were going for it, but we held on to record a famous victory and boy did we party that night. It was obviously a kick in the teeth that the cup was presented to us in some dimly lit back room, because we deserved better than that. I wasn't privy to everything that had gone on beforehand but some real horror stories had started to emerge and my first hope was that all our supporters were safe from harm.

The consequences of the aftermath of that game were that we were banned from competing in Europe the following season and that was a major blow to the players. We were gutted about that. Imagine not being able to defend a major European trophy. Again, Willie Waddell worked his socks off in trying to persuade UEFA to lift the ban, but all they did was to reduce our two-year sentence by 12 months.

At least a couple of us still managed to get 'abroad' that summer as after our win in Barcelona wee Bud and I popped into Clachan Travel, near Jim Forrest's pub on Paisley Road West, to book a break in Jersey for Sue and I, and Bud and his wife Margaret. And what a time we had.

As an aside, I won't divulge how much our bonus was for winning the European Cup Winners' Cup but let's just say it was enough to buy me a brand new Cortina GT, and I was delighted with my purchase.

We were all resigned to missing out on the thrill of European competition, until someone came up with the idea of a European Super Cup, competed for by the reigning champions of Europe's two major knockout competitions. Ajax were the holders of the European Cup and our interest was piqued at the thought of playing them home and away. UEFA agreed it was a worthwhile idea but decided that because we were banned from all European competitions for a year, they couldn't sanction it. They said they would reconsider the idea in 12 months.

A couple of months later, someone at Rangers decided to resurrect the idea as part of our centenary celebrations of 1973 and contacted the Dutch masters. Thankfully Ajax agreed and what followed was two fascinating and highly entertaining games, enjoyed by players and supporters alike. It was a genuine pleasure to play against what I would term the perfect football team. Ajax were simply outstanding and at times it was difficult to remember that you were actually playing against these footballing geniuses, and not just there to admire them.

Cruyff, Rep, Krol, Neeskens, the Muhren brothers, Haan, etc. The list of household names seemed endless, and more than 57,000 fans were at Ibrox for the first leg. I played in that game but was forced off just after half-time with a hamstring injury. Still, it was a great pleasure and I thoroughly enjoyed the occasion. It's probably one of the only times I didn't mind being substituted as I could admire their play from the bench.

I think Derek Johnstone summed them up perfectly when he said, 'They have the individual personalities but still combine brilliantly as a team.' Davie Smith was equally impressed after the game at Ibrox and he was waxing lyrical in the dressing room about the visitors' performance. And when a classy footballer like him spoke in reverential terms then you took notice. It was also Tom Forsyth's first game at European level and we all agreed when big Tam said it had been such a privilege to play against Ajax. It's fair to say most of the lads were in awe of them.

They were a wonderful side and I think we all learned from the two games. I know I did. They hardly wasted a pass and did everything with the greatest of ease.

We lost the first leg 3-1 at Ibrox, with Rep, Cruyff and Haan on the scoresheet, and Doddie getting our goal. The second leg took place eight days later in the Olympic Stadium in Amsterdam and I was gutted to miss out through injury. But it was still a privilege to be there, and while Ajax were again in great form, we also played very well and pushed them all the way. This time it ended 3-2 in favour of the Dutch, but twice we were in front and it took a goal from the great Johan Cruyff to seal victory.

The matches also gave me an opportunity to renew an old friendship with someone I had gotten to know a couple of years earlier. Johan Neeskens was a superbly gifted player who I had first come across when Scotland played the Netherlands in a European Youth Cup tie at Ibrox. We lost 1-0, with Johnny Rep coming on as a sub to score the game's only goal, but I bonded with Johan after that game and when he was over for the first leg of Rangers v Ajax we had a good natter. He told me he was very impressed with Ibrox and he thought the crowd was fantastic, but I never did quite get round to enticing him to come play for Rangers.

When we went to the Netherlands for the second leg we hooked up again and this time I invited him over to Scotland for a holiday. He accepted and came over for a week that summer. We had a brilliant time and I enjoyed showing him all the famous sights in Scotland, and he reciprocated by inviting me over to the Netherlands for a break.

We got on well and I thought a lot of him as a player. He admitted he was the strong man of that Ajax side but he could also play a bit. He was very skilful, like the rest of the team. He was 17 when he joined Ajax and he raved about the path they had to the first team and what was expected of them. It was an education for me too. Unfortunately, I didn't get to play against him in those matches because he missed the first one due to injury, and I missed the second for the same reason.

I had been touch and go, fitness wise, for the game in Amsterdam, but Jock Wallace thought it more important that I was ready to face Morton at Cappielow a few days later – although I wish he hadn't bothered. In all my time playing in Scotland, that was probably the worst game I'd played in terms of the ferocity of the challenges we faced. We were simply kicked off the park by a group of thugs.

I felt that over the two matches against Ajax, we had not only been representing Rangers, but also Scotland, and as a proud Scotsman you want to do your best. We came up just short against the Dutch but at least we were allowed to play football. In Greenock, the two points were all important as we battled with Celtic and Hibs for the title. We were top of the league and that day Celtic lost to Airdrie, while Dundee held the Easter Road side to a draw. Now we had to beat Morton, but it was always hard to get a win doon the water. It's also easier if you have your health!

I was at centre-forward in place of Derek Parlane and we scored early on. Twenty minutes later I picked up a ball out wide (yes, I was a wandering centre-forward) from John Greig, headed for the byline and I just knew that the defender was going to clatter me, but I managed to get my cross in and Cutty

Young swept it home for our second. Once our physio had filled in the stud holes on my leg with polyfilla, the game was restarted and Alex MacDonald was the victim of a shocking challenge. Tam Forsyth was then targeted and it was starting to get out of hand. Straight red cards would've sorted out the nonsense but in those days you had some referees who were reluctant to brandish even a yellow.

Minutes after the bad challenge on me, I set up Tommy McLean and his shot hit the bar, but I copped another set of studs. With just shy of half an hour on the clock, another Morton player left his mark and I knew my day was over. The manager was going ballistic on the sidelines and ordered a stretcher for me, but there was no way I was giving that shower the pleasure of seeing me carried off, so I struggled back to our dugout. Graham Fyfe replaced me and as I neared big Jock, he came over and gave me a bear hug. He patted me on the head and said, 'That's my boy.' We won the game to maintain our challenge but there were more than a few bruised bones as our coach rolled out of Dodge City that night.

6

Tam's Scottish Cup Thunderbolt

I'VE ALWAYS maintained that winning the European Cup Winners' Cup was the highlight of my career, and that will never change, but in terms of that season, and the bigger picture, it was probably one of my lowest points in the game. It was my fourth season at Rangers and should've been a period when I was kicking on and becoming a first-team regular, but nothing could've been further from the truth. I did play 34 games, and one could be forgiven for thinking it was quite an accomplishment to make that number of first-team appearances for a club the size of Rangers. It was, but it wasn't. We played 56 competitive matches in 1971/72. Only Peter McCloy played in every single one – a fantastic achievement. But I missed more than 20, and that wasn't down to injury, but to a loss of form or, to be more precise, because I was confused and conflicted. Don't get me wrong, when I was given the nod to play in Barcelona I didn't let anyone down – but by then I had worked out what my role was. I know that sounds daft, but it's completely true.

Before the start of the 1972/73 season, I gave an interview to a Scottish newspaper and suggested that supporters would see a 'new Alfie Conn this season'. I know, typical tabloid fare, but there was more than an element of truth to it. The previous season, I probably played a lot of games on the back of some decent performances in 1970/71. Because I really struggled, and it didn't take Willie Waddell and Jock Wallace long to realise that. I'm sure the Deedle kept faith with me because he knew I was desperate to do well for the team – and he knew I was capable. So did I, but despite trying everything, it just wouldn't happen.

I then heard the words no player likes to hear, 'You'll be in the reserves this Saturday!' But I couldn't grumble – they had been more than fair with me, and patient. And instead of simply banishing me to the second team, big Jock took me aside and spent a good deal of time with me. He told me to make good use of my spell in the reserves and NOT to use it – like some did – by going through the motions. He advised me to try slowing my game down, and then speeding it up. He told me to play defensively, to play in the middle, to play a more attacking, forceful game, coming from behind as often as possible on the lookout for scoring chances.

So, during each reserve match, and in practice matches, I got my head down and worked hard at my game. I tried all the different styles and methods suggested by the gaffer, and I knew that Jock was with me every step of the way. He helped me out as much as possible with advice, and when you knew he was taking such a keen and personal interest in you then you certainly didn't want to let him down. The other side of the coin was that I realised I must be worth saving if the big man was investing so much time in me.

So what was this big crisis I was suffering? It was all about my role in the team; my style of play, to be more precise. I had lost my way and didn't know what suited me best any more. Was it going forward all the time, looking for a shot at goal? Or playing behind the midfield, or slowing my game down much more, or playing up front? I didn't know, and that's where Jock was worth his weight in gold. He was a master in situations like that, because he noticed things that others might have missed. But the moment I dropped into the reserves I took the opportunity to do a bit of soul-searching. I took his advice; I wasn't going to mope around and decided to apply myself fully. To be honest, that was my way, so it wasn't a huge culture shift. I started to train even harder than before. If I'm being honest I was never the best of trainers, although with big Jock in command, training had become much more enjoyable. Still, I knew within myself that I could give far more. And the result? I soon learned that my best style of play was going upfield, as far as possible when the occasion demanded, almost like an extra forward. In the thick of the action – which I thoroughly enjoyed – and anything less on my part would've been a cop-out.

Playing behind the midfield, for instance, just didn't suit me. I wasn't in the game often enough. It was the same when I tried to operate as an orthodox midfield man. Again, I didn't feel involved enough. But the new role really suited me. It allowed me to tackle, pass the ball, come through for shots, defend, do anything in fact which would help the team. I suppose it was something like a roving commission in the middle of the park, and I loved the freedom it offered.

In football back then, there was a natural way for your career to go. You were scouted from any number of crack juvenile clubs and if lucky enough you signed an S – schoolboy – Form for a professional club. I was so fortunate to sign for Rangers and I had my time in the reserves. I made my European debut at 16 and was being labelled 'boy wonder'. I was only human and so it is difficult to ignore talk like that. Anyway, after playing loads of games for the first team I should have been moving my career forward and, after claiming a jersey in the first team, perhaps even looking to stake a claim for a Scotland place. But it was one step forward and two back, so I had found myself in the reserves and pretty far out of the first-team picture. Yes, it was soul-destroying, and perhaps even embarrassing, although I wasn't the first to suffer such ignominy. One of Jock's buzzwords was 'character', and that's what was required here. Thankfully I was made of pretty good stuff and once I chased the initial bout of 'woe is me' from my head I knuckled down and set about sorting out my problems, many of which were mental. That was confirmed when I finally got the form back and the happiness I felt was palpable. There really was nothing quite like playing for the first team.

I was one of these guys who would come off the park and assess whether or not I had contributed in a positive way that afternoon, whether it be with an assist, a goal or even by linking play and creating chances. In early November, we travelled to Dens Park on league duty, and it was a ground I liked. It was a tousy affair, as usual, and with just 20 minutes remaining, and trailing 1-0, we were doing everything we could to grab at least a draw. Picking up the ball in midfield, I dribbled past four defenders before smashing it into the top corner. I was delighted with the goal, and it got us a point. Quite astonishingly, in the days that followed it was being hailed as the greatest goal ever seen at Dens Park.

Saturday, 6 January 1973 was another afternoon I enjoyed tremendously. We were three games into an incredible run of 16 successive league wins when we played Celtic at Ibrox. We had played them just once so far that season, in the league at Celtic Park, and lost 3-1, so revenge, as well as maintaining our good run, was foremost in our minds. Some 72,000 crammed into Ibrox and the majority were roaring us on. We knew that a good result would mean we could have a real go at the title. Celtic, Hibs and ourselves were the main contenders as 1973 got under way.

The police had recommended a noon start, in a bid to lessen any potential trouble, but Rangers vetoed that and the game kicked off at 3pm. There was no Jock Stein in the Celtic dugout as he was in hospital following a heart scare just after Christmas, and it was the first time our new Centenary Stand had been used.

We went ahead after McCluskey hauled wee Doddie to the ground and the referee pointed to the spot. Derek Parlane scored from a rebound – after Evan Williams had saved his initial kick – and that gave us the boost we required. But Celtic equalised when a Dixie Deans shot took a crazy deflection off Davie Smith and left Peter McCloy stranded. We felt a grave sense of injustice as we had easily been the better team, but it was time to roll up the sleeves and show some character. Right up until the death it was a tousy contest but when I noticed Cutty Young make for the byline, I knew exactly what was coming. I broke my neck trying to get into the box and rose to power a header past Williams. The feeling was immense. The moment the ball hit the back of the net I ran straight over to our supporters to celebrate with them – but little did I know that my 'over-the-top' celebrations would have a negative impact on Derek Parlane.

The win helped us leapfrog Celtic into second place, one point behind Hibs, although Celtic had a couple of games in hand. The game was also notable because our supporters stayed behind long after the final whistle to sing our praises – and we could hear them from the bath!

Fast forward three months and we were playing Ayr United in the Scottish Cup semi-final at Hampden. We won 2-0 to set up an Old Firm showdown the following month, and Derek scored both goals. After his second he ran over to the fans to take their acclaim – and he was booked for ungentlemanly conduct. It was a complete nonsense. He wasn't antagonising the opposition support so he was furious, and no wonder. After the game it was explained to us that the football authorities had introduced a new rule – ungentlemanly conduct – after the way I had celebrated the winner against Celtic on 6 January. Derek had become the first victim of 'Alfie's Law', as I jokingly referred to it, although it was no more than a killjoy rule designed to suck the life out of the game by banning players for celebrating with their own fans.

What the authorities couldn't do, though, was stop us being Gilbert O'Sullivan fans. Let me explain. Back in the day, Alex MacDonald and I were secret fans of the Irish singer. I enjoyed his records in the early '70s but wee Doddie took it a step further – he knew the words to all the hits and would sing them at Ibrox!

I remember my cousin Tony getting in touch to say that his band were supporting Gilbert at a gig in Manchester and he asked if Sue and I would like to go. Sue was really keen, but there was a problem. I couldn't go to see Gilbert O'Sullivan and not tell wee Doddie, as I knew he'd be furious at missing out. I called Tony and he said he could get me four tickets and backstage passes, so off we went down to the gig and had a great time. After the concert, Tony took us backstage and we met Gilbert. He was a nice guy and Doddie was in his element. He and his wife, Christine, had a great time. Later that night we went to a swanky Manchester city centre bar for a few drinks. Tony was telling us he'd known Gilbert for a few years, and when the singer had been struggling he had helped him out by giving him gigs at the Empire Ballroom in London. When Gilbert hit the big time he'd repaid Tony by hiring his band to accompany him at his concerts.

We had a ball and journeyed back to Glasgow the following day on a high, with all the lads keen to hear how the gig had gone. While we were chatting, the Ibrox commissionaire said, 'Alfie, there's a call for you. If you'd like to follow me.' The lads were shouting, 'Gilbert wants you to do backing vocals on his next song!' It was Tony and he said, 'I meant to say we're up in Glasgow for a concert next week, if you guys would like to come again.' I thanked Tony and said we would, and then I was thinking, 'He could've saved us a 400-mile round trip if he'd told me sooner!' But the four of us went to the concert in Glasgow and this time we were invited back to Gilbert's hotel. We had a great night and he remembered us from the Manchester gig. We were now confirmed Gilbert groupies and he gave Sue and Christine autographed copies of his new album as well as a book he had just brought out. By all accounts Tony said he hadn't changed a bit since hitting the charts, which was music to my ears. Sadly, it didn't stop Doddie singing his songs at training!

The next time Tony invited Sue and I to a gig was a few years later when we were living in London and I was playing for Spurs. He called and said, 'You'll never guess who my band and I are supporting at the Royal Albert Hall?' I had a couple of guesses before he said, 'Frank Sinatra!' I was gobsmacked. 'I suppose you won't be able to get us tickets for a massive gig like that?' I asked, almost in defiance.

'Of course I will,' he laughed.

On the day of the gig, a Saturday, Sue went shopping for a new dress while I headed for Filbert Street, home of Leicester City. It was a tough, tousy game and while going for a high ball I ran straight into my team-mate, Steve Perryman. The moment I hit the ground I was out cold. Steve had also taken a knock but I definitely came off worse as his head caught me just above my left eye. I received attention on the field before being stretchered off. The doctor continued to assess me in the medical room but it was off to hospital for me – and I still have the scar to this day. I was kept in hospital for a couple of hours before being released with concussion and told not to go anywhere with bright lights for the rest of the night! When I got home Sue was still sitting there in her lovely new dress but sadly Frank would have to go on stage that night without us.

But I'm getting ahead of myself.

Victory over Celtic in the new year game handed us a terrific platform to get our season back on track. We were second, albeit having played three games more than Celtic, so the only thing we could do to help ourselves – and keep the pressure on our rivals – was to keep on winning. And that's exactly what we did. Falkirk, Kilmarnock and Morton were dismissed as we made it five wins out of five in January. We had only two league games in February, which we won, and also progressed to the quarter-finals of the Scottish Cup by seeing off Dundee United and top-of-the-table Hibs.

With Dad at Turnhouse Airport, Edinburgh after he'd been away playing for Hearts. We're the dad and son second from left – although I'm sure you recognised the trademark frown!

Dad and his cannonball shot.

The Terrible Trio – Conn, Bauld and Wardhaugh

Fashion statement: not long after I'd signed for Rangers

In action for the Gers

Taking a breather…

Off to see Gilbert O'Sullivan – with Doddie, his wife, Christine, and Sue

Relaxing with Doddie in France before the European Cup Winners' Cup tie against Rennes

Flying high: en route to the continent

Career highlight: celebrating with the lads and the Cup Winners' Cup

With my Old English Sheepdog Blue

At the Rangers Rally with Doddie and DJ

Mum and Dad got me the best ever cake for my 21st

My very own mini Ibrox proved the icing on the cake at my landmark birthday

That goal! Scoring in the 1973 Scottish Cup Final was a huge thrill

Celebrating our Scottish Cup success

Sue and I after our engagement

Match of the Day: Our wedding in the capital

Sue looking radiant on our wedding day

March was a complete wash-out for me personally. I had suffered another injury and there was talk that I might miss the second part of the season, but I was determined that wouldn't happen. I'd picked up a knock in a league game at the end of January, was on the bench for the Scottish Cup tie against Hibs the following month and then missed the whole of March. But the lads racked up five terrific victories in the league that month to stay in contention for the big prize. We had also set up the Scottish Cup semi with Ayr United after beating Airdrie. And here was I, sitting at home wondering if I was going to have a part to play in this exciting end to the campaign. Well, the answer was an emphatic YES. It was my 21st birthday the day before the semi against Ayr, but the perfect present was a place on the bench for the Hampden match. I was delighted to be back.

One of the reserve games I played in the run-up to regaining my fitness was against Hearts at Ibrox. Dad was there watching, but for once he was forced to sit on the fence. I was a sub for Rangers, and wearing the number 12 jersey, while the sub for Hearts – and also wearing number 12 on his maroon shirt – was my brother Bobby. It was quite the family affair. To complete the coincidence, both of us got on, and that was the first time we had played against each other in a competitive match. Oh, and Rangers won 3-1.

Any game time was valuable and 48 hours after my actual 21st, we were due to play Hearts at Tynecastle. I was delighted to get on as a substitute and play my part in our 1-0 win, which set the tone for my birthday bash that evening in an Edinburgh hotel. After being injured for so long things were definitely looking up. I then played in our last four league matches, the first two of which we won. On 28 April, we travelled up to Pittodrie for a tough game against Aberdeen. I managed a goal, but the 2-2 draw seemed to have killed off our faint hopes of winning the title. True, we were neck-and-neck with Celtic, but their superior goal difference was always going to see them over the line. We beat East Fife 2-0 in our final league game, at Ibrox, and I scored again, but the bigger – and most important – picture was that the league was lost by a single point.

There was one game left to play – the Scottish Cup Final against Celtic at Hampden Park – and games didn't come much bigger. My aim was to make sure I was in the best possible shape for that one, and hope that manager Jock Wallace – who had taken over after our success in Barcelona – thought I was worthy of a place.

The cup final was due to take place seven days after our final league game, and as we were still trying to shake off the bitter disappointment of coming up just short as Celtic racked up their eighth successive title. They had lost out in the League Cup to Hibs, so our aim was to ensure that the honours would be evenly spread among the country's three form teams.

Our preparations for the final were impeccable, and Jock left nothing to chance. When he read out the team on the morning of the game at breakfast and I was given the number ten shirt I was delighted. This would be my first Scottish Cup Final, and I was determined to make the most of it. The build-up on the day was electric and the moment we walked out on to the Hampden pitch before the game we were greeted by a sight which I don't think I'll ever fully get my head around. There wasn't an inch of available standing room on the vast terraces. I had scanned the old ground before my foot had even brushed the turf and what greeted me was almost beyond comprehension: a mass of heads, bodies, all 122,000 of them. Packed together like sardines; half in blue, half in green. Both sets of fans bursting a lung to make themselves heard. The noise was completely off the scale and was easily the loudest I've ever heard at a game.

We lined up to meet Princess Alexandra, which was an honour, and with the formalities over it was down to business. Our supporters in the covered traditional Rangers end were in tremendous voice and there was a definite feeling that it would be our day. Celtic were pre-match favourites – but the tide was turning and I sensed that. Now we just had to make it happen.

It wasn't like the theatre, where the noise dies down the moment the performance begins. Bedlam reigned well into the game and after 45 pulsating minutes of frantic action, the scores were tied at one apiece. Kenny Dalglish had given Celtic the lead and Derek Parlane had equalised with a bullet header from an Alex MacDonald cross.

At half-time, big Jock told us he was happy enough with our performance and asked for more of the same in the second period. He noticed I had been struggling a wee bit towards the end of the first half, and asked how I was. I was able to answer his question just 17 seconds after the restart. Cutty Young picked up a George Connelly clearance and arrowed a long, searching ball from inside his own half in the general direction of Derek Parlane. The moment I realised Derek was getting a touch I was off and running. Pure instinct had taken over. Billy McNeill still had a good few yards on me but he was never catching this fleet-footed kid. I took a touch, the Celtic skipper attempted a last-ditch lunge, but it was too late. I had nicked it past him and was off into the sunset. Forty-five yards from goal, now 35. McNeill was slumped on the ground and could only look on in anguish as a despairing run from Jim Brogan, attempting to halt my progress by any means imaginable, was doomed to fail. All that stood between me and glory was composure – and goalkeeper Ally Hunter. But Hunter was just a fraction late in leaving his line and I had the run on him. One touch to leave McNeill trailing in my wake and another to slide in and hook it past Hunter. That was all it took. The composure was never usually a problem and on this occasion it didn't desert me. In real time the ball zipped into the net from 16 yards. In my mind's eye it took far longer, but the moment it left my right boot I knew it was a goal.

The strike came at the traditional Celtic end, but I wasn't interested in showboating. I wanted to celebrate with my mates – and that feeling was off the scale. It wouldn't be too much of a stretch to say it was the greatest feeling I'd ever encountered in football. Think about it. I was 21 and the official attendance for the final was 122,714. Sadly, we will never see crowds like that again.

After going 2-1 in front, George Connelly equalised with a penalty, and then on the hour came one of the most bizarre goals I've ever seen. Dead-ball expert Tommy McLean clipped in a free kick, which was headed on to a post by Derek Johnstone. The ball ran along the line and hit the other post before Tam Forsyth stood on it and it somehow rolled agonisingly over the line. It was Tam's first goal for Rangers – Jock's first trophy as manager – and my team-mate would admit later that he almost missed it. I can vouch for that; I was standing right behind him at the time. My heart was in my mouth so I'm not sure how Tam felt. Our supporters were able to celebrate a cup win AND the culmination of a wonderful 26-game unbeaten run, which had started the previous December.

The lead-up to my goal contribution that day would come back to haunt me a few years later but at that moment it helped us win the national trophy for the first time since 1966. It was also the last 100,000-plus crowd in Scotland. I recalled my old man telling me of the time he played in front of more than 130,000 at Hampden.

It was the 1956 cup final and Hearts beat Celtic – and the players celebrated with a nice fish tea in Edinburgh's West End Cafe. I loved listening to all his stories and had been mesmerised when hearing about the size of the crowd that afternoon, so to experience something similar was mind-blowing. But like my dad, I'd been able to shake off the nerves and perform to the best of my ability, and the goal I scored is something I will cherish for ever.

Oh, and Dad scored the clincher for Hearts on his big day at Hampden, which was one of the few similarities in our careers.

Just a couple of weeks after the cup final, Sue and I were due to fly out to Canada – courtesy of the Toronto Rangers Supporters' Club. I was loving life as a Ranger and this was one of the best perks of the job. The secretary had contacted me just after Christmas and told me of his club's plans for their summer celebration. A golf day and dinner dance would be the highlights, and he asked if I would be the guest of honour. I was delighted to accept, and Sue decided it would be far better than watching me play for Rangers in the pouring rain. I had to remind her that she'd only ever seen me play twice!

We were really excited ahead of the two-week trip and when it came to leaving the house I had my doubts that our suitcases would even fit into the taxi. Sue had packed for all eventualities. Maybe one of those eventualities should've covered not being allowed on the plane. We arrived at the airport in plenty of time, relaxed and looking forward to our first visit to Canada. We went straight to the check-in desk so we could then chill while awaiting the call for our flight. Chill?

Our flight tickets had been paid for in advance by the guys in Toronto, but we were told that even though we were booked on the flight, we wouldn't be able to travel. I don't profess to be Einstein but I didn't understand what was going on. The staff at Prestwick Airport said they had no notification that our return tickets had been paid, and until we could get confirmation we wouldn't be able to fly.

I eventually got through to my contact in Canada, despite it being the middle of the night there, and he confirmed that it had been paid. Fortunately he was able to give me a reference number and I handed it over. It seemed to take an eternity for the staff to process it as they explained that their computer didn't recognise the booking. They then suggested we go home and come back the following day and hopefully the computer would've recognised it by then. We were exasperated. I insisted we were flying that day and we were asked to take a seat. Probably ten minutes later – but it seemed a lot more – we were told that we were good to go and the staff member did that fake smile thing and said, 'Have a great trip!'

The flight was scheduled to leave in less than an hour so we had to get our skates on. From being relaxed on arrival at the airport we were now up to high doh, but the moment we got on the plane we were fine, and a couple of drinks later we had a laugh about our near miss. We had a brilliant time in Toronto. It's such a beautiful city and the supporters' club committee went all out to make sure our stay was just perfect. The golf day was so enjoyable, and a huge success, and the charity dinner raised lots of money for great causes. We were treated very well indeed and despite a dodgy start, the trip was a roaring success.

I had a couple of weeks at home before the slog of pre-season training began and another trip to Gullane. The aim was to get us in tune not for the season's curtain-raiser, the Drybrough

Cup, but another assault on the league and the European Cup Winners' Cup. I played a bit of golf in my time off. No, make that a lot of golf. In those days it wouldn't have been uncommon for me to play THREE rounds on the same day.

When we got back, it wasn't all hard work and sweat though as the players' pre-season head tennis tournament was in full swing. Now this was something that EVERY single player took seriously, so much kudos to those who emerged victorious after the week-long competition. But it all boiled down to the final on the Friday after training and as the crowd gathered round to cheer on the participants, a silence fell as Jock Wallace and Willie Thornton entered the arena. Not to worry, though, as they were merely there to add their encouragement. And so the final began: John Greig, Alex O'Hara and myself vs Doug Houston, Graham Fyfe and Sandy. Let battle commence.

Sandy and co. got off to a flying start, and looked easy winners, until Greigy typically rallied his men to a terrific fightback. Then, in a grandstand finish, Doug, Graham and Sandy clinched the title after extra time. It was all tense stuff but you would've paid money to listen to the 'encouragement' from the spectators – far less the action! And don't think for a moment that we were happy with the runners-up spot.

I didn't know it at the time, but my final season in light blue would be a disappointment. It started the way it would continue with an uninspiring draw at home to Ayr United in our opening league match, and kind of ended with me on the treatment table suffering from a serious cartilage injury. The bits in between, in hindsight, weren't much better. A win over Celtic, in the League Cup, and a couple of European ties were the standout moments.

Jock Wallace had won his first trophy as manager the season before, and that had led us to believe that the big man's appointment would bear regular silverware. And it would – but just not straight away. We were impatient, the supporters were impatient. We were Rangers, and we wanted to win things now. But while you could see the building blocks slowly falling into place, the 1973/74 season would do nothing to swell the contents of the trophy cabinet, and that was disappointing.

After the Ayr match, we lost three of our next five league games, which – although no one would ever admit it – effectively left us playing catch-up in the league. It was a real downer, especially as the three losses occurred at Ibrox. Was nothing sacred any more?

We finally hit a bit of form in mid-October and big Jock had us going along like a steam train. We racked up five wins and a draw in the league as well as home and away victories over Ankaragücü in the European Cup Winners' Cup. Both games against the Turks were an absolute nightmare to play in, though. I had never been to Turkey before flying over for the first leg in Ankara. The trip got off to a decent start as we were staying in a nice hotel and the staff were courteous and friendly. And then it was all downhill from there.

When we arrived at the Ankara 19 Mayis Stadium for the first leg, we didn't receive the friendliest of welcomes.

Apparently the stadium was named after the date on which a famous revolution began, although it might have been more appropriate to rename it after the date of our Euro battle! Before the action began, each player was presented with a lovely bouquet of flowers, roses, I think. Perhaps they should have thought of giving us Red Spider Lilies, better known as the death flower! We were kicked from pillar to post – and back again, and all the while the Polish referee struggled to control the violent Turks. We were subjected to a new low of gamesmanship and outrageous tackling, and when the ref had the cheek to book me for retaliation on one of the home players, I could only shrug my shoulders and laugh.

We were on top from the start and the Turkish players – along with the 45,000 home supporters – probably knew that it would take something they didn't possess for them to go through, so they took out their frustration mostly on my legs. There was barely 60 seconds on the clock when one of them went straight through me from behind. I collapsed in a heap out near the touchline and Jock and his coaching staff later admitted they thought my leg was broken. I had treatment from Tommy Craig for almost FIVE minutes but I was determined I was going back on. These thugs didn't scare me. And revenge wasn't just sweet, but almost instant. With 11 minutes on the clock I scored the opening goal of the game. Cutty Young skipped down the left and sent over an awkward bouncing cross, which I managed to clip into the net. When I celebrated, I made it clear to the Turks that I wouldn't be intimidated by them. That was a sweet moment, and maybe daft.

With an hour of the game played, I had the ball in the net again, but it was ruled out for offside. Not to worry, though, as Tommy McLean scored our second just moments later and we were on easy street – but only as far as qualification for the second round was concerned. The home side stepped up their thuggish antics and I was forced to show off my hurdling skills as one defender after another came flying in.

We were never so relieved to hear a final whistle blow and the first thing I did was to acknowledge the small pocket of Rangers fans – around 25 had followed us to Ankara – over on the far side. They were fantastic and along with the British Embassy staff, they made as much noise as they could.

While in Ankara, I believe our directors and members of the press were entertained at the embassy building, which I'm sure was nice, but personally I couldn't wait to get home. The ambassador was apparently a former pupil of Hillhead High School, in Glasgow, and a big Rangers fan. As we were leaving the stadium that night we were all presented with a Turkish rug. I would have much preferred them to keep their rugs in exchange for not kicking us as much.

The following morning we were up early and preparing for the five-hour drive to Istanbul, before catching our flight from the city's main airport. It was far from the most luxurious – and also one of the hottest in the world – so the club decided we should take a bus tour of Istanbul to save us hanging around the airport. It was enjoyable and we were shown parts of the old wall which used to surround the city, before going to the Blue Mosque – which we thought had been renamed just for us! It is a spectacular building and the hallowed shrine of all Muslims, who face Mecca when they pray there. One tradition which we all had to adhere to was taking our shoes off before we went in – and you can imagine the wisecracks that spawned. After that we visited a huge bazaar, which had stalls selling everything you can imagine, from souvenirs to more rugs than I'd ever seen in my life.

I was happy to get home, though, and even happier when the second leg was over. We thought the Turks might be on their best behaviour a fortnight later at Ibrox, but it seemed they had doubled down in their brutish antics – and even Tam Forsyth was targeted by them. Big Jock had warned us before the game not to get involved, and to try our very best to remain cool in what would be difficult circumstances, which was easier said than done. The gaffer clearly wasn't thinking like me and knew exactly how they would behave. But even he admitted he was shocked by what was in store for his players. We were battered, bruised, kicked and crunched by our opponents as football took second place to feuding. We did manage to keep our heads remarkably well in such a torrid atmosphere and only one player was booked. That would be me. Two Turks were sent off and more were booked. They tackled as though they were scything grass.

During one particularly bad spell in the second half it would have been easy to have played them at their own game and got stuck into them. The tackling had become so bad – and downright dangerous – that it was a realistic proposition, but we regained our composure and did well to calm it down.

That said, the tackle – sorry, assault – on Tam Forsyth was one of the worst I've ever seen. The Norwegian ref produced a red card, and it was just as well. Wee Doddie was also assaulted, and then Doug Houston was subject to a really nasty one, for which his aggressor was ordered off.

John Greig got a couple of goals, and Alex O'Hara and DJ were also on the scoresheet as we limped, battered and bruised, into the hat for the next round.

And the draw was less than kind as we came up against a very strong Borussia Mönchengladbach side. We were completely outplayed over in Germany and lost 3-0, which gave us little hope of rescuing the tie at Ibrox. We gave it a go, though, and I remember the journalist Ken Gallagher telling me that the normally super-confident German press went awfully quiet when I had us in front after ten minutes. We would go on to win the game, after goals by Bomber Jackson and Doddie, but Borussia scored twice to win 5-3 on aggregate.

Ten days before Christmas, St Johnstone arrived at Ibrox for a league encounter and we were looking forward to keeping our good run going. What was disappointing, though, was the emptiness all around Ibrox when we trotted out the tunnel to start the game. Just over 8,000 were inside the ground, and the overall feeling was one of eeriness. Was I back in the reserves? Anyway, we got going and right from the beginning I had a feeling that we were going to be unstoppable. I scored my 12th goal of the season and the supporters inside the ground were delighted. It was early on and seemed to demoralise Saints a bit. There would be further goals from Cutty Young, wee Doddie, Derek Parlane and Davie Smith. It was an overwhelming victory and one that gave the fans hope as we approached the festive season. Sadly for me, that was the only season I'd see, as an injury that afternoon proved more than costly. In fact, it more or less finished my Rangers career.

The game against Saints was going according to plan, until I took a heavy tackle from one of their defenders in the first half. I was struggling a little but nine times out of ten you can 'run it off', and I thought that would be the case. I even believed that if I could struggle on until half-time, the break would do me good and give Tommy Craig a chance to work on it. The gaffer asked how I was and I told him it was painful, but that I'd give it a go without taking any daft risks. The second half began and the ball came to me almost straight away. I took a touch and it was agony. I was in so much pain that I just crumpled to the ground. I knew right away that it was serious.

I hobbled off and took a seat on the bench, before going into the treatment room and lying on Tommy's table. He had a look at it and it was thought the best option would be to see how it was on the Monday morning. It was an uncomfortable weekend and on the Monday I struggled into Ibrox. Tommy seemed hopeful that with a few weeks' rest I'd be OK for the 5 January game against Celtic, and I know Jock Wallace had his fingers crossed for that one too.

Alex O'Hara took the number ten jersey for the next couple of matches and we won both, but the Celtic game at Parkhead was edging ever closer and I didn't think I had a hope in hell of playing in it, and I said so. Believe me, if there was one game I wanted to play in – one team I wanted to beat. Well, this was it, but you know your own body. I had as much chance of playing in it as I had of leading Scotland to a World Cup win.

I wasn't the only one pig sick about it. The gaffer told me I'd be a big miss as I had been playing well. It was nice to hear, but at that point I don't think there was any consoling me. I hated missing games, but I knew in this instance there was nothing anyone could do. Patience was the best policy, but god how I hated saying that. Rushing back after cartilage trouble was the worst thing any player could do.

I went into Ibrox to keep an appointment with the club doctor, but I think everyone feared the worst. I know I certainly did. After the meeting with the doc and the physio, we were all in no doubt what had to happen, I was going under the knife. Yeah, it's part and parcel of being a footballer – more so in the 1970s – but it was still a sore one to take. I knew exactly what was in front of me, and it wasn't the first time I'd suffered a nasty injury around the festive period, but this was the worst. The gaffer was hoping I would be out for just a month, but yet again my body was telling me otherwise. I reckoned a couple of months. There's nothing lonelier than a cartilage operation and all that follows, but that was the diagnosis and I had to get on with it.

I was admitted to the Victoria Infirmary in Glasgow just after the new year for the operation and in my first post-op review I was assured everything had gone according to plan. And the first visitor up to see me was our physio, Tommy Craig. He asked how I was, handed me a bag of grapes and started to chat about my post-op recovery. There was a man who loved his work.

To compound matters we had drawn with Partick and lost to Celtic over the Ne'erday period, which did our title hopes no favours at all. But all I could do now was look forward to when I would be able to play again, and it looked so distant on the horizon that I couldn't quite see any sign of a comeback. My mind was starting to take over and I knew I had to fight the negativity and do my best to stay focussed.

I liked Tommy as a guy, but no matter how important his job was, I wasn't ready to talk rehabilitation. I was barely 24 hours out of theatre and Tommy was the last guy I wanted to see. My next visitor was more welcome, as he didn't want to talk about anything medical. Kenny Dalglish was an opponent on the park, but off it he was one of my best friends. I always remember his face when he popped in to see me for the first time since I'd had the op. It had been about a week and I was sitting up in bed with a pretty nurse on either side. Kenny saw this, but didn't clock the *Rangers News* photographer hidden by a hospital screen. His jaw just about hit the floor. And then he noticed the snapper. It was one of those light-hearted moments you need when you've been through something traumatic. I must admit, nurses Tinney and Robertson were a more welcome sight than Tommy.

Lots of my team-mates from Ibrox had been up to see me. It was great to see guys like Colin Jackson, Cutty Young and Johnnie Hamilton because they brought a bit of normality to my situation and we would have a laugh. Joe Mason would also visit with Tommy Craig and the variety was often good.

But the most regular visitor was Kenny and the second time he visited he came bearing gifts. He brought me a portable television and a transistor radio, and boy was I grateful for both. But that just illustrated how solid our friendship was, as well as his generosity. We had become good pals in the late 1960s when we played together for the Scotland youth team a few times. We just clicked and remained good mates. While we were playing football we would meet up socially and thoroughly enjoyed each other's company. When we came up against one another on the football field, that friendship was put to one side. Trying to gain the upper hand for our respective teams always took precedence. We had a lot of shared interests and probably had similar personalities. The only difference being we came from different cities.

After the operation, and as soon as I was able to have visitors, Kenny came in every other day. The time after he brought me the TV and radio, he noticed that I had started to lose weight –

nearly a stone – and on the following visit he brought me a steak dinner. His father-in-law owned a restaurant near Hampden and he would pop in before the visit and pick something up. The restaurant was only five minutes from the hospital so the food was always hot. On one occasion he even visited me after he'd just played for Celtic. It was all brilliant for relieving the boredom, which was my biggest enemy during that particular recovery. It was murder sitting there all day without being able to move and nothing really to do. From the moment I went into hospital, what I craved most was a train ticket back to Fife. I knew that getting out of hospital was really just the beginning of the road back – a road which would more than likely take a couple of months, but I wanted to take those first steps in Fife.

I had plenty of time to think while I was in hospital and I spent a lot of time poring over my injury record. It was baffling why it always seemed to happen around Christmas and new year. This was the third year in a row and it didn't get any easier. I was beginning to think I was jinxed and it started to prey on my mind. But this latest one was by far the most serious. One of my favourite competitions was the Scottish Cup, and the ties started in January, which I was seldom fit for. I also had my goals like every player, and getting an under-23 cap for Scotland was one of those ambitions. And when your manager goes out of his way to tell you that you'd been playing well, then you hope the Scotland selectors are listening. But at that moment my sights weren't set on anything so ambitious. I was looking forward to the time when I could simply kick a ball again.

A couple of days before I was discharged from hospital I had a surprise visitor. It was the disc jockey from Hospital Radio, and we had a chat for about half an hour. Do you remember that old BT advert, 'It's good to talk'? Well, that was me while I was in hospital, and it was great to see a new face. Just as the presenter was leaving, he said, 'Is there a record I can play for you seeing as you're getting out soon?' My choice was 'All Right Now', by Free, and we both had a laugh at how appropriate it was.

The moment I was told I could leave, I headed home. I wanted a few days in Kinghorn before starting the light physio work that Tommy had laid out in a detailed plan (just walking to start with). It wouldn't be too long until I was travelling into Ibrox most days to use the gym and work on more detailed fitness plans, but that could wait.

I'd had the operation on 9 January, and by the end of February I felt that a comeback wasn't too far away. I had put in the hard yards and was looking to reap the benefits by pulling on the boots again. That meant another trip back to the Victoria Infirmary to see if they would give me the all-clear to resume playing. Twelve weeks had passed since I had kicked a ball and the doctor had warned against pushing myself too much too quickly. After being out so long, I was only too happy to take his advice.

And then the big day. I was told I was playing against Morton's reserves and I was like a young kid about to make a long-awaited debut. Truth is, there would only be a few hundred fans in attendance, but this was my cup final. I had decided to shy away from any tackles and just see how long I would last and, more importantly, how I would be the next morning. I did exactly that. It was a Tuesday afternoon, it was miserable and quite chilly, but I was walking on air. Apprehensive? You bet, but small steps for man and all that. On the Wednesday morning it was quite painful. Nothing unusual there, but it did stiffen up a bit and again I was told that was perfectly normal. I hadn't tested it too much, as it was more about testing ME. I knew that making tackles would come in time. I had no psychological issues with the leg, and I knew it would stand up to a tackle, but only when it was fully tuned up and ready for one. I was determined to do things right as I don't think I could've coped with another spell like that on the sidelines.

As soon as I knew I was to have the op, I had set myself a target, and I stuck to it, give or take a few days. That was one thing that pleased me. I didn't just lose my first-team place and a cartilage, but also a lot of weight too, so I had to put that back on. It was only when I went into Glasgow city centre to get measured for a new suit I realised just how much weight I'd lost, although bulking up was something I quite enjoyed.

A few days after my comeback match, I played against Hibs reserves at Ibrox, and the crowd was larger than it normally was for a reserve game. To think that a lot of supporters had come along just to see how my recovery was going made me feel good. Again, I took it easy for the most part, only exerting myself at specific times during the match.

I had now taken part in training sessions with the first team, bounce games at the Albion and a couple of reserve matches. I suffered no ill-effects and as far as I had been told, I had come back quicker than most from such a serious cartilage injury. I had appreciated the two reserve games I'd played in, something I would've taken for granted before, but it's only when you're injured you realise what you're missing. The spell in hospital had been bad enough, but there's nothing worse than getting treatment morning and afternoon and knowing you won't be playing on a Saturday.

Before the injury I had been having my best season in front of goal and had even been leading Derek Parlane in the scoring charts, but naturally he started scoring again and drew level with me on 12. He then scored seven in two games to streak well ahead. But goals were the last thing on my mind after my latest comeback match. This time it was against Clyde's reserves, and even though I felt the leg was getting stronger, I managed to pick up a dose of flu and was in bed for a week. I started to believe the stories about curses.

One of the things I had missed most about not playing was my relationship with our supporters. I'd be playing against, say, Dundee United or Aberdeen, and would often look up at the crowd if there was a lull in play, and recall when I used to stand in the Rangers end, singing the songs and having a laugh with my mates. I know I was lucky to make the leap from terracing to pitch, and I worked so hard to make the pro grade, but I'd like to think I never lost that connection with the supporters. For me, that was as important as any connection with my team-mates. I also fed off the energy of our fans and on many occasions they pulled me through the last ten or 15 minutes of a game.

I was equally at home with a foot on the ball running at the opposition, or crunching into a tackle to win the ball back. Some folk would say there wasn't much of me when I was a kid, but that never stopped me from competing for a 50/50 with some scarily big defenders. I could be as tough as them at times, but I always played the game as fairly as possible.

As 1973/74 wore on, it was quite clear that I wouldn't be making any significant contribution to the first team again that season. The injury had been a bad one and recuperation had taken as long as it wanted. We won our last four games but still finished third in the table. Another big disappointment. There was one small moment of comfort for me, which as time went on would become extremely significant. It arrived on the afternoon of Saturday, 27 April and we were at home to Dumbarton in our penultimate league game. The title race was over and we were resigned to second or third spot. I was named as substitute, potentially my first appearance since December, and when I replaced Derek Parlane I raced on to the pitch and played my usual game.

Little did I know that it would be my final appearance in a Rangers jersey.

Jock had made no secret of the fact that he had signed Ally Scott to replace me, not put pressure on me, as I had first thought, but that was the big man's prerogative. When he had become manager we hadn't always seen eye to eye. In fact, we clashed more than a few times. I always believed my best position to be in midfield, but Jock thought otherwise and wanted to play me up front. It wasn't a position I enjoyed, but he was the boss. Jock had been in charge for two seasons and he was slowly putting his stamp on the team. There were further changes during the summer months and you could see the way he wanted to go. I knew that the coming close-season would be an interesting one, and I was prepared for every eventuality. Well, almost every one.

7

Earning my Spurs

THE 1974 World Cup was over and memories of Grzegorz Lato and Gerd Müller were fading rapidly. I watched most of the tournament as I had done since I was a kid. There was something magical about the competition when you were a youngster and lapping up all the big names that you only really saw on television. A couple of days after the showpiece final – in which host nation West Germany defeated the Netherlands – attention in the papers switched to the domestic Scottish season, and the usual blanket coverage of the Old Firm. There were reports that Willie Waddell and Jock Wallace, as well as Celtic manager Jock Stein, had been over in Germany enjoying the finals, but now that they were back they would be fully focussed on fine-tuning their respective squads for the forthcoming campaign.

Celtic had just sold Davie Hay to Chelsea, so had money in the bank. Rangers, meanwhile, would be mulling over an enquiry from Aston Villa about one of their midfield players – namely me! I only occasionally read the papers, but anything I missed I was usually told about quite swiftly, despite an absence of mobile phones in those days. Believe me, the jungle drums beat just as efficiently as any superfast broadband.

This may all have been taking place around half a century ago but I reckon it was the start of Scottish clubs beginning to cash in on their bankable assets. Celtic had picked up a cool quarter of a million for Hay, and there were more clubs in England willing to take a punt on players from up north. Waddell and Wallace were aware of this and were ultimately tasked with keeping up with the Joneses.

Aston Villa had managed to get out of the Third Division so they were looking to improve their squad for life in the second tier. Rangers had put a price tag of £140,000 on my head but at the time I knew nothing about any interest from Villa. It was the same as the two bids the club had apparently received from Sunderland boss Bob Stokoe. I knew nothing about them, or that Rangers had valued me at £140,000. I was 22 at the time and I'm sure I fell into the category of 'bankable asset', despite missing a large chunk of the previous season with a cartilage injury, and requiring an op. I suppose there were two ways of looking at that. Would teams think I was injury prone, or would they reckon I would be fit and raring to go, and that they would be getting someone hungry to play again?

I had started pre-season at the same time as the other players, officially, anyway. Truth is I had been doing what I could as soon as it was safe to, post-operation. And maybe a little when it wasn't safe! It was great to be back in among the boys and during pre-season there were no thoughts in my mind of playing my football elsewhere. But we weren't in Europe that season and we all knew that the club would have to get their extra cash from somewhere. Sure, there had been rumblings of discontent from yours truly, but as far as I knew I was staying put – for the time being at least.

Pre-season training had been going well and everyone was feeling optimistic as the season crept ever closer. The only negative was the impending doomsday trip to Sweden. Don't get me wrong, Sweden is a lovely place, and I thoroughly enjoyed playing pre-season games there, but no one in their right mind would enjoy what big Jock had in store for us. We had been before. The Hindos training camp was in the middle of nowhere: Stalag 13 they used to call it. We would go on these lengthy cross-country runs. It was utter madness, like something you'd see in a film showing the extremes of army training. There would be half a dozen of us lying on the ground with a full tree trunk lying straight across us. It was ten times worse than Gullane. It was a Swedish international runner who took us for cross-country, and he was a tough taskmaster. I was dreading it, and could still picture him standing there, the year before, with this whistle in his mouth. But when he blew for the run to start, I had other ideas. Off we went on the road to nowhere while a few minutes after we'd started, I'd go over on my ankle and start making this big fuss. He's over like a shot and I'm sent back to base camp for treatment. Result. I was hoping that on this occasion he might have something milder for us in mind.

But I received a strange call from Willie Waddell the night before we were due to fly out to Gothenburg.

'Meet me at Glasgow Airport at such-and-such a time in the morning. You're not going to Sweden.'

'Right, OK.'

That was the extent of the call, as the Deedle wasn't big on chat. No more information, just an instruction. *The Times*'s cryptic crossword was often easier to work out. The following morning I was there bright and breezy and I knew we were going to London, because we were standing in the check-in queue for the London flight, but still I had no idea why. I had a small hunch – which would turn out to be wide of the mark. Sounds crazy now, but in those days we did things differently. I didn't have an agent so we handled situations as they arose. And the time it took us to fly from Glasgow to London was the time I got to process this potential career change.

A couple of weeks beforehand I had met Manchester United manager Tommy Docherty at the Buttery restaurant in Glasgow. The meeting had been set up by my journalist pal, Ken Gallagher. The Doc had been due to go on holiday and told me he wanted to take me to Old Trafford and that he would be in touch when he got back. So I was thinking we were going to speak to the Doc. But I always remember as the plane is landing in London, I'm thinking, 'Why didn't we just meet in Manchester?' (I was later told that the Deedle had refused to deal with Tommy Docherty.) I really had no idea of my final destination. Mr Waddell and I walked out into the concourse of the airport and there was a guy waiting on us – Eddie Baily, Cockney as they come, and he shouted to us. 'This way, gents,' he said. Eddie was Bill Nicholson's assistant. He then turned to me, shook my hand, and said, 'Welcome to Tottenham!' I thought, 'Tottenham, interesting.'

Willie Waddell hadn't said much on the plane, just sat there reading his paper for most of the journey, and any chat was just small talk, so this was a revelation. My first thoughts on a potential move to Spurs were also interesting. I wasn't imagining a packed White Hart Lane, lining up alongside their star players or potentially playing in an FA Cup Final. No, I wasn't long married and Sue and I had recently moved into a house in Kirkcaldy. We'd just finished decorating and now we would have to move house all over again. How would she take it? Rangers had obviously sold me to Tottenham and hadn't said a thing about it. I get these days that players probably have a bit too much say in what's going on, but I would have liked the courtesy of the management getting me in and saying, 'We've received a bid from Tottenham and we're happy with it. Would you like to go there?' I knew nothing about any move until Mr Waddell's instruction to meet him at the airport. In hindsight, it was a poor way for the club to conduct its business.

Anyway, off we motored from the airport to White Hart Lane, and by this time I had a million thoughts racing through my head. When you're up in the air and can see nothing but clouds, not much is reality, but once on the ground in busy London it's a different story. We arrived at the ground and were ushered straight up to Nicholson's office. He seemed friendly, which instantly put me at ease. He wasn't your stereotypical gruff Yorkshireman, but he was no fool either. We got straight down to business and Bill and Willie Waddell were quickly into their stride. There was lots to discuss and I sat there interested in what they were saying, and awaiting my opportunity to input into the conversation. The meeting started at around 11.30am and an hour and a half later we stopped for lunch. It had developed into a proper three-way conversation and I was glad to be included.

When we returned to the office, it was more of the same chat and we eventually got round to discussing my contract. It turned out to be far more in-depth than I could ever have imagined. But I suppose the bottom line was the wages. At that time, Rangers paid a basic weekly wage of £60, while Celtic offered £10 more. When Bill Nicholson said, 'Right, son, you'll be on £200 a week,' I was inclined to ask to borrow his pen. I couldn't believe the figures being discussed – but the section on bonuses had still to come, and that provided quite a shock.

At this point, Willie Waddell was sitting observing but remained silent. I would love to have known his thoughts on whether he believed some English clubs were paying far too much, or if he was embarrassed that any club could offer three times more than a huge club like Rangers.

Anyway, I was delighted by my new wages, and then my new boss said, 'Obviously there will be bonuses, appearance money etc., then there are the crowd bonuses, and those are linked to our home attendance figures.' 'Crowd bonuses?' I said, with a puzzled expression on my face. 'Yip,' he answered. 'You get so much per thousand up to 19,000, and so much per thousand up to 29,000, 39,000, etc.' That shocked me, probably because I'd never heard of such a thing. It was up to us to entertain, win games and get the crowds in. Looking back, it was a sensible approach by Spurs.

To illustrate what this meant in terms of wages, we would play Nottingham Forest, a lower-division team, in a cup tie in my first season, and we drew at their place, but they beat us in the replay at the Lane, and my bonus was in excess of £200 – and we lost the tie! It was made up by a crowd bonus and the appearance money on top of that. More than 50,000 had watched both games. So, going initially from £15 a week at Ibrox, and £60 at best, to quadrupling your wages plus all your bonuses was just crazy stuff, but I wasn't complaining. At that precise moment, money had taken over. It was king, and the emotional price of leaving Rangers had yet to surface.

Bill Nick told me he had been watching me for two years – since Spurs had played Rangers in a pre-season friendly at White Hart Lane. I took that as a real compliment as he was one of the great managers of his generation.

A few moments after signing the contract, he said to me, 'You'll be wanting to phone your wife, I suppose, and tell her the good news!' But I wasn't so sure Sue would see relocating to London as good news. She was a home bird and I was apprehensive about making the call. We had been married in the May, and it was only July. But that was the way of it. I was the one earning and I suppose that was the all-important factor. We had to follow the work.

Bill Nick offered me his telephone to make the call. I dialled the number and awaited the connection. 'Hello, is that you, Alfie?' Yes it was me, here we go. 'Eh, I've got some news for you, Sue. I've just left Rangers and signed for a new club.' Silence, and then, 'OK – which club?' 'Tottenham Hotspur, we're moving to London.' More silence. And then, 'London, oh, nice.' And that was that. Thing is, at the time I had a cousin who lived in London and he had a big band. He had been at our wedding in the May, and I'll always remember him saying, 'Why don't you sign for Tottenham and you guys can come and live near us in London? Think of the fun we could have!' And a few months later it was a reality. How spooky was that?

Around an hour so after the deal was done, there was a press conference at the ground and Bill Nick said, 'I am delighted that we've managed to sign the boy. We know all about him and realise he is a player of great ability. He likes to play in midfield, moving forward, but he is flexible and that suits this team. There will be a medical examination in the morning but we don't anticipate any snags. We are very, very happy that Alfie has agreed to join us.' (For my medical the team doctor was on holiday and I was seen by his brother. The doc told me later that I should never have passed, but that conversation was just between the two of us.)

Bill shook me firmly by the hand and you could tell it wasn't stage-managed for the papers. I could feel the warmth. He said to me, 'All being well, son, you will make your Spurs debut at the ground where your dad played with such success for many years. We've fixed up a pre-season friendly with Hearts.' This man knew his stuff. In contrast, Willie Waddell shook my hand but it seemed bereft of emotion, but that's just the way he was.

When I got back up the road Sue and I had loads to talk about. I told her all about my surprise visit to London and everything that had transpired; my contract, the wages, bonuses, signing-on fee, etc., and she said, 'What about houses, any idea where we'll stay?' I told her we would be going down in the next week to ten days and that we could start house-hunting right away. Meanwhile, the club would put us up in a hotel. Sue was originally from Edinburgh and I knew she was happy in Kirkcaldy, but despite it being a big move, she embraced it fully. Being the positive person she was, she looked at it as a new adventure and she absolutely loved London, taking to it so quickly. It's strange but we weren't in the centre of London much. We eventually bought a house in a wee place called Turnford, near Hoddesdon. It was only five minutes from Spurs' training ground in Cheshunt. We were there more than we were at the Lane so it made sense.

The training ground at Spurs was top-notch – so different from the facilities we had at Rangers. Previously we'd turn up at Ibrox on a Monday morning and get one set of gear – socks, jockstrap, shorts, top, jersey and that was for the week

– no matter the weather, rain, hail or snow. After training each day we hung it all up on a metal coat hanger, with a basket underneath. And on a Friday the socks were like concrete – an offensive weapon. It was little wonder that no one would tackle each other as the smell would've knocked you down. You also got a tracksuit but you were only allowed to wear it on the short walk from Ibrox to the Albion training ground, and you then had to take it off.

My first day's training at Spurs was a double session. It was at White Hart Lane and after the first stint we went into the dressing room and all the players were getting stripped and throwing their gear into the centre of the room. I'm still sitting there with my gear on. Pat Jennings was next to me, and I said to him, 'Why are the players chucking their stuff on the floor? How will they know what's theirs?' He looked at me and said, 'Alfie, you get clean kit for every session.' When I told him what happened at Rangers he genuinely couldn't believe it.

I was a Spurs player now and it felt good. Tottenham were a big name in the game and had paid a cool £140,000 for me, so that was a ringing endorsement of what the manager believed I had to offer. Even before my cartilage injury I hadn't been a regular starter at Rangers and had asked for a transfer during the winter. But while I was happy at my new club, it did take me a while to get over leaving Rangers. The night after I got back from London, my mum had a party at home in Kirkcaldy. I was never much of a drinker but at one point I slipped out into the back garden with my Rangers top on, a can of beer in my hand and I sat there on my own with the tears running down my face. I didn't want to go, but felt I had been put in a position where I had to. Willie Johnston, Colin Stein, Graham Fyfe and myself all left within a year. The team that played in the Barcelona final didn't play one game together after winning the trophy. When you're a kid and play for the team you supported, the emotional bond is strong, and I struggled for a while to let that go.

Willie Waddell had chucked it and a new manager wants his own players. Big Jock liked guys who could run and work. Bud and Steiny leaving didn't influence my decision to seek something new, that was down to one of Jock's signings, the player that had supposedly been brought in to replace me. We all have an idea of our self-worth and I didn't think Ally Scott was as good as me. And I still believe that. I had nothing against Ally but he was playing and I wasn't. That wasn't my decision, that was one for the manager. I could disagree with it all I wanted, but I couldn't change it. The only thing I could do was bide my time or leave, so I slapped in a transfer request. Then it's a game of poker. If the manager wants to keep you he'll find a way of letting you know, even though it might not come directly from his mouth.

But to give you an idea of Jock's mentality, we were playing at Ibrox one afternoon – against Ayr United, I think – and I was on the bench. We had been poor and it was a tough watch. With 20 minutes to go big Jock told me to go out and get warmed up. The minute I go out and start running up and down the track, the crowd start shouting for me. Ten minutes later, I'm still running up and down the track, and then Jock calls me over, and I'm thinking, 'OK, get stripped, get on that park and make a difference.' And my zip is half down by the time I get back to the dugout. And big Jock shouts, 'Get back in, you're no' goin' on!' I said to him, 'What was the point of that?' And he replied, 'Listen to the crowd, they were booing us, and now they're cheering – you've done your job!'

I don't think Jock was surprised when I asked for a transfer, but the Deedle still had a big say on everything that happened at Rangers, even though he wasn't manager. Big Jock had moved into the hotseat, but any contractual matters you had with the club were handled by Waddell.

To ask for a transfer you just chapped the manager's door and said, 'Can you put me up for sale, I want away?' and he'll either tell you to put it in writing or he'll agree on the spot. Eventually I was told I could go, but then for a time it looked like I was getting back in the team, and when that didn't happen I told myself that I had to go – for the sake of my own sanity. If truth be told, when you ask for a transfer you're actually hoping the manager says, 'No, I want you here and I want you to fight for your place.' You want a reaction, a positive one, so when he says you can go, there's no way back.

I was gutted to leave Rangers – the tears that night in my mum's garden told the full story. Everybody who knew me knew that Rangers were still my team, and that never changed, even according to some fans who insisted I did the dirty by eventually moving across the city, but to me Rangers were still my team – even though I was now a Spurs player.

And in one of my first games at the Lane, I realised just how special the Tottenham fans were. It was Alan Gilzean's testimonial against Red Star Belgrade and on a bitterly cold night more than 22,000 turned out to honour the original King of White Hart Lane. Gilly was on his way to a new career in South Africa but not before his adoring fans had an opportunity to say goodbye. I decided to enjoy the occasion and in typical Gilzean fashion, he flicked home the opening goal. I then went on a mazy run through the Red Star defence and was brought down. Cyril Knowles took the spot kick and scored at the second attempt. It was the perfect send-off for a legend, and for yours truly, the best way to say 'hello' to the north London faithful.

Even though I was delighted to have joined a club the size of Spurs, the start to my English career was anything but a great success. It took me a while to break into the team, and while I wasn't so naive as to think I could walk straight into a side with players such as Martin Chivers and Martin Peters up front, I did think my chance would've come a lot sooner than it did.

I was the last player Bill Nicholson signed for Spurs. He was a Tottenham legend but had perhaps endured one rebuild too many and had decided to step down just a few games into the season. He suggested to the board that they appoint Johnny Giles and Danny Blanchflower in his place, but they had other ideas and the job went to Terry Neill, the former Arsenal man.

It initially proved unpopular at the Lane, and it was a bit of a disaster for me.

Apart from some bounce games and friendlies, I made my competitive debut in mid-September in a midweek League Cup tie at home to Middlesbrough. I replaced Keith Osgood in the second half and we lost 4-0. The home fans in the 15,000 crowd were furious and they let us know. When we returned to the dressing room Neill gave us a rollicking, and it was fully deserved. I must've made quite an impression as it was fully three months before I featured again for the first team.

It was soul destroying but I did my best for the reserves although on occasions I let my frustration get the better of me, and in one second-string match I was sent off for arguing with the referee. It was the fifth red of my career – all for chirping away at the man in the middle – and I wasn't best pleased with myself. I was having a bit of trouble with my fitness and it was getting in my head. It had taken me some time to get fully over the knee injury, and Sue and I had just found the house we wanted, so at least that was a weight off my mind.

Once again I had a manager who made it clear that he preferred those who worked hard over so-called flamboyant players: those who liked to take on defenders in an effort to create opportunities. My second sub appearance was far more successful and I came on for Chivers as we beat Newcastle United (look out for that name!) 3-0 in a rare league win. I was back in the second team the following week as we lost 4-0 to Ipswich. The season was lurching from one crisis to another and we were soon dancing with our demons near the foot of the table.

Three days after Christmas, Colin Stein and his Coventry City side visited the Lane and left with a point, courtesy of a typical Steiny goal. Sadly I was miles away playing in front of three men and a dog for the stiffs, so I didn't get the chance to see my old team-mate. I'd be lying if I said by then I wasn't becoming disillusioned. On 4 January, Nottingham Forest and Spurs fought out a dour 1-1 draw in an FA Cup third round tie at the City Ground. On the Monday morning after that game, two of the senior players, Pat Jennings and Cyril Knowles, asked for a meeting with Neill. He welcomed them into his office but what they had to say shocked him, and me when I found out about it. Pat and Cyril told the manager they thought I deserved a chance in the first team, as I had been training really well and turning in good performances for the reserves. It was such an amazing thing for them to do and I suppose Neill had no alternative but to accede to their request as the team was struggling and he needed a spark from somewhere to help save our season.

I made my first competitive start for Spurs on 8 January 1975, roughly six months after joining from Rangers. It was the replay against Forest and even though we lost 1-0, I felt I had played reasonably well. Probably as well as could be expected for someone with only a few minutes' top-flight action under his belt, and so far into the season.

Saturday, 11 January was the day my Tottenham Hotspur career came alive. We travelled up to St James' Park, in the north-east, the night before our vital league match against Newcastle. I say vital because we were struggling at the wrong end of the table and needed something from the game – if only to help us believe in ourselves. It soon turned into a day that would live long in my now fading memory.

Some 40,000 fans packed into the stadium and we were on it from the first minute. We were 4-0 up at half-time and I had scored twice. On the hour I completed my hat-trick to put us 5-1 ahead. It was a dream come true and our travelling army of fans were in raptures as the game finished 5-2 in our favour. My fellow Scot, John Duncan, was on the scoresheet, as was Cyril Knowles.

I became a permanent fixture in the team, but the heavy win at Newcastle proved a false dawn and we lost our next three to Sheffield United, Everton and Stoke, games we really wanted to be winning if we were to move away from the basement. And on it went, with just a single point from our next six. It was an unmitigated disaster and try as we might, the results were appalling. We had a team meeting and a few home truths were discussed. We won our next three games to give us a great chance of staying up – but we had to maintain that standard of performance and, more importantly, keep on winning. We lost 3-2 at Turf Moor against a handy Burnley side. We had three matches left, starting with a home shoot-out with Chelsea. A crowd of 51,000 crammed into the Lane and saw me get my second goal in three games as we won 2-0. We knew that a win against old foes Arsenal at Highbury would keep us in the First

Division, but they were also scrapping for points and although we gave it a real good go, we lost 1-0 in a titanic struggle.

Everything would now come down to the last game of the season: Tottenham v Leeds United at the Lane. Leeds had little to play for. They were guaranteed a top-ten finish, but the sting in the tail was that this Leeds team was packed full of scrappers, were the reigning league champions and had also qualified for the European Cup Final. Probably not the type of team we wanted to play against as we fought for our lives. But Leeds it was, and we prepared the best we could. At stake was the future and reputation of Tottenham Hotspur FC, who hadn't been relegated since 1935.

As usual, our home ground was packed to the rafters – with the gates reportedly closed at 6.30pm – and we got off to the best possible start. I was weaving my merry way through the Leeds defence when I was fouled 20 yards from goal; Cyril Knowles slammed home the free kick. We were 1-0 up at the break but really came alive in the second half. We played some nice stuff in and around their box and I managed to slip Martin Chivers the ball and he fired home our second. Things had just become a little more comfortable.

On the hour mark, Steve Perryman was pulled down in the box and Cyril converted. Time to get the cigars out. Well, almost. I decided to have a bit of fun when the ball made its way out to me in the channel. I sat on it and urged my opponents to come and get it. Not my proudest moment, although it fired up the fans again and they started chanting my name. Billy

Bremner took exception to my showboating and mouthed some sort of threat, but I was playing to the gallery, and the gallery was loving it. God knows they hadn't had much to cheer about that season. Joe Jordan pulled one back, but I then got into a decent position near the Leeds goal, and although I thought I had dragged it a bit too close to the touchline, I decided to have a go and when I saw the ball nestle in the back of the net that was me. Straight up to the supporters and giving it big licks. That was the moment our magnificent fans decided I was heir-apparent to Alan Gilzean's throne, and the 'King of White Hart Lane' song reverberated around the Lane. It was magical. That's the only way I can describe it. I was the happiest player alive, although I had one task left to complete that night. As we walked up the tunnel I headed for the away dressing room, knocked the door and apologised for taking the piss. Thankfully I was forgiven.

After that game, the *Daily Mirror* wrote, 'Tottenham's heroes were left-back Cyril Knowles, centre-forward Martin Chivers – who was recalled after two months out in the cold – and Alfie Conn.'

Five weeks previously our chairman, Sidney Wale, had said that only a miracle could save us – and that miracle happened that Monday night. It was an incredible end to the season for the club, and for me personally. At one point it looked like I might be leaving Tottenham without even managing a top-team start – and ended with me on the throne. Luton and Chelsea were relegated as a result of our late-season surge and we could head off on our holidays knowing we had at least achieved something tangible.

As an aside to the game against Leeds, Willie Ormond had come down to watch Billy Bremner, and was an interested onlooker as I decided to park my bum on the ball. I was told by a member of the Tottenham staff, who had been sitting close to Willie that night, that he said, 'Oh, that'll do for me!' To be honest, I couldn't have picked a better game to turn on the style, with the Scotland manager watching. Leeds had a fantastic team, and they knew how to win – although not that night!

Another reason I enjoyed being at Spurs was the freedom it gave me from the Ibrox style police. I liked to play with my shirt hanging over my shorts, socks at my ankles and my hair and sideburns as long as possible. I remember someone saying to me, 'Oh, yeah, that iconic look you had going on with your hair at Spurs.' I'm not sure it was iconic but it was definitely 'me' at that time in my life, and it was the 1970s. On the flip side, I remember reading a letter from a woman which appeared in the *London Standard*. In it she said, 'He's a nice footballer but the hair is quite the scruffiest I've seen!' That made me chuckle.

But it was the London of that era and my cousin Tony, of the psychedelic jazz-rock combo the Tony Evans Association, played the type of stuff that we loved. We'd very occasionally go to see them play at the Talk of the Town. And, once, on Sue's birthday, Tony took us to a swanky place called the 21 Club and he paid, thankfully, as it was four weeks' wages just for the prawns.

8

If the Cap Fits …

THE COMMOTION surrounding our successful last-gasp attempt at preserving our First Division status had died down and we had each gone our separate ways at the end of a very draining season. I hadn't kicked a ball in earnest before January, but the second half of the campaign had been so intense that it felt like I'd played the full season. At one point relegation had seemed such an inevitability that when we completed the great escape, it felt like we had really achieved something. Truth is, we should never have found ourselves so deeply mired in the brown stuff. But after the last ball was kicked, Sue and I headed off on holiday for a relaxing week by the pool. After that, we drove up to Scotland to spend some time with our respective families.

One day, Sue was at her folks' house in Edinburgh while I popped over to Limekilns to see Mum and Dad. I was relaxing in the living room, probably chatting about my first season in England, when the sports section of the Scottish news came on.

'Manager Willie Ormond has announced his squad for this year's Home Internationals, which, for Scotland, starts on Saturday, May 17 in Cardiff against Wales.'

The living room fell silent. The newsreader announced the Scotland under-23 squad first, and I was in it. That was a big thrill. And then he announced the full Scotland squad – and I was in that too, which was an even bigger thrill. I wasn't aware you could be part of both squads, but I had a smile as wide as the nearby Forth Estuary.

I'll never forget the moment the graphic showing the full squad appeared on the TV screen and my dad was extremely animated, but somehow I remained calm. Dad shouted, 'Elizabeth, come and see this,' and my mum came rushing in. Despite my relaxed demeanour, it was a lovely moment to see my parents so happy and so proud of me.

The players named would have the honour of representing Scotland in the 1975 Home Internationals series, the oldest international football tournament in the world. It was quite an honour and I looked forward to the beginning of the competition. Before the first game we all received our official blazers and ties. If we didn't win it, we would certainly be the smartest-looking of the squads. The first game was against Wales, and naturally we were all hopeful of playing in that. When the team was announced on the day and I wasn't in it the first thing I did was to congratulate the guys who were. It was obviously disappointing not to even make the bench, but I was sure my turn would come. I was still part of the squad and watched on from the stand inside Ninian Park, in Cardiff, as the teams fought out a 2-2 draw. My old Rangers team-mate Bomber Jackson got one of our goals.

Next up was Northern Ireland at home and again I was hopeful. On this occasion, I was named as a substitute and realised I was one step closer to fulfilling a boyhood dream. There were 65,000 at Hampden that night and I was buzzing. It was an incredible feeling, although my only disappointment was the absence of the great George Best. I would've loved to have played against him. He was my idol, and simply head and shoulders above everyone, and when someone like Pelé says that Georgie was the best he'd seen, you tend to listen. Best always seemed to play for the sheer enjoyment of the game. He loved taking players on and you always had the feeling that his number one priority was to entertain. There was one game I recall, when he turned out for Northern Ireland against Scotland in Belfast and single-handedly tore the Scots apart. He was a genius – a once-in-a-lifetime player. A crowd-pleaser. All these things and more.

I was only 23 at the time but I'd already racked up a fair bit of experience and handled the occasion of my first cap well. I've always been that type of person. I'm usually quite chilled and the only time I ever got nervous was before a cup final. But any other game was OK, even wearing that famous Scotland shirt. I'm pretty sure we all travelled down to Wales together, stayed overnight and then back up to Glasgow after our draw with the Welsh. We were booked into a hotel in

Glasgow for a couple of days before the Northern Ireland game, and then stayed overnight until we were due to head south to Wembley.

I'd played at Hampden a few times, in cup finals etc., but it didn't feel any different going there with Scotland. I was obviously delighted to get a cap and represent my country but I wasn't fazed at all.

But that was put to the test after 65 minutes when Willie Ormond turned to me and said, 'Out you go and get warmed up.' That was the moment I knew I was likely to get on. I was hoping it wouldn't be another big Jock Wallace moment! With just under half an hour remaining I was champing at the bit to get on. When it happened, it was such an incredible feeling, and I got an amazing ovation from the crowd. I don't know if the demographics have changed nowadays but I'd say that back then more than half the crowd were Rangers supporters. It certainly felt like it.

We won 3-0 and the mood in the camp was positive. We had a chat in the dressing room after the game and were reminded that we had another big game on the Saturday, and that we should go easy on ourselves. Despite just having cruised to victory over Northern Ireland, we were already desperate to be in the mix for the game at Wembley and weren't about to do anything to jeopardise our individual chances.

We had one light training session the following day before heading for the bright lights of London on the Friday morning. If I remember correctly we were slight favourites to beat

England, which was quite something. I lived in London at the time so it felt like I was going home.

I got on well with Willie Ormond. He was a nice man as well as a very good manager. He had played many times against my dad. Willie was part of Hibs' Famous Five, and my dad was one of Hearts' Terrible Trio! Willie was a big Hibs man. He didn't complicate things, and he didn't tell us all to do this or that. 'Here's the team, lads. Go out and enjoy yourselves.' Nowadays they're out with iPads, clipboards and lecturing subs for ten minutes before they finally get on the park. Willie kept it simple. Players know their jobs. In the days leading up to an international, there are many occasions on which they receive 'instructions', so there's really no need for chapter and verse before running on to the pitch. You just want to get out there. Sure, if a situation has arisen during the game, and you're going on to counteract something or someone then a few words are usually enough.

Mid-morning on the Saturday, we were sitting down to our pre-match meal at a London hotel when a deathly hush fell over the entire room. The manager was about to read out the team. Everyone reacted differently. Some stared at him intently, as if trying to will him to call out their name. Others pretended they were only partly interested, but we all had one thing in common. We were desperate to run out at the iconic Wembley Stadium with that Scotland shirt on – but knew that only 11 could.

It was every schoolboy's dream to play for Scotland at Wembley. Mr Ormond went through the team. Kennedy,

Jardine, McGrain, Munro; that's four jerseys gone already. Seven to go. McQueen, Rioch, Dalglish. My mate Kenny has the number seven jersey. Good for him. Right, four left. Come on, Mr Ormond, don't let me down. And then he said it. 'Number eight, or inside-right, as we used to say,' and he looked at me and said, 'Alfie!' He just said my name, I'm in. I was so grateful. The other names were a blur, although, for the record they were Parlane, McDougall and Duncan.

After our pre-match meal, I was walking out to the hotel foyer to clear my head and digest the news just as my dad, brother and grandfather were walking in to see me. I got a bit emotional as we embraced, but it was great knowing that they'd all come down to support me.

I don't remember much about eating lunch, or of packing my bag and jumping on the coach for the short ride to the stadium. I hadn't played at Wembley before and when we arrived at our destination the butterflies were starting to kick in. I was hopeful that this 'nervous energy' would dissipate as soon as the game started, but we'd see.

We were welcomed by a high-ranking official from the Football Association and shown to our dressing room. Again, everyone handles these occasions differently and I wasn't as bad as I thought I might be. I'd only ever seen Wembley on TV but it was an incredible sight in the raw. From sitting on the bus peering incessantly at the Twin Towers to hopping off and walking into the stadium and through to the dressing room, it was everything I'd dreamed of and more. Everything seemed built on a bigger scale than your normal football stadium. We were all pro footballers who thought we'd seen it all, but our eyes were wide open.

There were a few short of 100,000 there that day and it really was a sight to behold. In those days everyone was standing, and the place was rammed. The teams walked out side by side and I was next to World Cup winner Alan Ball and when we emerged from the tunnel this almighty roar went up. I swear, I had never heard anything like it. Ball just looked at me and said, 'This is supposed to be our f**kin' home game!' I reckon we had at least 70,000 in that stadium. It truly was a picture – as was Bally's face. It was a pilgrimage in those days for our supporters. The moment they arrived home from the Wembley weekend they started saving up for the next one in two years' time.

I didn't look upon England as the enemy. They were standing between us and victory and we had to do everything we could to beat them, but that was the same as any team we played. England weren't special. As Bally said, it was like a home game for us with that incredible support, so we had nothing to fear. I got on well with Alan. He was a passionate Englishman, just as we were all passionate Scots. It would be his 72nd and final cap for England.

I might only have played a couple of times for Scotland, but I've been to quite a few internationals and the Scottish supporters are always fantastic. They will put up with anything as long as you give 100 per cent for that jersey. Before kick-off, I was nervous, and I knew it was all about handling it as best I could. Nerves have ruined many a fine player and I was determined not to be one of them. I played alongside guys who had to throw up before a big game or they would struggle to keep it together. Once they had been sick, they were usually OK.

We knew fine well that the hopes of 70,000 Scots were resting on our shoulders, and as we lined up to meet the dignitaries we would do our best not to let them down. With all the pre-match distractions out of the way it was down to business. The moment the game kicked off the nerves had gone. We had a game of football to win – but we didn't exactly get off to the best start and were one down early on.

Stewart Kennedy got pelters after that game but I don't think he did an awful lot wrong. England's first two goals were screamers, so there was nothing he could do; nothing any goalkeeper could have done. At half-time we were 3-1 down, as Bruce Rioch had scored a penalty for us, but we still felt that we could beat them.

Willie Ormond was relatively quiet at the interval but urged us to go out and salvage something from the game. We didn't capitulate in the second half, but it seemed like everything they hit went between the posts. Probably the most positive moment I had that day was when we were 5-1 down and tens of thousands of Scots started singing my name. Despite everything, that was a real 'wow' moment for me. In the first half I'd hardly kicked the ball. I had a couple of half-chances, but at half-time I was angry with myself and had decided I was going for it. This was a huge opportunity and we couldn't surrender meekly. I was walking back out the tunnel, still furious at the way the first half had gone, and I thought to myself, 'F**k it, I'm going to give this a right go.' I was taking players on right, left and centre. Ultimately, I would get past most but it was usually a case of one too many.

I certainly didn't get any grief from the Scotland supporters after that game. When the final whistle sounded I found myself standing beside Alan Ball, as fate would have it, and we shook hands. There was no gloating on his part and we swapped shirts. We were about 40 or 50 yards from the tunnel and two England players had started running towards it. They were targeted by 'projectiles' and wee Bally took one look at what was happening and said, 'I'm walking off with you, Alfie.'

I hadn't noticed the missiles and asked him why. He said, 'Because when you're walking off, they'll stop throwing bottles and cans and I'll get in without getting hit!' He wasn't daft. And that's exactly what happened.

Apparently, Kenny Dalglish and I were the only two Scots to receive pass marks in the following day's newspapers. I didn't read the papers the next day so my dad must have told me. A pal of mine and I were talking about that game fairly recently and he asked if Brian Clough had ever tried to sign me, and I told him that not to my knowledge, although that wouldn't have been a surprise in those days. He said that Clough had spoken about me in almost reverential tones during the live TV broadcast of the Wembley game.

It was my second and final cap for my country and while the results were clearly mixed, I will always be grateful and proud that I pulled on the dark blue shirt.

That night, my cousin Tony, the big band leader, helped organise a night for the Scottish team at one of the Mecca clubs, the Empire Ballroom, in Leicester Square. All the players were invited but after the result we'd just had I decided quite early on that I wasn't going – I was still pig sick as we left the dressing room and walked straight out of the stadium. I jumped into the car with my dad, brother and grandfather and drove up to Luton, just to get away from London. We booked into a small motel about an hour north of the capital and went inside. My dad waited until we got into the room and he said, 'Look, son, I know you're not in the best of moods, and I completely get that, but you really should be at that function tonight. Your cousin has organised it for the players and it'll look bad if you don't go.'

I knew he was right but he understood why I hadn't wanted to go, so I agreed that we should drive back down to London and show our faces. It wasn't like it is now, with so much traffic that your car barely moves a few yards in 20 minutes, so it was a relatively stress-free journey. I parked up and we went into the ballroom. Trying to put on my best fake smile, I hooked up with the other players and we had a few drinks. People were coming up and saying that 5-1 wasn't a true reflection of the game and that we should hold our heads high. I wouldn't say the drink was flowing but we'd had one or two, and after a couple of hours the mood had lightened ever so slightly, but we were still hurting – big time.

And then it all kicked off – big time!

One minute we were standing in little groups, chatting among ourselves, and also to a lot of the Scotland supporters who had managed to gain entry. I had gone up to the bar for a round of drinks when all hell broke loose. In a matter of minutes, no, make that seconds, the bottles were flying and folk were punching lumps out of one another. The Empire Ballroom had turned into a war zone – for one night only. A lot of the empty screw tops were being directed at the stage, and next thing I know Tony is at my side and pleading with me to get up on the stage and appeal for calm. I did as I was asked and just as I leapt up the steps to the stage a bottle whizzed by my head and smashed off the wall right next to where the band had just been playing.

I'm a confident enough guy but I'm no UN diplomat, so I didn't want to start waving my arms in the air and appealing for everyone to calm down, but I had to do something. I stepped up to the mic and asked everyone if they would stop throwing bottles and fighting, and I said that no one was more disappointed than the players. I mistakenly believed that the trouble had started because of the defeat we'd suffered. Within a minute or two my charm seemed to be working, although a few of our punters were shouting and gesturing towards one guy in particular. It quickly transpired that a band member had been holding up five fingers on one hand and one on the other and laughing at our supporters. Some of them had tried to laugh it off but once it all kicked off it spread like wildfire and while half of the participants didn't know why they were fighting, the mood in the camp allowed it to take hold very quickly.

We managed to get it all calmed down, and the rogue band member was 'ushered' off the stage and out through a back door, but the place was such a mess that the manager of the club had no alternative but to shut for the night. It was a shame to see such a beautiful venue so messed up.

The Joe Loss dance band had the residency in the Empire and when he moved on my cousin's band got the gig. It was a prestigious venue but that night, sadly, it all went wrong. Tony was already a successful band leader, and when the Empire gig came up, to fulfil the contract, he split his band in two, with the other half continuing to play regularly in Monaco. Tony and I were great friends and lived just ten minutes from each other in London. But that night we just shook our heads and hugged, before we once again set off for our motel.

We had the Sunday off but had been told to report to Glasgow on the Monday afternoon for some sort of debriefing. For some reason I didn't hear Willie Ormond say that we were to meet up, and as the mood was pretty low, no one was really talking. I might have gone straight into the shower and missed it, I don't recall. But our under-23s were training at Lesser Hampden on the Monday afternoon, so I went along to that. When I walked in the gate Jock Stein was standing close by and came straight over. 'What are you doing here?' he asked. 'You're supposed to be meeting up with the big squad.' I told him I didn't know that, and so he asked if I wanted to train with the 23s. I said I did, got changed and I trained at Lesser Hampden.

Scotland were due to play Romania the following Saturday, while the 23s had a game in the same country. The under-23s were in action 24 hours beforehand. I was in the squad for the big team, but Jock met with Willie Ormond to ask if he would allow me to play for the 23s, as they still had a chance of qualifying for the latter stages of the European Championship, and he agreed.

I played for the 23s and we beat Romania, but I suffered a dreadful injury. One of the home defenders tackled me and I landed awkwardly. My Achilles tendon took the brunt and I was in agony. I had genuinely never felt pain like it, and had quite lengthy treatment on the pitch before being carefully moved into the stadium's medical room, where our doc continued to work on me. He could tell by the shape of my ankle and heel that it was a bad one. Strangely, though, the longer I remained on the treatment table, the more the pain lessened. The doc spoke to me about the incident and asked what I remembered of it. To my mind it had been an innocuous challenge, and it was more the way I had landed that did the damage. He agreed, and while the pain was off the scale at the time, it was starting to calm down. When the game finished, and I realised we had won, a kind of euphoria had taken over and I was able to get back to London OK the next day. I went straight home, put my feet up and convinced both Sue and me that I would be fine for the start of pre-season training, which by now was just a few weeks away. She seemed more sceptical than me, but then again she usually was, and with good reason.

By the time pre-season was upon us, I had forgotten all about the injury, turned up on the first day back and we did our usual roll call. We spoke about what we had been up to during the close-season, any international or charity games we had played and any knocks we think we might have taken. I remembered the heel injury in Romania, and it was logged.

We trained and everything seemed fine with the ankle and heel. I wouldn't say I was a big fan of pre-season but I did what I had to as it definitely helped once the cold weather and heavy pitches kicked in. Our fitness levels had to be good and I'd like to think mine always were. We were having the usual banter during training, but I sensed that something just wasn't quite right, although it was hard to put my finger on it. And then it all came out. It always does, doesn't it? The manager had given me the OK to miss our close-season trip to Majorca to play for Scotland. But when it came out that Neill had awarded all the players who were in the Balearics a pay rise – that was everyone in the squad except me – I was furious.

I asked for a meeting with the gaffer and told him I wanted the same as the other guys, nothing more, nothing less. I didn't want to be treated any differently, but unfortunately I waited and I waited until I reckoned he was just taking the piss. That was when I went back in to see him and handed over a written transfer request. I didn't want to leave Spurs because the fans were terrific, but I clearly wasn't going to stand for being singled out in a negative way either, so that was my decision. Pay me what the others are getting or I'm off. I had been forced to take a stand.

Just 24 hours later I couldn't believe the reaction as news of my request was in the public domain. The club switchboard was jammed with hundreds of calls complaining that it was disgraceful that they were allowing me to leave. The supporters became my biggest ally in my fight for financial parity and that forced the club into speaking with me about my wages. Honestly, I was so humbled that I wanted to personally thank every single person who had taken the time to call and make their feelings known. But the ball was still firmly in the board's court – they had to show fairness. If they were reasonable and made a decent offer, I would bite their hand off. I didn't want to go anywhere.

The manager didn't handle my request well. He knew that I was getting less money than everyone else yet it didn't seem to bother him. We had been back at pre-season a couple of weeks, I had spoken to him a few times and he had never cracked a light about the wage rise he had given to the others. If he felt that I didn't deserve it for some reason he should have told me why, rather than act like everything was normal. I had also spoken to a couple of board members whenever they visited the training ground, but they too were tight-lipped. We didn't have agents in those days so I had to deal with it myself. The manager told me he'd sort it, but he didn't.

When I handed the transfer request to him, he looked at it and said, 'What's this?'

'It's a transfer request.'

'Why?' he asked.

'Because I've lost trust in you.'

He looked at me as if I had just landed from the moon.

'Come on, gaffer,' I reasoned, 'I've asked a few times for the same as the other lads, and clearly, for whatever reason, it isn't going to happen, so I'll go elsewhere and see what I can get.'

'So, it's all about money with you,' he said, rather disparagingly.

'It's why we all work, obviously,' I said. 'But this is about more than that, and you know it.'

Well, nothing ever did get sorted out with a pay rise, and as usual a couple of pre-season friendlies had been arranged and that was that for me. In the first of these I came down again on the Achilles and once again the pain was off the scale. I was carried from the field and knew right away it was the same pain I had experienced in Romania. The physio was on it in a flash and a few minutes later the club doctor had joined us in the medical room. It wasn't looking good. In fact, 50 years later it is still incredibly painful if I touch it or knock it against something. It has never healed properly.

Fate had once again decided to intervene in my career; this stop-start glamorous life that frustrated the hell out of me. Apparently, the Achilles is the strongest muscle in your body but obviously that was two knocks on it now and something had to give. The pain was excruciating. When I reported to White Hart Lane the following morning the doctor said he was booking an appointment for an X-ray at a clinic in Harley Street. It was the sensible thing to do, but when the prognosis came back, and the surgeon said my Achilles had completely gone and that the only viable option was to operate, otherwise my career was over, I was straight into hospital. There was no keyhole surgery in those days and so I was in plaster for five months and out of football for just short of a year.

I was distraught. The season previous had ended positively and I had just represented my country at Wembley. It seemed like the football gods had been smiling on me, but now this. I was in a dark place, and then a message arrived from an unlikely source. Roy McFarland, the Derby County and England defender, had suffered a similar injury and been out for nine or ten months. I got a lovely message from him, giving me some hints on how to deal with the injury and the aftermath of the operation and his words were gratefully accepted. He told me it was a serious injury, a career-threatening injury, but only if I didn't fight and get the better of it. That advice and his words of encouragement were exactly what I needed to hear at that time, and Roy will never know how much they helped me.

I thought back to the game at Wembley and although it had been a disastrous result for the nation, I hadn't done myself any harm. A week or so after that game I had been chatting to my dad on the phone and he started to recite part of a newspaper article. It was something like, 'Alfie Conn, the new boy, made several sparkling second-half runs, which almost seemed like a mark of defiance against the dominant English side.' I laughed to myself as that was exactly how it had gone, although I wasn't sure how this reporter had known what I was thinking. I was angry, frustrated and felt for our magnificent supporters. If we were going down, I was going down fighting, and that's exactly what I did. And then someone said to me, 'Did you know that was Scotland's worst defeat at Wembley since they lost 9-3 in 1961?' Cheers.

I was always proud of my dad for winning a Scotland cap. Folk reckoned he should have had more, but representing your country at anything is an honour. It was always my ambition to follow in his footsteps, so when it happened I was grateful to Willie Ormond for making that dream come true. If kids had worn replica tops when I was growing up, I might've had a Scotland jersey in reserve – but I would've cut about with a Rangers top on. That was the team I supported and followed. In my day you would come in from school, get changed into your old clothes and straight down the park for a kick-about. It was almost mandatory. Most boys pretended they were some big-time player or other, but I was George Best or Jim Baxter, weaving my way in and out of the opposition defence.

But for the moment, memories were all I had. There was no playing, nor even watching, as I couldn't go to any games. Total rest had been prescribed and the team doctor would've gone ballistic had I ventured anywhere near White Hart Lane on a Saturday afternoon. For the first two or three months it was all about keeping the weight off the Achilles. I missed the entire 1975/76 season: that's how bad it was, and I didn't handle it well at all. There was very little I could do after the operation as I had this huge stookie on. I was sitting on my backside most of the time – and anyone who knows me knows that isn't me. Total rest. I did my wife's head in. Can I get a wee cup of tea, a wee sandwich, hen? 'Can you not get back to work?' she would ask politely! It wasn't just that, we had a dog as well and I couldn't take it for a walk, so I'm afraid Sue was also on doggy duty.

The club kept in touch with me the whole time. The doctor, physio, etc., and then when I got the walking plaster on I was able to go into the ground and that's when I started doing weight work. It was the training ground, which was five minutes from my house. My pal would take a day off work to drive me to the complex, which was really appreciated. I met some great people when I was at Spurs, despite not being the greatest at engaging with people. I'm more of a listener than a talker, while my wife was the opposite. Sue would meet up with the other wives and girlfriends, and developed some great friendships that way. She got on with people really easily. She loved life, loved a laugh, and would sit and chat to folk for hours on end – but she was no mug. I remember Spurs invited all the players and our wives to a big charity event at London's Grosvenor Hotel. We were sitting having a drink when Sue said to me, 'I know his face,' and she pointed to this guy who was standing quite near our table. I said, 'That's John Conteh, the boxer, and he's just won the world title.'

She said, 'Do you think he would sign my programme?'

I said, 'Let's go and ask him.'

There were quite a few non-football celebrities there that night and Sue had decided to see how many signatures she could get on her programme.

So, up we went, and she said, 'Mr Conteh, could I have your autograph, please?'

'Certainly,' he said, and he signed the programme, right across the whole front page.

She looked at it and said, 'Could you not have made that any bigger?'

He didn't say anything, but turned away, and as he did, he mumbled something to the person he was with, and they both looked at Sue.

My wife jumped on it and said, 'Excuse me, who do you think you're talking about?' I grabbed her immediately and said, 'Right, let's go, I'm not getting knocked out by a world champion!'

That was one thing about Sue – she wouldn't back down from anyone.

This sounds crazy, but the only time I ever really challenge anyone is when they call me Alfred. I was christened Alfie, and that's what my mum and dad always called me. I know it sounds pedantic, but if I'm in the doctor's surgery and they call out, 'Alfred Conn,' I'll say, 'My name is actually Alfie.' Yeah, it does sound pedantic!

9
Scotland Calling

THE WORST thing that happened to me at Spurs was Bill Nicholson deciding to spend more of his time in the garden. That was a hammer blow. I had been at the club for less than three months and the inspirational titan who had signed me was gone. Sue and I had settled into our little corner of London so effortlessly that we worried for a bit how things would go. 'What if you don't get on with the new manager, Alfie?' Managers come and go as often as sponsors these days but this was the 1970s and Bill Nick had been at White Hart Lane since 1940 – aka for ever. Sue knew how much I liked Bill but I assured her everything would be fine. It had to be as we had some great friends in London and I loved White Hart Lane. I was also amazed at how quickly I had struck up a special relationship with the supporters, and while this sounds really corny, London was home.

I was married at the time, so I wasn't like one of the single players who went down to London and got involved with the bright lights, clubbing, celebrity lifestyle, etc. I think in the three years I was there I was only in the West End half a dozen times.

Bill Nick's departure happened so quickly. There were no cheerios or goodbyes. One day he was there, the next he was gone, but he kept in touch with me throughout my time with Spurs and his encouragement was first-class. 'Keep working away, Alf, your turn will come.' It was such a boost that he still believed in me. He was a managerial legend at Spurs, having been in charge from 1958 to 1974, as well as 17 years a player. He stayed in White Hart Lane – never moved house. He was Mr Tottenham, and no one else comes close. I still maintain that Bill would have been brilliant for my career and Sue and I would probably never have left London if he'd stayed on. But he didn't, and his replacement, Arsenal man Terry Neill, waltzed into the club with his own masterplan on how we should take the next step. Most people I spoke to reckoned the only steps Neill had in mind were the few he would eventually take across north London to his spiritual home at Highbury. But he was our manager and I was his player. My second season at the Lane had been a complete washout and I was fit and raring to go for my third term. And then the manager left, inevitably for Highbury.

It was July 1976, and pre-season was in full swing. Bertie Mee had been in charge of the Gunners for ten years, after being the club physiotherapist, but he had been a success and won the First Division and FA Cup double as well as Arsenal's first European trophy. When he announced his resignation, I think we all knew who the favoured candidate would be. The majority of Neill's career had been spent as a centre-back at Highbury and it was no real surprise when he was confirmed as their new manager.

So who would be my third Spurs boss in as many seasons? Who could properly replace Bill Nick, the club's greatest ever manager? Keith Burkinshaw had been sacked as a coach at Newcastle United before being appointed as Neill's assistant a year later, and word started to filter through that he was favourite to land the job.

I think it's fair to say that Neill had never quite taken a shine to me, but the one thing he never had a problem with was motivating the players. He was excellent at that. But I had been thinking 'new manager, new broom', although nothing could've been further from the truth. 'Same old, same old' would've been a more fitting mantra. Keith was announced as Tottenham's new manager and that was that. While he was assistant, we had never really seen eye to eye, which was a great shame because I was so happy at Tottenham and wished for nothing more than being able to play my part in bringing success to the club. When Keith was appointed manager, I was fit, available for selection, and ready to help the team, but I was never really given a chance to stake my claim for a place. To illustrate my point, in that third season I kept myself in tip-top shape, because you never know when the call might come, and it came in mid-December when Manchester City visited the Lane.

It was a couple of weeks before Christmas and one look at the pitch would've had modern-day referees running for the hills. One end was covered in ice, while the other was merely bone-hard. We didn't know which type of boots to wear but the bottom line is there wasn't a single moan from any of the players. I always recall Steve Perryman losing the toss, and we were given the bone-hard end to defend, and Steve saying afterwards, 'If I'd won the toss I would have chosen to defend the ice in the first half!' Anyway, we were 2-0 up at half-time and had played some really good stuff. We had signed Peter Taylor for £200,000 from Crystal Palace and in this game, the first time we had really played together, we hit it off big time. Sometimes you just get that with a team-mate, you click for no apparent reason. Peter scored both goals that day and he played a great one-two with me for his first, in which he waltzed around two defenders before crashing the ball home. Glenn Hoddle was playing just behind us and everything seemed to click. I thought there was a good chance that we might get many more outings together but sadly it proved to be a false dawn.

The whole season, in fact, would be one of great disappointment, for me personally, and for the team. We should have done so much better with the players we had, but in another, more sinister way, the players we had were partly to blame. A few of the guys wielded far too much control in the dressing room and that's never a good thing. As we moved into the third quarter of the league programme you could see exactly where we were headed – and that was the Second Division.

In my last few months at the Lane there seemed a determination to make it a Londoners-only club, but history proved that such a plan would be doomed to failure. The great Spurs side of the 1960s, built by Bill Nicholson, was probably the closest there has ever been to an all-British side, with the likes of Danny Blanchflower, from Northern Ireland; Bill Brown, Dave Mackay and John White from Scotland; and Welsh players Cliff Jones and Terry Medwin. But that thinking had been pushed into the background, and when centre-half Willie Young and I were dropped we had a pretty good idea why it had happened, so we asked for a meeting with club chairman Sydney Wale. He seemed happy enough to meet us but when asked outright if we were out of the team because we were Scottish he refused to answer – and I took that silence to mean we were right. Somebody at the club didn't like us – but that certainly didn't apply to the fans. They could not have been any better to me had I been born in Tottenham High Road.

Get this, though. When it came to appointing Terry Neill's successor, the players were asked to vote on it. Everyone took part, even the junior players, but it was not a secret ballot, just a page with 'for' and 'against' Keith Burkinshaw columns. Naturally the majority weren't going to vote against the appointment when they saw the ballot was so open. And it was such a snap affair that Pat Jennings, the senior professional, wasn't even at the meeting when it happened. Maybe it was because the players had such a big say in his appointment that Keith seemed to give in to them too often.

The signs were soon there. During our pre-season tour of West Germany, the manager called a team talk one night.

After all we were abroad to get these types of things sorted out before the new season. But some of the lads wanted to go for a drink so the talk was cancelled and we all went to the pub instead. Too often I felt as though the players did what they wanted in training, and I include myself. There are times when everyone needs to be pushed, but my opinion is that the manager simply wasn't strong enough to get in our faces and tell us to get on with it.

As the season wore on, and our position became increasingly desperate, the backbiting became more vicious. We had a team talk after a disastrous 1-0 cup defeat at Cardiff, but what did we sort out? Well, we spent nearly an hour and a half discussing why I hadn't challenged for three balls in the air! The following day there was another meeting. I wasn't there, because I had been dropped for the game against Queens Park Rangers, but again I was the target – this time over throw-ins.

That was when I knew my time was up. Everyone was struggling, but whoever was dropped took the blame, to save others taking their share. I do accept some of the burden for Spurs taking the drop, even though I hardly played, but I was part of the first-team squad for most of the season. That said, there are others who should've taken far more responsibility, although that burden might have become so heavy as to weigh them down.

At the time, I didn't go along with all the talk that it might be a good thing if Spurs were relegated. I don't think there are ever positives in a situation like that. Most people knew that our squad simply wasn't good enough, despite having a potentially world-class player in Glenn Hoddle. The fans deserved so much better, but were badly let down. I get that every club, at one time or another, will face a crisis, and it's how they come out the other side that's important, but when we were going through our crisis it was hell on earth as you could see what potentially might fix it, but the malaise was too ingrained in our dressing room for anything to really make a difference.

While I flirted between playing for the reserves, being on the bench for the first team, or watching from the stand, it was clear that the writing was on the wall for me personally. Nothing had changed with the introduction of Keith and it felt like if I ever wanted to play football at a good level again I would have to move. There were few alternatives, although an upwards glance at the Second City proved interesting. Birmingham was a place that had 'almost' played a big part in my football career, although I never quite made it there. When I was leaving Rangers I was told that Aston Villa were serious about signing me. It was an interesting proposition. Ron Saunders had just left Manchester City to take over at Villa Park and had wanted to make me one of his first signings. Villa were in the second tier of English football, and that was an issue as I wanted to play in the top flight. They were definitely a club on the up but having been at an institution the size of Rangers for six years, I wasn't sure that I wanted to play for a team in transition. Saunders was an excellent manager, but there was a good chance it could be some time before Villa established themselves in the top flight again.

Interestingly, Birmingham City were now showing an interest, and a respected ex-Leeds United player, and a man who would go on to become a manager AND a minister made his move to take me to St Andrew's. Willie Bell, born in Johnstone, Renfrewshire, had enjoyed a successful playing career with Leeds, Leicester City and Brighton. Willie played in the Leeds team that had a reputation for being tough, but in 200 games he was only booked once. I recall reading in Norman Hunter's book, 'Willie was one of the bravest men I have seen in my life. He never blinked, nor flinched – he just went for it.'

In those days players were seldom privy to conversations between rival managers, even if the topic of conversation was YOU. Willie had apparently identified me as the player he wanted to inject new life into his stagnant Birmingham team. As usual, we found out most of our info from the newspapers, and Willie was quoted as saying, 'I see Conn as the type of player who could strengthen our squad, so I'll make an enquiry in the morning.'

I had missed the first six league matches of the season but was included for the game against Norwich City at the Lane. A Glenn Hoddle goal salvaged a point, but it was still a poor result. I had been in and out of the squad, used mostly in friendlies or League Cup games and I didn't feel part of the first-team setup. I felt it might be better if I was off the books. I knew of the interest from Birmingham and was sure there would be others keen to take a chance on me. A couple of days after the initial report, Willie was quoted as saying he was 'watching the situation carefully and would go to watch Conn play'.

However, the same newspaper suggested that Bell was playing games and using me to appease his supporters, who were demanding new signings. Keith said the same thing, and the final paragraph read, 'The situation may be resolved soon – with Conn settling his differences and coming off the Tottenham list.'

My position on the move, if anyone had bothered to ask, was that it would've taken a very good offer to tempt me away from Spurs. It's true that I wasn't a first-team regular, and that the entire situation was getting me down, but I wasn't a quitter and still believed I had something to offer the club. And then the papers down south discovered that my dog was called Blue. And just like some in the Scottish press, insisted it was inspired by a certain football club.

One headline rang out, 'Alfie Conn and his dog Blue don't know whether they're coming or going to Birmingham.'

Truth is, my dog's name was inspired by neither Rangers nor Birmingham City, but by my favourite character in my favourite TV programme – *The High Chaparral*. I suppose it didn't help that the character's full name was Billy Blue Cannon! I loved watching cowboy programmes when I was younger, but that was by far my favourite even into adulthood.

As time moved on, and nothing came of the reported Birmingham switch, I decided it would be better for my career if I left Spurs. I still wasn't playing and while in my heart I didn't want to move, my head was definitely saying 'go!' Sue and I had a good chat about it one evening and I told her there was apparently a bit of interest from other clubs in England, but she wasn't keen on remaining down south. We both loved where we stayed in London, and had fitted seamlessly into the lifestyle. It was perfect and we had a great balance between nights out and nights in, so we decided that if I had to move from Spurs – and wasn't going to another London club – then we should get back up the road to Scotland. It was a watershed moment in both my career and our lives.

I rang my trusted journalist pal Ken Gallacher and told him of our plans. I know he put the feelers out at both Old Firm clubs – probably the only two in Scotland who could afford the transfer fee Spurs would ask. Keith Burkinshaw then let it be known that if I were to sign for another team in England they would demand a fee of £130,000. But if I was heading back to Scotland they would accept half that. I guess I was moving on, then.

So, we'd decided on Scotland and realistically that meant Glasgow. As a Rangers supporter and ex-player, I was keen to move back to Ibrox, although there were a couple of reservations. More so over the way I had left the club, after feeling surplus to requirements. Some folk say you should never go back to your old club, but I've never been particularly superstitious.

News that I wanted home was out there, and now it was up to the clubs. Of course, that was out of my hands, so I played the waiting game. I was at Spurs, a great club with a fantastic tradition and, as I'd showed against Norwich, I was ready and willing to play whenever called upon, but Keith had made it perfectly clear that going forward I would be a squad player. I wanted and needed more than that. At 24, and with a couple of seasons behind me in the English top flight, I was sure I could've done a good job for him, but that was by the by. I had completely fallen in love with Tottenham Hotspur, and whatever happened in the coming days and weeks, that would never change.

The days and weeks were long and frustrating, and I had another run in the reserves. Hereford United's second string visited the Lane one night and the usual sparse, soul-destroying crowd were there to watch. As we lined up for the start of the game, you could hear individuals talking in the main stand. It was like playing in a public park. I didn't know it at the time but this would be my final, inglorious appearance in the famous Tottenham Hotspur shirt. And guess what – yes, I managed to take the hump. Put a football strip on me, show me a ball and I'll give everything I have; doesn't matter if it's against Real Madrid in the European Cup Final or Hereford United in a meaningless, mid-table reserve game. From what I remember of that evening, it was decent fare and I had set up a couple of chances for our centre-forward. Then, and with just a few minutes gone in the second half, our manager whistles and starts waving at the match official. 'Ref, substitute!' And naturally we all start looking over to the bench. 'Alfie,' he shouts, 'off you come.'

I'm not going to lie, I was seriously pissed off. Is this how far I had fallen? Being subbed off in the opening minutes of the second half against Hereford reserves? As I stomped around the track towards the bench, I was eyeing the manager furiously. Enough was enough. He was getting both barrels. As I neared the dugout, and was just about to let go, he said, 'There's someone to see you in the office, Alf. Good luck, mate.' That stopped me in my tracks. I smiled and headed straight up the tunnel and through the back to the office. From the angle I was approaching, there were no windows in the office, so I had no idea who was 'demanding' to see me during a game. Automatically, you think of your wife and family. But when I opened the door, the first thing I spotted were the rosy cheeks of my former Scotland under-23 manager, and that was something I definitely hadn't been expecting. Jock Stein. Arguably the most revered manager in the history of the Scottish game. Now, this was quite something. Think curveball and multiply it by infinity. I smiled and said hello, and Jock returned the compliment. Was he just passing White Hart Lane and had decided to drop in for a chat about the old days? Nope. He said he had been given permission to use the manager's office and in we went.

First and foremost, I wasn't aware that Jock had been at the game, and my initial thought was that he had come all that way to watch a reserve match and I took that as a big compliment. I was sat across the desk from this legend and he said to me, 'I'd love you to come to Celtic. I know it's a big deal and probably a lot to process, given the years and the success you had at Rangers, but for my part I've spoken to the players and they're quite happy for you to come. I would like you to come.'

It was a surreal moment. Anyone who knows the history between Rangers and Celtic would immediately throw up a thousand red flags. But take the two clubs out of the equation just for a moment and think Jock Stein. Think of his managerial qualities, and the impact he'd had on me as my under-23 coach. It was a real question, and I answered it as best I could.

'Well, if you want me to come, I'll come.'

We talked contracts and he told me that the deal was initially for one month only, to give me every opportunity to prove my fitness. He then looked me in the eye and said, 'Are you fit, son?' I said, 'I am.' And that was the end of the fitness chat.

He said, 'Well, there's just one more thing to sort out before we agree to things formally. I like to think I know a player when I see one, and I think you're a player, but the one thing that worries me is that good players, and I mean, right good players, they get their hair cut a certain way. Short back and sides. Neat, you know what I mean?'

At the time my hair seemed longer than Rapunzel's. Had I been locked in a room at the top of the Tower of London I could've used my locks to escape. I liked it long as it somehow added to the flamboyant alter ego I had assumed at Tottenham. It was more than just my trademark – I thought I suited it! I told Jock that if he had a policy about long hair, or even if it was a preference that his players should have short hair, then I would get it cut. 'Great,' he said, 'I've booked you an appointment at a top hair salon in such-and-such a street. Tomorrow morning at ten!'

I had to laugh. This man didn't do anything by halves. It seemed that if he wanted a player, he went and got him. He told me that he had already spoken to Keith Burkinshaw and that I could come back to Scotland and the fee would be £65,000. That was the deal, and apparently Jock liked a bargain.

Once I got my head around the fact that I had signed for Celtic I think I was OK about going there. I told Sue that night we'd need to pack up again and she was fine about it. She was happy that we were going back to Scotland as that meant seeing her family regularly again. She told me that she'd really enjoyed London, and had made loads of friends. She would be sad to leave them but family trumps friends, and London was only a few hours away.

I'll say it here and now, but if Jock Stein had been manager of any other club, even Albion Rovers, I'd have gone there. Jock was the main attraction. I revered him as a coach and the thought of playing under him excited me.

I had a few days in London to sort everything out and then travelled up to Scotland to start training. It was a few weeks before I started to question if I'd done the right thing. I was starting to get a lot of abuse and some of it was hard to take. Sadly, it was everywhere. An innocent bystander may have thought I'd committed a heinous crime. At that time, my mum and dad had a house right on the water in Limekilns, in

Fife, and there was a walkway between their back garden and the beach, and they would get insults hurled at them by people who had gone there for that purpose alone. It was despicable. Maybe it was the done thing in those days but it was completely out of order.

The one saving grace was that Sue didn't face any abuse. She was well out of it, as she had no interest in football. I was never one for shirking anything in life but if Sue had received a hard time because of the football team I'd chosen to play for, that would've crossed the line. To be honest, the abuse never turned physical or violent, perhaps because I always tried to play it down. It was all mouthing, especially when there was a crowd. Speaking one to one wasn't so bad, and it seemed you could get a fair hearing.

I've now had almost five decades to process the facts surrounding my move to Celtic in 1977. And now I realise it all happened just a bit too fast. Jock Stein had clearly been talking to Keith about a potential transfer. The two managers had probably had at least a few days to process the information and everything else surrounding the move. Me? I didn't have that luxury. I was languishing in the reserves at Spurs, an iconic manager comes along and wham, I was swept away by the offer. As I said earlier, a journalist friend of mine had let it be known that I wanted to come back to Scotland, and at first there were no takers. Both Rangers and Celtic were aware that I would soon be available for transfer. It was then up to them if they wanted to make a move.

To rewind slightly to the week or so before I signed for Celtic, apparently Rangers supporters had been chanting my name at a match, so they clearly wanted me back in light blue. And so when I signed for Celtic I could fully understand why that must've been a massive kick in the teeth. I used to receive lots of letters when I played at Ibrox telling of how I was their favourite player. Now, I had gone from being the guy who was about to return to Ibrox, who went all Judas Iscariot and signed for Celtic. Could I understand the fury and the backlash? Now, I understand it 100 per cent. I completely get why supporters gave me both barrels every time I appeared at Ibrox in a different coloured shirt – and for many years afterwards. And now I see that not as a tirade of personal abuse directed at me for a single misdemeanour, but as a backhanded compliment from thousands of people who valued my previous contribution to the club so much that they were hurt when I signed for their rivals.

There were genuinely only two clubs who could afford the fee Tottenham wanted and they were Rangers and Celtic. But both were under NO obligation to sign me. Jock Wallace at Rangers was the kind of man and manager who had his own mind and would never have been railroaded into signing a player he didn't want, or might think wouldn't fit into the side he wanted and how he wanted them to play.

I think it's important to remember why I left Rangers in the first place. I wasn't wanted. I wasn't a first-team regular and another player had been signed to replace me. What type of message does that send to someone? But at the time it probably made sense for me to leave – for both me and the club. I could move to England, try something different, play in the first team and enhance my opportunity of playing for Scotland. And Rangers could cash in and strengthen the team. Win-win. So the last thing I wanted was to go back to that same environment. That was my predicament. Now, let's say Jock Wallace had come in for me and told me that a few years at Spurs had made me a better and wiser player, and that he saw a bespoke role for me in the team he was building. That would've been a game changer. I was still a Rangers fan – that hadn't changed, and never will. My heart would definitely have ruled my head and I would've chosen Rangers over Celtic, assuming both had been interested. Equally, had anyone else but Jock Stein been the manager of Celtic I would not have signed for them. Sue and I would have rethought our plans and would probably have tried to make it work in England.

Lots of ifs and buts and I suppose the bottom line is that Rangers didn't show any interest. That doesn't rankle with me or upset me, because you can't make someone want you. I had a wife, a kid and a mortgage and I had to work, so I chose to sign for Jock Stein. And now, nearly five decades on, I ask myself if it was worth the hassle I got and continue to get? Would I do the same thing if I had the decision to make again tomorrow? Not a hope in hell. Some things in life just aren't worth the grief, and this was one of them.

10

Crossing the Great Divide

TUESDAY, 1 March 1977. The deal was done and I was a Celtic player. Maybe I was just a tad naive about the fall-out from the move but I thought the noise would die down after a couple of weeks. How wrong could I be?

I had been languishing in the Tottenham reserve side and my hopes of getting back into the first team were diminishing week by week, which in turn was slowly destroying my soul. But Jock Stein had been keeping tabs on me and decided I was worth a punt. And being the shrewd man that he was, when he decided to make his move, it had strings. The Godfather of Scottish football made Spurs an offer they couldn't refuse. He knew Tottenham were keen to offload me so he agreed to pay £65,000 once I had proved my fitness, and so a loan period of one month was crucial to his plan. Show your fitness, Alfie, and we have a deal. I had pushed any thoughts of injury to the back of my mind as I was desperate to get playing again.

The papers north of the border were full of my shock move to Celtic. That wasn't a big surprise but I hoped that once the nation's bout of Alfiemania had dissipated they would leave me alone and move on to someone else. My only interest was in leaving the house in the morning and going to training, and then playing football on a Saturday afternoon. I wasn't really interested in how many people had played for both Rangers and Celtic in the previous 50 years – or becoming the most high-profile player to have turned out for both halves of the Old Firm. Notoriety was never my thing. When Mo Johnston made the headlines for choosing Rangers over Celtic in 1989, having previously played for the latter, a dozen years after my switch to Celtic, I quietly wished him good luck. I knew he would need it.

Jock had warned me in advance that he would be putting me up for the midweek press conference, as he knew I was keen to get it over and done with. I would rather have avoided it altogether, but that wasn't an option. Jock was up first and I thought his speech to the media was balanced and non-confrontational. He said, 'Alfie has signed initially for a month, but that's simply to confirm his fitness – nothing else. I'm delighted we have managed to get him and he will be in the first-team squad for Saturday's game with Aberdeen. We bought Alfie from Spurs because he's a good player. We didn't buy him to rile people because that would've been stupid.'

When it was my turn I told the press I was delighted to get back up the road, and that I had thoroughly enjoyed the majority of my spell in London but the time was now right, and my aim was to slip seamlessly into the training sessions at Celtic and hopefully make an instant impact. I said that I'd had great respect for Jock when he was in charge of the Scotland under-23s side and I meant every word when I said he was the best manager I had played under.

I was inevitably asked my opinion on how I would now be viewed by a large section of the Rangers support, and I said, 'I'm not worried about the reaction from them. I just want to get on with my career.'

In hindsight I was wrong to say that. Of course I was worried about the reaction, and for a couple of reasons. The first was that no player likes to be jeered. Football is an entertainment business and we like to think that if we do something good it will be rewarded by cheers. Let's be honest, most people prefer to be liked. It's not a prerequisite but it's far better than being barracked mercilessly.

The second reason was that I was still a Rangers supporter. On this point people can think or say what they like (I know), but I knew what I was and what I still am. I've been a Rangers supporter since I was old enough to know what it meant, and that has never left me. But I needed to earn a living. I had a family to support and having loyalties in football sadly doesn't pay the mortgage or put food on the table. Only one club had come in for me and that was Celtic, and I was happy to sign my name on the contract. But anyone who knows me well enough knows that I would never short-change an employer. Celtic were now paying the wages and I was all in. My aim – as always

– was to stay fit and fight for a first-team place, and once I achieved that, to fight to stay in the team.

My first day at training was a bit like your first day at school. I'm not really the nervous sort but I was definitely apprehensive rolling up to Celtic Park that morning ahead of my first training session. I drove into the main car park and sat in my car for a while. Did I come to the wrong place? It was three years after I'd left Rangers, but this seismic shift in my place of work definitely registered on my personal Richter scale. How could it not? I had walked through the front door at Parkhead many times as a Rangers player, and it was always something I enjoyed. We would get off the team bus and with chest puffed out, proudly wearing the badge, I would walk through the front door knowing that I was representing such a fantastic football club. Now, though, it was different.

I got out the car and there were quite a few Celtic supporters milling around and looking for autographs. One or two stopped me and asked for a signature. I smiled, signed my name and thanked them. I then walked through the front door and it felt very strange indeed. I never bought into the whole west of Scotland, Protestant–Catholic thing. It seemed more like a personal thing with me. I was a Rangers supporter, an ex-Rangers player who had enjoyed plenty of success over Celtic – and who had REALLY enjoyed playing against Celtic – and now I was a Celtic player. But walking through that door was like walking into another dimension. I was greeted by a man in a Celtic blazer and he showed me through to the Celtic dressing room. That short walk was also weird. 'Where am I going?' I thought briefly. 'Why have I signed for Celtic?' That was something I questioned a lot in the early days, and I came to the conclusion that I hadn't signed for Celtic – I had actually signed for Jock Stein. And there was a difference.

When I walked into the dressing room for the first time there was one voice I heard above all others – that of Rangers' nemesis, Johnny Doyle. His first words to me were, 'Here he is, the currant bun!' What an icebreaker. He was one guy I really hit it off with and we would go on to have a great relationship. In all the time I knew him, I think he only called me Alf just the once. I said to him, 'Should I be worried?'

He was often accused of being a bigot, but he wasn't. He was simply a Celtic man through and through, and there is nothing wrong with being a passionate supporter of a football team. We had a few of our own in my time at Rangers. Johnny christened me the 'currant bun' and not once did I take offence. He became one of my best mates at Celtic – and beyond my time there. We would wind the coaches up together. They would have these best of three competitions in training and the coaches would always write down the results. They would praise the winners of these head-to-head sprints and encourage the loser to do better next time. We were usually paired together, and Johnny would win the first one, I'd win the next, and then we'd cross the line together in the deciding race. It would drive them nuts, but it kept us sane.

When I visited Ibrox for the first time after signing for Celtic, I naturally turned right to head to the home dressing room, and all I heard was, 'Hey, currant bun, wrang way!' Johnny – who wore a Celtic scarf to every match – pointed to the left. Next minute he walks over to me, thrusts his scarf into my hand and said, 'Take that into the dressing room for me,' and in a flash he was gone. And I'm left standing in the foyer at Ibrox holding a Celtic scarf.

Even after I left Celtic I'd meet up with him at a wee place in London Road called Joe's Kitchen, not far from Parkhead, and we'd have a cuppa and a blether. He was never anything but very loyal to me and I'm convinced that had there been any dissent towards me in the Celtic dressing room then Johnny would've put them right.

I'll never forget the night I got a phone call in 1981 to say he had died. It completely knocked me for six. It was such an awful tragedy.

There weren't really any of my team-mates who I didn't get on with at Celtic. Danny McGrain didn't suffer fools gladly, but we got on really well. It's well documented that I was good friends with Kenny Dalglish long before I joined Celtic. He signed for Liverpool the same year I joined, but we had a few months together at Parkhead, which was good. Seemingly Jock Stein had gathered all the players together before I signed to tell them of his plans. He wanted to know if anyone had any objections, or if they weren't happy with the move. No one complained, and I took that as a vote of confidence in me.

Although the same couldn't be said for a few Celtic supporters. In my first game as a visitor to Ibrox, I hit the bar and the post and afterwards, when I spoke to a couple of fans, they said I had done it deliberately. I said, 'I'm not THAT good!' But I took it in the spirit that hopefully it was meant. I actually recall hitting that shot at Ibrox and turning to celebrate because I was convinced it was a goal, and then remembering that Ibrox still had square goalposts. Had that been the posts nowadays it would have been a goal. Mind you, had that gone in I was right up the tunnel!

But to rewind slightly to my Celtic debut, up at Pittodrie, we were in the lead in the title race although Aberdeen had proved something of a tough opponent that season, as Celtic had failed to beat them in three games – including the League Cup Final. I was clearly late to the party and thought Pittodrie was probably a decent place to make my debut. Aberdeen hadn't been on the best of runs so it was also an opportunity for Celtic to break their duck for the season. We travelled up on the team bus and when we arrived at the ground there was a healthy contingent of Celtic supporters waiting at the front door. I received a positive reception, which gave me one less thing to worry about.

Unfortunately the game itself wasn't quite going according to plan and just after the hour mark I was told to go out and warm up. We were behind and perhaps the fans saw me as the guy to go on and rescue a bad situation. It had also been a bad-tempered match, and a few minutes later I was standing on the touchline, stripped and ready to take my bow. George McCluskey came off. I was involved almost instantly in this whirlwind of a match but even though I had a couple of decent half chances, Aberdeen would go on to win 2-0. Jock Stein let the players know exactly what he thought of us dropping both points and on the way down the road the only positive for me was that a potentially awkward debut was now out of the way.

The following day in the match report, a journalist suggested I had done little to affect play, and he was probably right, but it was another column in the same newspaper that caught my eye. This opinion piece suggested I was 'exciting, gifted, if occasionally undisciplined'. So far, probably right. The writer suggested that my return to Scotland should have been applauded rather than derided, and that Rangers fans would be best advised to lay off me as it hadn't been my fault that Rangers hadn't tried to sign me. The piece went on to say, 'There was no reason to believe that Conn himself would have wished to come back to Rangers. Indeed, the opposite is apparently the case.' I had never once said that I didn't want to come back to Rangers. Now, whether or not a newspaper had (falsely) reported this as the case, the truth was I hadn't said it, nor ever suggested it.

I was being used to highlight the continuing unhealthy aspects of the Rangers–Celtic rivalry, and that wasn't something I appreciated. The article was seemingly calling out this unhealthy rivalry but in essence all it was doing was adding fuel to the fire ahead of my first Old Firm match. It was said that I couldn't possibly approach this date as just another game of football. That was true, but as Jock Stein reminded everyone, 'This game is not just about Alfie Conn, it is about improving your league position, about beating your opponents, about all the players.' But those words didn't sell newspapers and as the big game edged ever closer I did start to feel real pressure. It was also at Ibrox and the majority of fans would be those who had once cheered me. Celtic had held the upper hand that season and there was nothing to suggest it was about to change. On the morning of the big match, one paper wrote, 'Conn was a popular player at Ibrox because he was flamboyant, but he is now proving equally popular with the Celtic fans.' A blessing or a curse?

The game was upon us and I didn't sleep much the night before. When Jock named the team I was playing up front alongside Kenny Dalglish. It was a positive team and the hope was that we could take another step towards the league title. When Roy Aitken put Celtic in front, that target edged one step closer. There was just 11 minutes on the clock, and moments later I connected well with the ball and smashed a shot goalwards from 20 yards, but it flew narrowly past the post. Two minutes later my swerving effort cannoned back off the woodwork. I was getting closer. All around me it was bedlam – and I seemed to be the sinner-in-chief. My name was mud as far as the resident choir was concerned, but that didn't make me want to try even harder to shut them up. I just tried to ignore it and concentrate on the game, as difficult as that was. In some ways it was a backhanded compliment as the Rangers supporters in the 51,000 crowd were furious that I wasn't playing for them. Perhaps others who had taken a similar path wouldn't have been met with the same fierce criticism. That's what I told myself, anyway.

My old strike partner, Derek Parlane, equalised for Rangers on 20 minutes, and then late on he edged Rangers in front, and that was the moment all hell broke loose. There was still 11 minutes to play when Rangers went in front, but it was as though the roof had fallen in. A relatively calm Old Firm game became bonkers as Celtic fans fought with one another and dozens of fans spilled on to the field. Cans and bottles were flying through the air and it took the police – and Jock Stein – five minutes to restore an uneasy calm. The big man came flying out of the dugout and headed straight for the Celtic end. As fans fought with police, Jock threw himself straight into the middle of it all and began remonstrating with those still on the park.

When play finally restarted, Aitken equalised and even though wee Doddie had the ball in the net for Rangers, it was ruled out for offside. It was actually a relief to get into the dressing room after that one. It might seem that on 99 per cent of occasions, the players are in no danger whatsoever, but all it takes is for law and order to break down and we have a big problem.

After that match, the papers were full of the crowd trouble, my part in the game and Doddie's cancelled effort. For a few days there was no let-up and everyone was having their say. Then, in the middle of all the post-game post-mortems came this oasis of calm: an interview with a well-known figure from my past – and it reaffirmed that I had made the right decision by signing for Jock Stein.

Don Revie was asked his opinion on the move and he gave a candid answer. I'll never forget it. He said, 'Alfie Conn will become one of the greatest footballers in Britain … if he remains with Celtic.

'It is fair to say that the 25-year old failed to fulfil his immense potential at Tottenham. He is now with Celtic on a month's trial, and I am convinced he will truly blossom if they decide to sign him permanently.'

It was a joy to read, and not just because it was saying nice things about me, but because it wasn't related to any of the nonsense that had been spouted incessantly since my return to Scotland. In my opinion, Don Revie always tried to look at football in a positive manner. He continued, 'Jock Stein is one of the best managers when it comes to bringing the best out of players. Over the years I have lost count of the footballers who have performed better for Stein and Celtic than any other team. Two who come readily to mind are goalkeeper Ronnie Simpson and inside-forward Bertie Auld. They were regarded as past their best when Stein signed them from Newcastle United and Birmingham, but both produced the best form of their careers with Celtic.'

Don also brought up the time he had my name on a contract, but ripped it up when Rangers came calling. He then spoke about me having a difficult time at Spurs, through injuries and other reasons, but still believed I was a good fit for Bill Nick's team. He added, 'Conn is an exciting forward, possessing the control and pace to go forward with the ball and take on opponents in tight areas. But he hasn't always made the most of his talent, and that is where someone like Stein comes in. He has a refreshingly simple, straightforward approach to coaching, and this is reflected in the football of his teams. They are well organised, and perform with drive and enthusiasm. Stein has always been a great believer in attacking football. His teams go for goals on opponents' grounds as well as their own.'

My thoughts exactly. And there was no denying that Jock's attention to detail was always meticulous, and Don Revie also believed that it was quite often the small things that made a difference. He said, 'We lost out to Celtic in season 1969/70, in the semi-finals of the European Cup, and Stein didn't miss a trick. Before the first match at Elland Road, he agreed that Celtic should not wear white socks as these might clash with Leeds' all-white strip and accepted our offer to supply another set. As our trainer Les Cocker offered 12 sets of blue stockings, Stein shouted, "You must be joking, there's no way we're going out there in Rangers colours!" He knew that his supporters would've berated him for it, but it was these things he spotted, even in the white-hot atmosphere of a European semi.'

Appearance was also everything to the big man, as witnessed with his 'request' that I get my hair cut to an acceptable length.

There were few blips in the run-in to the championship and a 3-0 defeat at Motherwell apart, the title was wrapped up with several games to spare. Nine points was the winning margin over Rangers with Aberdeen a couple further back. The game which clinched the trophy was at Easter Road against Hibs. It was packed out, as you would expect, and the supporters had to wait until the hour mark for the goal which won the league. I picked up the ball out wide and whipped in a cross which Joe Craig fired home. There was delirium on the terraces, which was just as well, because the Hibs chairman, Tom Hart, had banned the TV cameras, so as far as I know the only people to see the title-clinching goal were the fans present on the day. There were no mobile phones in those days. I was pleased to get the assist as I'd missed a decent chance in the first half.

The league was in the bag and I'd played in more than a dozen games, so I felt like I'd contributed. I had also arrived in time for the latter stages of the Scottish Cup and routine wins over Queen of the South and Dundee, which set up a final against who else but Rangers. The build-up to the final was predictable, 'The name will be logged in the *Guinness Book of Records*: Alfie Conn, the only player in the history of the game to play in successive Rangers v Celtic Scottish Cup Finals on opposing teams.'

Fair enough, as I suppose it was newsworthy, and it was said that no other player in the 103-year history of the competition had ever won a medal with Rangers and Celtic, but here I was four years after doing it for Rangers in an Old Firm final. I was just glad that I had already played against Rangers since arriving back in Scotland from Tottenham and hoped that might dilute the ire directed at me from the Rangers supporters. I admit to being concerned about the reception I would get from both sets of fans before the match at Ibrox, but they had their say. They shouted and they chanted and got it out of their systems, and I vowed to block out any noise at Hampden on the big day.

The Old Firm match was the greatest game in the world, certainly that I'd played in. The 1973 Scottish Cup Final is a day that lives long in the memory: 123,000 inside Hampden and a five-goal thriller to delight and excite. We won 3-2 that afternoon and it was bedlam at the final whistle. I played for Spurs against Arsenal, but it wasn't in the same class. For the latest instalment in the history of the Old Firm, it was just a pity that the crowd was limited to around 50,000 as such an occasion deserved more than double that. After all, it was the fans who made it what it was. It was also the first time the cup final would be televised live, which was bound to have an effect on the size of the crowd.

The build-up to the game was as usual spectacular, as it seemed the whole country had gone cup final crazy. We were in demand for TV, radio and press interviews as well as loads of stuff with sponsors. When the big day finally arrived we followed a routine I was well used to, having played in a few Hampden cup finals. In the dressing room before the game, Jock Stein didn't say too much. He chose his words carefully and used the time up until kick-off wisely so that no one had too much time to overthink things.

When we walked out on to the pitch the noise was incredible, with both sets of supporters contributing to a colourful and spectacular atmosphere, despite the wind and driving rain. I looked all around the ground, drank it in and then prepared for kick-off. Jock Stein proved the master tactician on the day and ditched his cavalier style of football to ensure Rangers' big guns didn't get as much space or see as much of the ball as they would have liked. Jóhannes Eðvaldsson stuck to big Derek Johnstone like a limpet. The marking was tight, in fact, too tight at times, and there was little room on the pitch for the creative players to thrive. The end result was a rather unglamorous game for the neutral – and the millions of viewers tuning in at home.

There was one moment of real controversy, and it took place in the 20th minute. Celtic were awarded a corner and I went out to take it. Stewart Kennedy, the Rangers keeper, had saved an Andy Lynch header, but had given himself quite a whack after smacking off the post. While he was receiving treatment, I stood with the ball in my hands, waiting to take the corner. Any noise coming from behind was jumbled, and I was focussed purely on hitting a good corner. As the trainer made his way off the pitch, I placed the ball next to the corner flag. I looked up to see where everyone was and then hit an absolute beauty to exactly the spot I was aiming for. Up went the heads. Big Roddy MacDonald met the cross with his head, and then all hell broke loose. In went 'Shuggy' Eðvaldsson to hit the ball, Kennedy dropped it a yard off his line, desperately Jardine and Johnstone were guarding their goal line and the ball came back off the big Icelander, appeared to hit Johnstone on the hand – and referee Bob Valentine whistled (although no one heard it) and pointed to the penalty spot. No VAR, no four-minute delay, just a good old-fashioned decision to give a spot kick. Was it controversial? Yes, it was, as I've seen it back on TV and I'm still not convinced it was a penalty. But as a footballer you don't question a decision that's given your way and Lynch dispatched the kick to give us the lead – and the cup.

We were probably the better team on the day, although there wasn't a lot in it. I'd had an early chance when I broke through the heart of the Rangers defence but smashed my shot off Kennedy's knees. Late on, we had one more chance of note to double our advantage. I found Danny McGrain out wide with a raking pass. He hit the ball low and hard across the box and Paul Wilson, with the goal at his mercy, completely missed it. Craig was at the far post and had a great chance, but Kennedy saved and Bomber Jackson cleared.

There were a few unsavoury incidents at the end of the game but the cup had been won, although it was just a pity that after an hour and a half, it came down to a moment of controversy. After we returned to the dressing room, Jock Stein was giving a post-match pep talk when we were told by an SFA official that we would be allowed back out on to the pitch to do a lap of honour. We looked at one another and got to our feet. Danny McGrain grabbed the cup and out we went, but there were still hundreds of Rangers fans in the stadium. It wasn't one of the SFA's better decisions but we took a half lap of honour anyway. To finish the season with a league and cup double was special, and at that moment I must admit that I believed I had made the right decision.

11

A Season of Two Halves

FOR MY first pre-season with the club Jock Stein had decided to take us to Singapore. We would do a certain amount of training, play some bounce games and take part in the World of Soccer Cup, an international tournament featuring the host national team, as well as Arsenal and Red Star Belgrade. Singapore was a wonderful place to begin our preparations. It was a working holiday but we still got to see a wee bit of the place and it was stunning.

After starting off my Celtic career with a league title win (albeit I'd arrived in March) I was really looking forward to the new season, especially the opportunity to get some meaningful work in with Jock and his coaches, but before we had even boarded our flight controversy hit, and it involved my friend and team-mate Kenny Dalglish. Kenny was in dispute with the board and it ended with him refusing to travel to Asia with us. By the time we returned he would be a Liverpool player. It wasn't the best of starts to our pre-season jaunt halfway around the world but as professionals you get on with it.

We faced Singapore in their national stadium, and with the sun splitting the sky and the home supporters out in force – the attendance was around the 50,000 mark – the atmosphere was electric. As I looked around the stadium just before kick-off I remember thinking how fortunate I was to have witnessed some of the things I had in my life, and some of the interesting places I'd visited as a result of being pretty good at football. On this occasion, we knew that Red Star had defeated Arsenal 3-1, so up for grabs was a game against the crack Yugoslav side. We were on top form that day and everything came together nicely as we won 5-0. I scored twice, and Tommy Burns, Shuggy Eðvaldsson and Bobby Lennox were also on target. We were pretty pleased with ourselves but in the final we played poorly and lost 3-1 to Red Star. No excuses but we wilted in the 90-degree heat and the 60,000 crowd hailed the Yugoslavs at the final whistle. Had we missed Kenny? What team wouldn't miss such a world-class player?

From Singapore it was another long-haul flight to Australia, where we were taking part in a second competition. Once again we were up against Arsenal and Red Star, while an Australian XI replaced Singapore. Our first game handed us a quick opportunity to gain revenge on Red Star, and this time the searing heat was replaced by a far milder climate in Melbourne's Olympic Stadium. It might have been a pre-season tournament but it was a cracking match and ended in a 1-1 draw. Sadly, near the end Pat Stanton was sent off for retaliation, when he took exception to being punched in the face!

From Melbourne we moved on to the Sydney Cricket Ground, where I was once again up against old foes Arsenal, and they remembered me from my time at Spurs, despite my cropped hair. That game was played at breakneck pace and we won 3-2, but the only thing I really took from it was yet another injury.

After the match a few of the players went out for drinks, although Arsenal had explicitly banned their guys from doing so. Malcom Macdonald and Alan Hudson decided to grab a few pints and paid the ultimate price by being sent home by the club. It was a real pity because it wasn't a crazy session, but just a couple after a tough 90 minutes.

Our final game, which I missed, was against the Aussie national side and we scraped the decision by the odd goal in five and that meant a place in the final of the competition – against Red Star Belgrade! For this one it was back to Melbourne and we didn't give Red Star a sniff, finally getting one over on them by winning 2-0. As a result, the club pocketed £20,000 and then named a new captain in the wake of Kenny's move to Anfield. Danny McGrain was announced as skipper and it was a popular decision with everyone at Celtic.

Looking back, it came to pass that the World of Soccer Cup in Oz would be the last trophy Jock Stein would win for Celtic. We thought this jaunt would have us in fine fettle for the season ahead, but little did we know what was around the corner. I was fit for the start of the season, Kenny had gone to Liverpool in a £440,000 deal, and some of the money from that transfer was used to strengthen the squad. And then it all went pear-shaped. Our first game of the season was against Dundee United at Parkhead. The league flag was unfurled and in retrospect perhaps it should've been a red flag. The match itself was a huge disappointment and finished 0-0. Pat Stanton and I suffered knee injuries and while I would recover (of sorts) from my knock, Pat's injury would all but finish his career. It was a sad way for such a glorious career to end. Pat was a lovely guy but, more importantly, a terrific footballer, and my heart really did go out to him. It also went out to our supporters because our next four league games ended in defeat – to Ayr United, Motherwell, Rangers and Aberdeen. After five matches we were at the bottom of the table with a solitary point. And this coming in the wake of a double-winning season.

At the start of October, we beat Hibs 3-1 but lost Danny McGrain to injury, and he would miss the entire campaign. Suddenly we were minus Dalglish and McGrain and I just don't think the quality, or belief, was there and that made for a long season.

Later that month we faced Wacker Innsbruck at Celtic Park in the third round of the European Cup and were looking good at 2-0, but with 14 minutes to go (and just after I came on as a substitute), I was fouled by Werner Schwarz. He was booked, but I was carried off. The Austrians pulled a goal back to give themselves real hope for the second leg, which they won 3-0, and once again I was on the treatment table. My legs were getting a pounding and it was starting to take its toll.

But you stop feeling sorry for yourself when you meet someone far worse off than you, and that was the case in the new year of 1978, when I had the pleasure of meeting one of the most inspirational kids around. We were up in Aberdeen to face the Dons in a league game and as usual arrived long before kick-off time.

When we got to the ground and jumped off the team bus, I saw Dons manager Billy McNeill grab a hold of Danny McGrain. Thinking nothing of it, I headed to the dressing room with the rest of the lads. A few minutes later, Danny came in, shouted, 'Alfie,' and beckoned me over. He had a quick word with Jock Stein and the gaffer nodded to me. Outside, Danny said, 'There's a young lad who's just had his arm amputated and he's a big Celtic supporter. You and I are his favourite players apparently,' and he laughed. We walked to the boardroom where the young lad, James, was waiting with his family. When we opened the door, and James saw us walking into the room, his eyes filled up and he became so emotional. It was quite a moment. He told us that he'd been a goalkeeper for a boys' club but had been in for an operation and ended up losing his arm. It was obviously a seismic event in his life, but he said cheerfully, 'I still play football with my friends, although I don't go in goals any more!' Despite being from Aberdeen, he was a lifelong Celtic fan and he was a great kid. He told Danny and I that we were his favourite players, and just then his older sister, who had remained silent throughout, said, 'I'm a Rangers fan, and you used to be my favourite player, Alfie!' Danny looked at me and laughed, and I didn't quite know what to say, so I said thanks!

We lost that game 2-1, and it came in the middle of a horrendous run of five straight defeats that well and truly sunk us. At that point no one believed that we were capable of holding on to our title – least of all us.

The final match of an abysmal run was at Celtic Park when we hosted St Mirren. There were 20,000 present, which meant big gaps on the terraces. We got a free kick, about 23 yards from goal. We had been practising free kicks at training all that week, as it was part of our drills. It was between Ronnie Glavin and I to take it, but I said to him, 'The way that wall is set up is perfect for you to have a shot.' So, Ronnie had a go but stuck it well over the bar. After the game, big Jock was going through us, especially Ronnie, and said, 'You practise free kicks all week and that's what happens.' I butted in and said, 'Gaffer, it was me that suggested Ronnie hit it because of the way the wall was set up.'

We had lost 2-1 and that was that. For starters, the look Jock gave me would've turned milk. He took the huff because I'd sided with Ronnie and refused to speak to me for a week. Perhaps he was starting to feel the heat, but I always felt that if I'd something important to say I should say it.

We played back-to-back league games against Hibs at Easter Road in the April. The title was long gone by this time and the cracks were beginning to show. In the first of these, poor Ronnie got it in the ear again and it wasn't really his fault.

We were struggling, big time, and Ronnie was injured. Big Jock was going through us all at half-time and no one knew where to look, and then halfway through this tirade the door opens and in walks Ronnie. Jock looked at him and shouted, 'Aye, you. You deserted a sinking ship, didn't you?' And that was the end of the team talk, as we all got up and got back on the pitch. A wee bit early, but poor Ronnie had spared us more of the hairdryer treatment. Jock could be ruthless when he needed to be. We drew that game 1-1, and three days later we were back at Easter Road and lost 4-1. I don't know whether the knives were already out for the big man but a few weeks later, at the close of the league campaign, and we had finished fifth, there were real rumblings of discontent in the stands. Rangers had won the treble and we had suffered the embarrassment of missing out on a place in Europe, as Dundee United and Hibs grabbed the two remaining places. I think it was telling that for our penultimate home league match, we had a little over 6,000 in the stadium. The fans were voting with their feet and when that happens the writing is usually on the wall.

Despite the horrendous amount of injuries I suffered throughout my 16-year professional career, this was undoubtedly my lowest point. To win the league one season and fail to even qualify for Europe the next was almost unthinkable, and it took a bit of time to get over. But if it was a disappointment for me, I can only begin to imagine what it must have been like for Jock. Remember, this is a guy who was a serial winner in his time at Parkhead: ten league titles, eight Scottish Cups, six League

Cups and a European Cup. He was used to winning trophies, so to finish mid-table in his final season must have been not only a career low, but a real kick in the teeth, personally.

It was announced that he would be leaving Celtic although many believed that he had been persuaded to stand down by the board. At the time it was reported that he was expecting to be appointed to the board of directors at Celtic but was instead offered a management position within Celtic Pools – which was really sad to hear, as he had done far more to further the club than those making the decisions. He rejected this position and was awarded a testimonial game against Liverpool. It's believed that at this match, the Liverpool manager Bob Paisley persuaded the big man to remain in football, and in August, 1978, he was appointed manager of Leeds United. Forty-four days later he was announced as the new manager of Scotland. That's football.

I had signed for Celtic for one reason and one reason only – Jock Stein. Did he live up to my expectations? He absolutely did. He was different-class as a person and a manager. He knew how to man-manage and his tactics were second to none. And when you sat and listened to him, his talks were riveting. We played Leeds in a friendly for Scotland under-23s at Hampden and to help us prepare for the game he took us down the coast to Seamill. We were told to be in the conference room for a certain time, as big Jock was giving us a talk. Anyway, he started to speak about the opposition, about what we couldn't let them do, and how they would try to do it. Almost an hour later he was still talking, and it flew in. Not one player had nodded off, or taken their eyes from the big man. Not only did he command respect, but he commanded an audience like I'd never seen before. He spoke a lot of sense, sure, but his talks were so interesting and that meant we lapped up everything he said. I used to wonder how folk could be taken in by some of the cranks in the world, but the power of speech is an incredible thing. I'd been in loads of dressing rooms where a manager would overdo it and repeat himself constantly, or talk about things that weren't relevant, but not Jock.

I also believed a captain's role to be an important one, and that they shouldn't be appointed just because of length of service. A good captain was vital during a game, especially if things weren't going your way. I played under Kenny Dalglish and Danny McGrain at Celtic and these guys were so good at motivating team-mates. At Rangers, John Greig was always urging the players on, which helps so much if you're starting to flag. And then you had wee Alex MacDonald, who didn't stop talking from start to finish. You had Sandy Jardine at the back, and Davie Smith, our Franz Beckenbauer. We talk about Harry Potter having a magic wand, but Davie was doing magic tricks with his left foot long before J.K. Rowling's fabled wizard creation.

When you play at the top level in Scotland, or at a high level down south, you inevitably work with the best the game has to offer. Everyone is an individual, and they all have different attributes. One of Jock's best qualities was as a human being. Nothing was too much trouble for him. He was also a very honest man, and when you know someone is being honest with you then you're inclined to reciprocate. It wasn't all about football with Jock, he was always concerned about how his players were in their private lives. His mantra was that if you're a happy guy at home then he would get the best from you on the pitch.

I had been struggling for a bit of form at one point so I went in to see him and I said, 'Gaffer, can you do me a big favour and leave me out of the first team for two or three weeks? Maybe put me in the reserves to see if I can get a bit of confidence back.'

His reply shocked me. 'If you cannot play in the first team then you're no good to me.'

So, I was in the first team on the Saturday and my form started to return almost immediately.

I didn't know this until the night he died, but not long after I had left his office, he jumped in his car and drove to my house. He sat down, had a cup of tea and asked Sue if we had any money problems, relationship issues, etc. He said, 'If you have, please let me know and I'll do what I can to help.' When Sue assured him everything was fine, he left, but not before saying, 'Don't tell Alfie I was here.' What a man he was.

Jock had the total respect of the dressing room. Guaranteed. I was only one full season with him at Celtic but I was in the game a long time and I never heard anyone say a bad word against him. Although … I believe he was asked by the board for his opinion on who should follow him into the hotseat at Parkhead. Thanks, gaffer!

I've always been a big believer that no matter what job we do, we all have the work-mates we get on with, or the boss that has it in for you because of one misdemeanour in a previous life. Some folk simply don't forget. Football is no different. It's just a job with a side helping of glamour, if you feel like indulging yourself. I retained many ordinary friendships well into my football career and like anyone else we would share stories down the pub. I had one mate who, no matter how hard he tried (in the beginning), just couldn't get on with his gaffer. He couldn't put his finger on it, and despite coming straight out and asking his boss one day, the reply he got was, 'I just don't like you!' Better out than in, I suppose.

When Billy McNeill arrived at Parkhead as Jock Stein's replacement, I wasn't unduly worried. Why should I be? I hadn't had any run-ins of note with my new manager and as far as I was concerned everyone was starting with a clean slate. Or at least that's how it should've been. But from the day and hour he walked through the front door at Parkhead with his stripes on, I got the feeling that I might be in for a rough ride. Call it intuition.

During McNeill's first season in charge, I was asked if, along with a couple of the other players and the manager himself, I would go to Yorkhill Sick Kids Hospital to visit some of the young patients. I had no problem with this. I had been up to Yorkhill a few times during my spell at Rangers, and as well as being a humbling experience, I knew that if my being there could help put a smile on a young face or two then it was something I was delighted to do.

The first ward we went into had young lads occupying each of the six beds. As it turned out they were all football fans and in the first bed we approached was a boy of around 11 or 12. He had stookies on both legs and looked a proper sight. He was a typical boisterous kid from that era, when the outside world was your playground and you jumped from wall to wall and got up to all sorts. There was never a thought of what might happen or where you might end up – like in a hospital bed.

Anyway, we walked over to his bed and he was beaming from ear to ear. For a few moments, he had forgotten all his pain and distress – his favourite players were standing in front of him. We started chatting and he said to me, 'Alfie, you're one of my favourite players, I've seen you play loads of times. How are you?' He was asking me! He then said, 'Could you sign your name on my stookies please – but I don't have a pen!'

I replied, 'Of course son. What have you been getting up to?'

The nurse accompanying us produced a felt tip pen and I proceeded to sign both stookies.

'Yes,' he cried out, and made a fist. 'I'm never getting these off now,' and he pointed to both stookies.

I laughed and rubbed his hair, and we were indulging in some chat when McNeill – perhaps feeling left out – stepped forward. He pointed to the plasters on both legs, and said, 'You'd probably still be able to run faster than Alfie here, even with your two stookies on.'

Pleased with his best efforts at a joke, he stepped back, still giggling away to himself.

I took a moment putting the cap back on the pen, handed it to one of my team-mates, and turned to face McNeill. I said to him, 'To be fair, I didn't have any problem with my speed when I ran past you a few times in the 1973 Scottish Cup Final at Hampden, especially at the start of the second half.'

That was it. A swallow-me-up moment for the other guys. They didn't know where to look, although it took a while for the smirk to leave my face. McNeill's earlier smile had gone, and he drew me one of his looks. The rest of the visit passed without further incident, although banter between us all was few and far between.

When we left the hospital, McNeill stormed off like a pacemaker in a distance race, and as soon as he was out of earshot, one of my team-mates said to me, 'Not sure that was the wisest thing to say, Alfie.'

I just smiled. I was quite nonplussed as I've always believed that if you can dish it out you should be able to take it back, irrespective of position. It's difficult to say if that quip was responsible for the way I was treated during my final season at Celtic, or even led to my eventual exit from Parkhead, or whether McNeill was simply exercising his right as manager to have the players he wanted in his team. He was a Celtic man through and through and perhaps he took exception to a Rangers man playing for his team. We didn't have an awful lot to do with one another during our time together at the club. I had less than a season under him, but he led Celtic to the title in his first season as gaffer so it's difficult to criticise his managerial abilities without sounding foolish.

My first season under big Jock had been an education, as well as enjoyable. He was a great manager to play under but when he decided to leave then my third season was always going to be something of an unknown quantity for me. It would be more accurate to describe it as a complete washout, and I hardly kicked a ball after a promising start to the season in which I scored ten goals. One of those was against St Mirren at Parkhead, when I managed to control a long, difficult ball before beating a couple of defenders, and the keeper, and knocking it into an empty net. I knew I was capable of goals like that, but there weren't an awful lot of opportunities in the first half of 1978 to prove my worth to the team. And that's what frustrated me more than anything.

It was the end of April when the manager told me I wouldn't be featuring in any more first-team games that season. The timing was strange, though. I quite clearly wasn't in McNeill's plans, which was fine, but there were still half a dozen matches left to play, and with Celtic eagerly chasing the title you'd think he might have left it until after the final game before booting me out of the first-team dressing room.

Perhaps he never got over the wisecrack at the kids' hospital, or maybe that's too simplistic an explanation. Maybe he just didn't fancy me, and as I said earlier, that's a manager's prerogative, but I felt that I hadn't been given a proper chance and that's what rankled with me. I played very few games for the first team, and just a little more for the reserves. I had my own seat in the stand and watched quite a few games from there. Occasionally I'd think, 'What the hell am I doing here?' And occasionally supporters would ask me the same question. I didn't have the answer, but I didn't get any grief from anyone, and that was something I appreciated.

I just got on with things and the day before the penultimate Old Firm league match of the season, which was an away game, but was to be played at Hampden as Ibrox was under construction, McNeill asked to see me. I knew I wouldn't be in the squad for the first team game, but he told me to report to Parkhead for the reserves. I wasn't surprised, but I nodded and went straight up to the directors' room, to watch a race. I was sitting minding my own business when Frank Connor came in. He was in charge of the reserves at the time, and he said, 'Alfie, you won't be playing for the reserves tomorrow, and you're not even on the bench. I would never do that to a senior professional player.'

It seemed McNeill had told Frank to make sure I stayed to the end, and that I wasn't to disappear early. Frank told me not to bother coming in and that he would cover for me. He was a lovely man, and someone I had so much time for. It was amazing the difference between the two men. I get that quite often a managerial duo have to be different, but this was exceptional. I didn't have any sort of relationship with McNeill, not on any level. Don't get me wrong, if he had something to say he would say it, and vice versa. There was never any need for third-party communication. If I had to sum up my relationship with Billy McNeill I'd say it was non-existent. I had one full season under Jock and I don't think I missed a game. I had gone from enjoying my football to the exact opposite when McNeill took over. Something I'd never done as a professional footballer was to phone in sick when I was perfectly fine – but I did that several times when McNeill was the gaffer.

I didn't travel to Hampden for the league match against Rangers, but I was contacted by a Scottish newspaper to give my thoughts on the game, and I predicted a draw. I felt that Rangers might suffer because they'd had to relinquish home advantage but that wasn't the case as they won 1-0. That game perfectly summed up the career of Alex MacDonald. He scored the only goal, a scrambled effort, but he absolutely bust a gut to get to the ball first, and that goal put Rangers right back in the title race. And they had wee Doddie to thank. Should Rangers win their four remaining games, they would win the title.

The season more or less came down to a straight shoot-out between the Old Firm at Celtic Park on Monday, 29 May. A kind of winner-takes-all. A few days before the game, I was sitting in my house in Coatbridge studying the form. The phone rang; it was McNeill. He told me to come in and pick my boots up. I said I'd be in at lunchtime the next day, but he said the only time I'd be allowed in was when the players had left for the day, so I had to wait until they had all gone home. Being denied an opportunity to say cheerio to my team-mates was, for me, disappointing, and petty on the part of the manager. I honestly don't know why he did it.

But I watched from the Parkhead stand; Celtic v Rangers, and what a game it turned out to be. Wee Doddie was at it again as he fired Rangers into the lead in just nine minutes. It was 1-0 at the break and ten minutes into the second half Johnny Doyle was sent off for aiming a kick at Doddie. Roy Aitken and Pat McCluskey had Celtic in front, before Bobby Russell equalised – and Rangers were in the ascendancy. But late in the game Colin Jackson put through his own goal and Murdo MacLeod clinched it with a fourth.

Naturally most of Celtic Park erupted in joy but I didn't feel part of the celebrations. How could I? I hadn't been involved through a mixture of non-selection and injury, so I hadn't really played a part in it – and one thing I'm not is a fraud. I won two medals in my time at Celtic but they're supposedly still at Parkhead. I phoned Ken Gallacher one day and asked if he could find out if my medals were still there, and if they were, if they could be sent out to me. He called McNeill, and he said, 'Tell him to come in and get them.' I said to Ken, tell him to go f**k himself – and that kind of finished it.

I knew my time was up at Parkhead before I was told. I was given the heads-up by a football journalist, probably Ken, so I was about as prepared as I could be. I was so far out of the manager's plans it wasn't real. I wasn't being disruptive. I was the kind of player who would turn up for training and just try to get on with folk.

There was one saving grace, though. As no player likes to think of themselves as being surplus to requirements, by being handed a free, there was one item deemed more newsworthy that week, which relegated my release to a few paragraphs. Margaret Thatcher was named as Britain's first female prime minister, so I should thank her for that!

Every successful footballer has his moment of glory. Some last a wee bit longer than others, but ultimately there is always a new star waiting in the wings to make his grand entrance. In what seemed like the blink of an eye, I'd played for Rangers, Tottenham Hotspur and Celtic, with a couple of international appearances for Scotland thrown in for good measure. But I was 27 years old and the injuries had taken their toll. I wasn't quite ready to throw in the towel just yet, but I realised that the calibre of team I'd be looking at from now on would never quite reach the heights of my first three clubs. I decided I would take a bit of time to have a good look at my options. Nowadays, the successful players cast a lucrative eye towards Saudi Arabia for their swansong, but that option wasn't around then.

There was one article which amused me slightly. It was titled 'Exit Alfie' and it said that I had cost £65,000 and played 57 times, which worked out at just more than £1,000 per appearance. The article continued, 'Celtic did their own budget yesterday and devalued the soccer pound by giving Alfie Conn a free transfer.' It also mentioned that I had made football history by winning league and Scottish Cup medals with both Rangers and Celtic inside four years, and then asked if I would now be motivated to prove Celtic had been wrong to release me by finding a new club and making a real go of it. Yes and no. The final paragraph suggested I was one of football's great crowd-pleasers, which was a nice way to finish.

I was at Celtic just over two years and I can look at it objectively now and say that for the length of time I spent at Parkhead it definitely wasn't worth it. When I signed for them I didn't know how long Jock Stein would be there, just like I wasn't expecting Bill Nicholson to leave Spurs after a couple of months. Players are well aware that managers usually like their own players in, and that's fine if you've had a few years out of it, but sometimes it's just the way the cookie crumbles.

12

And Moving On ...

AFTER LEAVING Celtic I wasn't quite ready to spend more time in the garden. Despite more than a few injuries during my career I still knew that I could do a job for someone at a good level. But there were issues. Like everything else in my career, nothing was straightforward. Billy McNeill didn't want me at Parkhead, and as he was going nowhere, then I was. Things had gone sour at Celtic and so there were no tears from me when I walked out the front door for the final time.

I was a bit fed up with all the politics involved in the game up in Scotland, and no doubt there were a few people who would have suggested I'd brought it all on myself after signing for Celtic in the first place, but that was of no consequence to me. All that mattered was that I find a new club, and I started looking around. England was once again my preferred destination; probably the only realistic destination at that stage in my career, so I was delighted when I found out that Derby County were apparently interested. Tommy Docherty was the manager of Derby and he was my kind of manager. I liked the no-nonsense way he went about his job and he was also a big success down south, where he spent his whole managerial career. Until I spoke to The Doc, I had been unaware that Billy McNeill had been placing hurdles in the way of me moving on. He had made it perfectly clear that he didn't want me, so why not just let me go? Docherty told me he had called McNeill and asked if I was available for transfer. McNeill said I was, and if he made an offer he would think about it. The Doc asked McNeill how much he wanted but the Celtic manager once again told Tommy to make him an offer. Docherty said to McNeill, 'Stop messing around and name your price.' McNeill refused, so any prospective move was put on hold. That was both frustrating and infuriating for me.

This would be the second time The Doc had tried to sign me. A couple of weeks before leaving Rangers, in 1974, I'd had discussions with him about signing for Manchester United, where he had been manager for two years. That definitely appealed to me and I was delighted when he told me he would be in touch with Willie Waddell as soon as he got back from holiday. Manchester was only a couple of hours down the road and United were known the world over. Sadly nothing came of that, and it was only later on that it was suggested to me that Willie Waddell had refused to deal with Docherty.

Now, he was trying to sign me again and I was really keen to get it sorted out, but I was still a signed Celtic player and therein lay the problem. And then out of the blue I got a call from McNeill and he said he was giving me a free transfer. That conversation was short, but I appreciated it and it allowed me to move on. But the timing was incredible. From the depths of despair to euphoric in the space of just a few hours. I called Ken Gallacher at the *Daily Record* and told him what had just happened, and he told me to leave it with him. Before I knew it The Doc was back on the phone. He asked me how I had managed to sort it out, and then invited me down to the Baseball Ground for a look around, a chat and to discuss terms. It was happening and I was delighted.

I headed straight down the motorway to the East Midlands and it was a really exuberant Docherty who met me at the front door of the stadium. It was a ground I liked the look of straight away and almost instantly had visions of being very happy there. I had visited the Baseball Ground with Tottenham and the atmosphere was always first-class. It was a tight ground and that gave the impression that the fans were right on top of you. It was my kind of ground. 'Landed on your feet here, Conn,' I told myself.

It was great to be back in the English First Division, and also quite a relief that I wouldn't be joining British football's 'brain drain' just yet. There had been a lot of talk about several experienced, mostly English, players leaving Blighty behind and heading across the pond to the States to play in their growing indoor league. It was something I had fancied for quite a while, and while I still fancied a crack at it in the summer, I now saw my long-term future at Derby.

As it was the close-season The Doc and I had plenty of time to chat about me, my injuries and how long I saw myself playing at a good level. As usual, I was completely honest and I think he appreciated that. I told him I'd had a few offers, one from Australia, as well as a couple of interested English clubs, but I made it clear I was now committed to Derby County. He liked that, and I think he also sensed that I genuinely liked the ground and that my enthusiasm levels for the new season were high. The old season had just finished and there was a decent break before pre-season training. On a personal level it was a relief to get my future sorted so early, which meant I could relax a bit.

Docherty knew I still had plenty to offer. It was only two seasons since Jock Stein had paid £65,000 to take me to Celtic, and it was common knowledge that The Doc was very much a fan of Stein. I didn't cost Derby County a lot, so the contract I received was generous, around £20,000 a year, which was a lot more than I was getting at Celtic. But the wages in the English First Division were usually more attractive than the money being paid in Scotland.

Of course, Ken Gallacher got the exclusive, 'Derby boss Tommy Docherty swooped last night to sign Celtic's free transfer Alfie Conn!'

Because of the manner in which my time at Celtic had ended, I wasn't the fittest I'd ever been, so I thought it might make good sense to perform a U turn and enquire about spending the summer in the United States, playing in their highly competitive indoor league, as it would get me up to speed far more than running along the beach at Kirkcaldy. I would also be earning, and that was a big attraction.

My meeting with The Doc drew to a close and he walked me down to the front door. He told me he was delighted that we had agreed terms and all that remained was to get me back down to sign my contract before the new season started. As his parting shot, he said, 'You know that I tried to sign you when I was manager of Manchester United?' I told him I knew that as we'd met at a restaurant in Glasgow. 'Ah, right,' he said, 'and I kept tabs on you when you were at Spurs. You're my kind of player, Alfie. You're just the personality player we need here at the Baseball Ground. The fans will love you. Go and enjoy the summer, whether that be in Fife or the States, and I'll be in touch to let you know when pre-season is starting.'

And with that, this enigmatic and colourful character disappeared back up to his office. My car was parked close to the entrance and as I opened the car door, I turned round for a quick look again at the stadium. It was a marvellous ground and I was so looking forward to getting started. Anyway, up the road, which took about six hours in those days and when I got in Sue was full of questions. 'I think you'll like it,' I said. It's a nice ground, the fans will look after us and the contract is attractive. I also spoke to Docherty about the best places to live, and he's put me right on a few things. I'm absolutely knackered so I'm going up to bed.'

That was on the Tuesday, but on the Friday afternoon, I got a call from a mate of mine to ask if I fancied going to the greyhound racing at Carfin that night. Hid dad kept greyhounds and he said, 'My old man has a dog running and he fancies it strongly. Are you coming?' It was very tempting, and in the end I decided to go. I met my mate just inside the entrance and he led me by the arm round to the paddock where the dogs were on show. 'Look at it,' he says, 'it's a beaut. I'm having a couple of quid on it, what about you?'

I was definitely up for joining him, and was looking at the dog's coat, his legs etc. when another of my mates appeared, and without drawing breath, said, 'Aw Alfie, that was bad luck about your man.' I had no idea what he was on about and told him as much.

'Tommy Docherty,' he said. 'Sacked.'

I couldn't believe my ears, and said to him, 'Are you sure?'

'One hundred per cent, mate, sorry, I know you were going there.'

It was a right hook straight to the gut, like big Jock Wallace used to do regularly to check you were doing your stomach exercises. I needed a minute. My transfer to Derby County was up in the air. My immediate future back in the lap of the gods. I had decided, just the day before, to call a couple of contacts in the US to see if they could get me over there for a couple of months, to tide me over before starting pre-season training with Derby. I had a feeling it would all work out perfectly, for once, and now this. I hadn't seen that one coming. I went straight home and told Sue. She was gutted for the family, but mostly for me. She knew what it meant to me.

We were still trying to come to terms with it a few days later when the telephone rang. Sue answered it and said, in hushed tones, 'It's Tommy Docherty.' Straight away he apologised. He insisted he hadn't seen it coming either, or else he would never have approached me. I believed him, and then he told me he had just been offered the manager's job at Queens Park Rangers and that he wanted to sign me. 'The offer still stands,' he said. I assured him I was interested, and that playing again in London appealed to me. Out the corner of my eye I could see Sue take an immediate interest in the call. We continued the conversation and then he said, 'The only thing is, Alfie, the chairman wants to see you play before he sanctions the signing. He remembers you from Tottenham and mentioned that you'd spent a lot of time in the treatment room. I know you're fine, but I suppose it would give him peace of mind, what do you say?'

I genuinely had no problem putting myself on show for the chairman. I knew I was fine, but then The Doc dropped another bombshell, 'We are just about to leave for a tour of South Africa and the chairman would like you to come along.'

My mind flashed back quickly to my dad, his invitation to go to South Africa, and it ultimately ending disastrously because he wouldn't go over there to sign the contract. Thinking on my feet, I said, 'OK, Doc. I'll go, but only if the club insures me. Technically I don't have a club so if I break my leg over there then I'm really snookered.' He understood completely. 'I'll get back to you in a couple of hours,' and he hung up.

When he rang back, within the hour, I could tell by the tone of his voice that it was a non-starter. 'Sorry, Alfie, he won't do it. I can't believe it. I've only just started at the club so I don't have much leverage. I'm really sorry, mate.'

I thanked The Doc for his interest and told him I'd have to decline his invitation. We were back to square one. When I told my dad about it he had a chuckle, but I suppose it was no laughing matter as I didn't have a club for the new season, and time was marching on.

13

Gone to the USA

MY DERBY dream was dead in the water and it was time to look for something new. I had some interest from England but with no disrespect to the clubs involved, they didn't excite me. I had to work, and it would've been a wage, but if you can feel enthusiastic about your work then all the better. And then the phone rang.

It was an Austrian agent, Herr Gartner, who lived in Spain, and who was in the business of recruiting players for a couple of Spanish clubs. He asked if I was interested in signing for Hércules CF, or Hércules de Alicante Club de Futbol, to give them their Sunday name. Was I interested in a team from Alicante? Of course I was. How could I not be interested in a team that called this beautiful Mediterranean port home?

Herr Gartner arranged for Sue and I to go over to take a look at the club, the area and the apartment that came with the job. I recalled my school days, and how the janitor always lived in the house attached to the school. Well, this was similar, but different. The club flew us over to Alicante and the agent met us at the airport. We had a chauffeur-driven car take us to the ground where the chairman was waiting excitedly to meet Sue and I. It was just one of these things but we hit it off with him right away and I was busy feeling that I'd landed on my feet. The chairman showed us around the stadium, and it certainly passed my test. We saw all the facilities and then we touched on the contract, and again it ticked most of the boxes. Sue and I were delighted, for multiple reasons. One, it was a chance to get far away from Glasgow after the disastrous end to my short spell at Celtic. Two, after the disappointment of missing out on a chance to play for Tommy Docherty at Derby, this was getting my juices flowing. I was also keen to get playing regularly again and felt that if I could resurrect my once swashbuckling style then the Spaniards would love it.

We shook hands with the chairman and Herr Gartner drove us the short distance to our new home. We stepped out of the car and stood there, staring at this plush apartment block. It was beautiful and the agent could see in our eyes that we liked it, and that made him happy as he was obviously on to a few quid if I signed. We walked around to the front of the building and took the elevator up to the fifth floor. It was as beautiful inside as it was out. I had a big smile on my face but if the truth be told, I was happier for Sue. She had put up with a lot of nonsense while I was at Celtic, indirectly, and this was payback. She deserved this more than anyone and the pleasure I took from knowing how happy she was gave me a warm feeling inside.

We had a good look around and then the agent said, 'Come, follow me,' and we left the apartment and summoned the lift. He pressed a button and the elevator took us down to the basement and we walked straight out and on to the beach. This was heaven. Sue and I looked at each other and the moment we shared told me that all the negativity of the previous couple of years had been well worth it.

We stayed in Alicante that night and went out for a lovely meal followed by a stroll along the front. It was simply gorgeous and we couldn't wait to get over there permanently. The next morning we flew back to Glasgow and back to normality – but not for too long, we hoped.

A week or so later I received a call from the agent who told me there was a little snag, but he was convinced it would all be ironed out. He asked for a little patience. I asked what the problem was and he told me not to worry. I pushed him for an explanation and he said that in Spain they had a two-foreigner rule but that one of their foreign players was injured and they saw me as the ideal replacement. I think the main issue was that the guy who was injured didn't fancy being replaced, and he was fighting it. He was under contract so I had some sympathy for his predicament. The agent assured me everything would be OK. I was concerned and while I tried to hide it from Sue, she sensed all was far from well and I told her what the problem was. We agreed we would give it another week and see then how the land lay. If the truth be told, neither of us had a particularly good feeling about it but we were prepared to wait and hope.

And then another call from the agent. This time to ask if I would go over to Alicante and play in a friendly match against a touring Mexican side, UAD Guadalajara. The president was keen to see me in action and as I was to be his marquee signing he wanted to make sure I was up to the job. I was OK with that so I made my preparations to fly out to the south of Spain. In a way it confirmed that Hércules definitely wanted me, but unfortunately the flight was delayed and I missed the opportunity to play in the game. It was very frustrating. I got to the stadium just as the game was kicking off but it was too late to take part. I was talking to the president and he introduced me to his opposite number at Guadalajara and he was asking me all about my situation. He said his side were on a tour of Europe and that their next game was in Seville. He asked if I'd like to play, and I said, 'Why not?'

Hércules were OK about it so I travelled to Seville, which is just under 400 miles from Alicante, and I was warmly welcomed into the dressing room by the other players. Before the game the Mexican manager gave his team talk, in Spanish, I presume, and then spoke to me in English, and that made me feel more at ease. Out we went for the game and Guadalajara were a decent side. I had not too bad a game and had one screamer of a shot that I believed was a goal all the way only for the Sevilla keeper to pull off a great save. Afterwards we were up in the players' lounge and the president asked if I'd like to stay with the team for the rest of the tour. He then said that if I played the way I had against Seville it would be a no-brainer and I would be offered a bumper contract once we got back to Mexico. And then I could send for my wife and kids! He had it all worked out.

My goodness, talk about things moving quickly. I thought back to signing for Tottenham, using Bill Nicholson's phone to call Sue to tell her we were moving to London. She'd taken it well, but somehow I didn't think 'Darling, we're moving to Guadalajara' would hold the same appeal, so I told the manager I only had enough clothes to last me a couple of days and that my wife was expecting me home. In truth, I probably bricked it. Sue and I discussed everything together, and made joint decisions, so that one wouldn't have been too popular, but we were a great team and she always had my back. True to form, when I got home and told her of the offer from the Mexicans, my intuition had been spot on!

So, after galavanting halfway across Europe I was still without a team. The trial had bombed, although I was a wanted man in Mexico (thankfully not THAT type of wanted man), and I needed to work. I was willing the telephone to ring to tell me that everything was sorted out at Hércules, but it was halfway through the following week that I received another call, one unrelated to Hércules. It was from a guy called Alex Pringle and he asked if I would be interested in playing in the relatively new Major Indoor Soccer League in the States. He was the manager of Pittsburgh Spirit, one of the six founding members of the league, and a club who played at the 17,000-capacity Civic Arena in a city of 300,000. The indoor league excited me, and I had been keen to learn more about it just before the

Derby County debacle, although I hadn't pursued it. Yes, Alex, I was interested, but it was a difficult one, because Sue and I had been over to Alicante and knew exactly what we were getting, where we would be living, etc. This new proposition involved something of a leap into the dark, and while we both liked to think that we possessed the true spirit of adventure, it was a bit more than the three-hour flight to Spain, and with two young kids we had a lot to think about.

The positive was that I knew of Alex. He was from Edinburgh and had played for the likes of Hibs and Dundee, so there was something there to build on, and he seemed super keen for me to go over to the States, telling me that he thought the indoor game would suit me to a tee. I told him I would get back to him asap and I phoned Herr Gartner for an update on the move to Hércules – and I immediately sensed his frustration. I got the impression that he still genuinely believed the transfer would go ahead, but he just couldn't tell me when. I told him of the counter-offer from the States, and that they wouldn't hold on for ever, so he vowed to get me an answer as soon as possible. I hadn't heard anything for a wee while so I sat down and discussed it with Sue and she insisted we should go for the Pittsburgh gig. I called Alex back and he sounded delighted.

Sue and I began to formulate our plans for moving to the States. The initial deal was for a year, so we rented out our house in Bishopbriggs and off we went. We thought that might be less radical than selling all our furniture! On the day we flew out it was our daughter Samantha's fourth birthday.

Steven was around 18 months and we were going on this great adventure. We were sitting at the airport waiting for our flight to be announced and I told Sue I was going over to the little airport newsagent to have a look. Imagine my surprise when I look at the back page of one of the newspapers and spot the headline, 'What's it all about, Alfie?' I think it might have been the *Daily Express*, but I couldn't be sure. I bought the paper and took it back to my seat. 'Some light reading for the plane,' I said, and showed Sue the back page. 'What now?' she said, as she let out a sigh.

I read this 'exclusive' about how I had been all set to join this Spanish side after leaving Celtic and had vowed to revive my career after 'flopping' at Parkhead. I had just begun to read this pile of rubbish when I started laughing. Sue looked at me with interest. 'What?' she asked. I told her that this so-called journalist, I can't even remember his name, had gone to a great deal of trouble to write a story that would show me up in a bad light, and had even got a quote from the president of the Spanish club, who said, 'Alfie who, I have never heard of him!'

Sue immediately butted in, saying, 'But we were over in Spain and he showed us around his club!'

'Relax, Sue,' I said, 'this numpty interviewed the chairman of Salamanca, and the club that wanted to sign me was Hércules!'

We both had a right good laugh and agreed that it was this journalist who had 'flopped' badly while trying to dish some dirt. It had backfired spectacularly and shown him up for exactly what he was, but the issue was that punters reading the story wouldn't know it was a pile of junk. Still, we laughed all the way on to the plane, tossing the paper in the bin before boarding – destination USA.

Pittsburgh is a beautiful city in Pennsylvania, close to the border with Ohio, and when we eventually touched down we were all quite tired from the journey and the kids were restless. Thankfully, there was a club official waiting to pick us up and take us to a hotel. It was great to relax for a day or two before getting involved in any club business – exactly what we needed.

First thing the next morning I went out for a walk in the city centre. It was a breath of fresh air strolling along the 'sidewalk' knowing you weren't about to get a mouthful from a disgruntled supporter. Just to be free of it all, even for a year, was such a relief. I love visiting new cities and thoroughly enjoyed exploring my new home. Fingers and toes were crossed that nothing would go wrong and that I could just get on with playing football. Ironically, onc of the only reservations I had was about just that, the football. It was six-a-side indoor stuff, the type you played with your mates on a Friday night. First and foremost, though, it was a job. I was supposedly at the peak of my career, and I was travelling thousands of miles to play indoor football. What happened to keeping an open mind?

Anyway, after a couple of days in the hotel we were introduced to our new house, and it was fabulous. Sue loved it, and it was everything we had hoped for. It had three bedrooms and a swimming pool, and Sue would be in there most mornings at half past seven, which illustrates just how warm it was. We were also given a lovely car, and two flights each back to Scotland to be used any time we wanted. The wages were also good so there were no complaints.

I was looking forward to getting started and we did a bit of training and practised together. Just like that we were ready to go. The Yanks have always known how to put on a show and opening night was full of the usual razzamatazz. The team we were playing had the former Chelsea player Alan Hudson in their ranks, and as we lined up inside waiting to go on, we acknowledged one another. Loud music then boomed from the super-size speakers and out we went to rapturous applause. And then it was time for the American national anthem. We had been well versed on protocol. Everyone would stand for the anthem and no one inside the stadium would be allowed to move around until it was finished. That meant Sue, who was in the bar with the other wives and girlfriends, missed the kick-off. They then weaved their way through the crowd to their seats, and once they had sat down, one of the girls said to her, 'Where's your Alfie?'

Sue took a good look around the pitch and sure enough I wasn't there. That's because around ten seconds after kick-off I had tried to turn with the ball, caught my studs in the astroturf and was on my way to hospital. TEN SECONDS! Still, I put it down to bad luck rather than an injury jinx.

While I was winging my way to the local medical centre, Sue was trying to find out where I was. When she was told I had been injured, she naturally started to make her way to the hospital. Before she got there, though, I was joined by Hudson. He had done the exact same thing and landed up in the bed next to me. What a start.

Throughout the league, the playing surfaces were laid on top of ice rinks. Wooden boards down on top of the ice, fixed and then rolls of cheap astroturf to finish it off. I could foresee a problem. Minutes after Alan I had started to talk, our goalkeeper Billy Michelow had joined us. What a carry-on. I ended up on the sidelines for around two months. I had been itching to get back playing after a week or two, but a doctor told me the knee wouldn't stand up to it so it was a frustrating period for me. The city of Pittsburgh definitely helped aid my recovery. As soon as I was able to walk, Sue and I and the kids spent lots of time getting to know our new neighbourhood and visited lots of great local attractions.

Once I was fit again, I must admit I took to the six-a-side game like a fish to water. I loved it, and we managed to go on a great run in the league, winning most of our matches and qualifying for the end-of-season play-offs. That was in no small way down to the form of an old Rangers team-mate of mine. Our manager, Alex Pringle, came to me one day and said, 'We're struggling a bit in front of goal, Alfie, do you know anyone who could come over and do us a turn?' I immediately thought of Graham Fyfe. We had spent five years together at Ibrox; he was a lovely guy but also a brilliant footballer. He was playing at Dumbarton, and had enjoyed a short spell in Australia, so I knew he wouldn't mind a bit of travelling. I called him and he was receptive to the idea. I passed on his number to Alex and before too long he was on a flight to Pittsburgh.

Graham turned out to be exactly what the team required and his goals were a major catalyst in us reaching the play-offs. Probably the reason Graham hadn't made more of his senior career in Scotland was because he lacked a bit of pace, but he was born for the indoor game, because once you had beaten your man you were clear, and the goal was in front of you. To give you an idea of just how much of a revelation Graham was, he won Most Valuable Player in the league that season – and MVP was the highest individual honour going. He scored goals for fun, but there was one opponent he struggled with.

A lot of the families would socialise together and Graham and his family spent a lot of time with Sue and I. On one occasion we had gone out for a meal and the problems started when it came to dessert. My son Steven was in his high chair and had a bowl of ice cream in front of him. It looked as though he was trying to ask Graham a question, and beckoning him to come closer, but when he did, Steven tipped the entire bowl of melting ice cream all over Graham's face. Everyone at the table was in hysterics and once Graham got cleaned up, he too couldn't stop laughing.

One of the things the club encouraged was for the married couples to invite some of the single players over for dinner once a month. We took our turn like the others and on the first occasion we had Billy Michelow and a young lad called Adrian Webster, who was over from England. I said to them, 'Tonight lads, we're going to be eating traditional Scottish food,' and both looked concerned. Sue and I served up mince, potatoes and peas and their attention turned to the plate. They cautiously started to dig in, and within five minutes both were asking for seconds.

The social side of things at the club was first-class, but importantly the balance was just right. We were able to live our lives and also help others who may have been struggling to settle in. Most things were geared towards kids so it meant there was little need for babysitters as Samantha and Steven normally came with us. We frequented a placed called Howard Johnston's, which did breakfast, lunch and dinner and normally we would commandeer a couple of tables. It was there that Graham received a faceful of ice cream!

The football was going well and making the play-offs was a big deal for the city. At the start of the season, we were playing in front of three or four thousand, but by the time we had put a winning run together it was difficult to find an empty seat in the Civic Arena. In the play-offs we were drawn against New York, whose big star was the Italian striker Giorgio Chinaglia, one of the greatest goalscorers of all time. He played for the Cosmos in both the outdoor and indoor leagues, and once scored seven goals in an indoor match against Chicago. We played the Cosmos home and away in the play-offs but lost narrowly on aggregate. Still, it had been a thoroughly successful season and the Pittsburgh owner was delighted. I must admit, I had really taken to the indoor game and was already looking forward to the following season. Sue and the kids were happy, and that meant I was too.

But, and there's always a but. That word has followed me throughout my career. No, haunted me would be a more appropriate description. Anyway, when I'd signed my initial contract with Pittsburgh, I had been advised to have a clause inserted saying that when the indoor season finished I could sign for a team for free and play the outdoor game in the summer, and then return to Pittsburgh when the indoor season resumed in the autumn. It meant I would be earning all year round, and in the US that was important. I didn't have too many good years left in me so I wanted to maximise my potential. And then Pittsburgh reneged on the deal, which was a massive game-changer.

San Jose Earthquakes wanted me for the outdoor season and I was keen to go down to California. I had talks with the owner of the Earthquakes and he invited me to play a couple of games. At this point, there was no conflict of interest, so off we went. Bill Foulkes was the manager of the Earthquakes and he had been in regular contact with me. He was a Manchester United legend and a very nice man. A survivor of the 1958 Munich air disaster, he went on to play almost 700 games for United including the 1968 European Cup Final win over Benfica.

Bill and I had a lengthy chat and he said he was keen to have me involved. They had a couple of games coming up and so I played in both. It was a good standard and also enjoyable. Sue and I were living in temporary digs in San Jose but it was really nice, the weather was great and we were living a good life. We would train in the afternoons due to the heat, sometimes as late as 5pm, but everything the club arranged was geared towards looking after the welfare of the players.

One afternoon I turned up for training and went into the changing room to get ready. I noticed a red handkerchief on my locker and thought at first that it was a joke, maybe one of my team-mates pretending that someone wanted to get romantic with me! I laughed it off and started to get changed, and then one of the American lads came over and said, 'Alf, that's not good, my friend.' I had no idea what he was on about and he explained that in the States a red hankie was a sign that you weren't required at the club. That worried me. I went straight out to see Bill and ask him what was going on. He said he didn't know, but would find out.

Ten minutes later I was invited to a meeting with a director of the Earthquakes. He told me that he had just learned that Pittsburgh had sold me to a team called Hartford Helions, and that I would have to leave. At that moment, there was a knock on the office door and in walked George Best, who I knew from my time in England. George said hello, the director asked George if he could come back in five minutes after we had finished our meeting. George said, 'It's nice to see you Alf, glad we're going to be team-mates,' but I told him I didn't think it was going to happen, and quickly explained the situation. He turned to the director and said, 'You're making a big mistake if you let this man go.' And with that he nodded to me and walked out. The director assured me there was nothing he could do. It was apparently a league rule that a waiver could be placed on a player, and that allowed other clubs to claim him.

I later found out that Pittsburgh hadn't been happy with me going down to San Jose, even though there was a cast-iron clause in my contract, which they had initially acknowledged. But I was a wanted man after a good season in the indoor league, and that proved frustrating for Pittsburgh because if that clause hadn't been there they could've charged a good few quid for me. It sounded like I was a victim of my own success. Many American owners didn't appreciate being challenged by players and so when I exercised my right to move to San Jose Earthquakes, Pittsburgh had placed a waiver on my head. Hartford took up my contract, wanted to charge the Earthquakes a fee for playing me, and the Earthquakes didn't want to pay. The upshot was that I was ordered to go to Hartford, which is in Connecticut, and apparently one of the coldest places in the US in the winter. Imagine how Sue took that news as she was lying on a beach outside our San Jose apartment topping up her tan. 'OK, dear, grab your thermals and big coat, we're going to Connecticut!'

I could picture her answer, and then I would have to tell her about the red handkerchief! What a day.

I called the manager at Pittsburgh but he said there was nothing he could do. He insisted he didn't want to lose me but said my insistence on playing for San Jose had irked the club. He knew all about the agreement I had in place but to me, the very fact that they could break that agreement on a whim was enough for me. I told him I wouldn't be going to play for Hartford or anyone else in America, and he said that decision would soon be taken out of my hands as I would be banned from playing anywhere in the States. 'That's that then,' I thought. As far as I know I'm still banned, and I'm in my 70s!

This crazy decision also impacted on a friend of mine and his wife, as they were due to fly out to San Jose to spend a couple of weeks with us. They had to cancel, and once again, Sue and I were packing suitcases and heading for the airport. There's no denying we were both completely gutted, but it was out of our hands. This time, though, we would be homeless when we got back to Scotland as we had rented our house out for a year, and the tenants still had a month of their contract to run. Unlike the Yanks, I wasn't about to hang a red handkerchief on their front door, so we moved in with a pal of mine for four weeks.

Career wise, I was becoming completely disillusioned with the game. It was such a roller-coaster ride of great experience, disappointment, great experience, etc. I was suddenly ruing the day I had decided to put all my eggs in the one basket, and give up on my education, because at this very moment I would've given up the game in a heartbeat. But when you're a kid it doesn't seem such a big deal, and when there are aspirations of having a career in football, you don't think the day will ever come when you resent not having some sort of alternative skills to fall back on.

14

Going Back to my Roots

DESPITE MY predicament, football and life had been good to me in the States, for a year at least, and as we flew back across the Atlantic I had only one thing on my mind, and that was getting another club as soon as possible. It was the close-season in Scotland, and probably the perfect time to pick something up. I was hopeful and positive and had vowed to weigh up my options as soon as I got home. Ideally, I wanted to put down some roots somewhere, hopefully for three or four years, but my injuries were well documented and so it was a case of wait and see. While Sue was busy getting schools sorted out for the kids, I was waiting on the phone to ring. I might already have mentioned that I wasn't the best at self-promotion so incoming calls would become my new best friends. It was the start of July and I was hoping to get something sorted out in time for pre-season training.

While I was playing it was often difficult to sort out the facts from the rumours, so you might hear of an attractive club seemingly being interested, and then you discover it was simply a figment of some journalist's imagination; a journalist who had a few column inches to fill during the summer. So that could be tough.

Once I had settled back in to life in Coatbridge, the first I read was that Airdrie – who had just been promoted to the Premier League – were interested in me. It was reported that manager Bobby Watson had made me an attractive offer. Really? But, according to the newspaper report, he would face stiff competition from Morton, Hibs and Arbroath. A couple of days later, the same paper reported, 'Arbroath have failed in a bid to land former Rangers, Spurs and Celtic player Alfie Conn!' If not helpful, it was certainly entertaining.

The following day, Airdrie were ruled out as my new employer – as 'Alfie Conn's future in Scottish football remained uncertain'. In the same report it stated, 'Alfie may go south!' Apparently I was considering offers from a couple of English Second Division sides. Oh, and I was now being referred to as 'a former pin-up player', which was quite a dent to my ego! But seriously, the next time I read a newspaper it proclaimed loudly, 'Alfie Conn has followed in his father's footsteps and signed for Hearts!' And, of course, this was true. I was bound for Tynecastle.

Throughout my career there were only a handful of journalists I truly trusted; Ken Gallacher, Jim Blair and Brian Scott being three that instantly spring to mind.

'Alfie Conn will be back in Premier League football in the new season. He completed a family double yesterday by signing for Hearts – 20 years after his father retired at the end of 14 years as a Tynecastle hero.'

I was pleased to sign for Hearts. They were a club I was familiar with, having been around the place as a child while my dad played there. I'd also trained with them before signing with Rangers, and alongside Willie Bauld junior, the son of another of the Terrible Trio. The familiarity, I felt, was a good thing for me at this stage in my career.

Just a week or so after arriving back from the States, I was asked through to Tynecastle by the manager, Bobby Moncur, and after chatting for half an hour I signed a contract. I was back playing for a top team, a Premier League team – albeit one who had just been promoted – and I couldn't wait to get started.

I was determined to make the most of this opportunity. Of course, I was delighted to be following in my father's footsteps. That was a big thing for me, but Dad and I never spoke about it. He had made a conscious decision to let me run my own career, and that was something I respected. And it meant there was less pressure on me.

I watched some of my first senior games at Tynecastle and I was always impressed by the atmosphere. The crowd were so close to the pitch and therefore the noise could be phenomenal. I had experienced it as an away player, but suddenly I was looking forward to the Hearts fans being on my side. My dad had joined Hearts as a youngster and had spent virtually his whole career at Tynecastle, so I wasn't going there to emulate him, as that would just have been plain daft. I was going there to try my best, and we would see where that took me.

I needed little persuading to sign for Hearts. They were a team with a fantastic history, and set on re-establishing themselves as a force in Scottish football. The fact that my dad played for them in the past had little bearing on my decision, but I had been determined to sign for a good team and that was exactly what I did.

But it wasn't long before the doubters were having their say. 'Will Alfie last a full match, never mind the season?' My injury record was there in black and white. I would never have tried to deny anything. God, no one hated that side of my past more than me. It was a topic of conversation when I chatted to Bobby Moncur, but it wasn't a stumbling block. While in the US, I had seen some of the best specialists in the country and they had given me an A1 rating. That was good enough for me and gave me the confidence to look for a new club safe in the knowledge that I wouldn't be conning anyone. There were a couple of offers from English clubs, but I felt it was time I settled in Scotland, and Hearts seemed a good fit.

We started pre-season training in mid-July and no one knew more than the players just what a vital season it was for the club and the supporters. Since putting pen to paper there had been a lot of press interest in me, and most of it centred on my past with both Rangers and Celtic. I was hoping that would become an ancient relic when the football began.

One of the first things we did was take to the tarmac for a lengthy road run, and I was paired up with one of my new team-mates, Chris Robertson. I had never played alongside Chris but we had a laugh about both playing in the Scottish Cup Final when he had come on as a sub for Rangers and I was playing for the opposition. We had both left the Old Firm behind, were both Edinburgh lads and here we were playing for an Edinburgh club.

Cammy Fraser would also have been a team-mate had he not left to join Dundee the moment I rocked up at Tynecastle. I hope it was nothing personal! He would be a loss, as he'd scored more than a dozen goals from midfield the previous season and had played a big part in getting the club back into the Premier League.

I was glad to see Willie McVie as a team-mate, let me tell you, as when he made up the half-back trio at Motherwell, alongside Peter Millar and Stewart MacLaren, I think his nickname, Chopper, was the kindest of the three. It was often said that no one got past this battle-hardened trio, and if they had the audacity to try, McVie would kick them up in the air, Millar would kick them while they were in the air, and MacLaren would kick you as soon as you returned to earth! It wasn't kind, but I used to laugh about it with Willie.

As far as pre-seasons go, I felt fit and ready to play because of the time I'd spent in the States. Pre-season training simply topped up the tank. At our press day I was as reluctant as ever to open my mouth, so I chose my words as carefully as possible. Rather predictably, most of the questions directed at me concerned either half of the Old Firm. I felt like telling the reporters I was now at Hearts, in case they hadn't noticed. It was tiring. I could predict the opening paragraphs, 'Alfie Conn admits he's something of a controversial character blah blah blah.' So when I got asked if my questionable work rate was the reason why I split opinion with supporters, I was impressed. My reply? 'My work rate isn't great, I admit that, and according to a lot of managers that's a cardinal sin.' But it was true, because I did most of my work on the ball, which often meant my contribution could be as little as ten minutes, which meant I would be out of the game for 80. But I still maintain that I was among a dying breed of players who took chances in trying to go past people. That will be why I was often called a crowd-pleaser. But it certainly wasn't rocket science. I had a bit of pace and good control of the ball. I would suss out early in a game whether or not a full-back was there for the taking and then I would try to make things happen. Don't get me wrong, I had the bruises on my shins and ankles to prove that at least I had tried. Perhaps I did things that a lot of players had had hammered out of them. I also managed to score quite a few goals for the clubs I played with, and that was something I enjoyed immensely.

I would always maintain that the people who paid to get into games were the most important. My view of that has never changed, but crowds were dwindling when I came back from America and the reason was simple: there was a lack of entertainers around. The likes of Aberdeen still had a couple of players who liked to have a go, and they were given a free rein by my old Rangers team-mate, Alex Ferguson.

At the pre-season press conference at Tynecastle I was finally asked how Hearts would fare that season, but I hated tempting fate, so I refused to answer. Maybe the reporters couldn't win! I think I said that survival was our number one goal, but some viewed it as negative. I thought it was realistic.

We started off with a friendly against a strong-looking Chelsea side and lost by the only goal. I had a 20-yard piledriver well saved in the final minute, or we would've snatched a draw.

The following day we were being linked with Willie Johnston, who was returning to Scotland after a spell playing in Vancouver. I was keen for that to happen as Bud was not only a talented player, but a great friend. He watched our match against Chelsea and then had talks with the gaffer, but at the 11th hour Rangers manager John Greig asked him to return to Ibrox and the lure of his former stamping ground proved too great. He was 33 at the time, and while Greig had promised him game time, his main reason for wanting Bud was to put pressure on a talented young winger whom Greig knew would make it to the top. This lad was ten years Bud's junior but had been virtually unchallenged for a starting jersey since he had signed. His name – Davie Cooper.

Bobby Moncur, a Newcastle United legend, knew that he would be hard pressed to outbid Rangers for the winger, who had joined Vancouver Whitecaps for £80,000, and also conceded that Bud's emotional ties to Rangers would be hard to sever, but he put his best case to Johnston and left it up to the player. Bud would join Hearts – but not for another two years, and I would be long gone.

I enjoyed the run out against Chelsea, but friendlies never did turn me on so I was looking forward to the start of the real action, the bread and butter of the Premier League.

We had one more challenge match to get out of the way, and it took place in Lurgan, Northern Ireland, against Glenavon. It finished 3-3 but was memorable for one of the many statistical coincidences football throws up from time to time. When my dad was playing, Hearts were largely successful, so his adversaries were the players of Rangers and Celtic. One in particular, Charlie Tully, lined up against my old man many times and they used to have real ding-dong battles. On one occasion, during a tousy affair at Tynecastle in front of 40,000, my old man and Tully were going at it hammer and tongs, and a newspaper report of the day stated, 'Celtic playboy Charlie Tully was fortunate to stay on the park for unbecoming conduct against Alfie Conn. The inside-left was booked.' It was apparently a big deal in those days to get booked, and shows the gravity of their individual battle. And Tully probably didn't know that my dad did a bit of boxing on the side. Anyway, it turned out that I was up against Tully's nephew, Brendan, when we played Glenavon. He was a handy player and scored, but thankfully there were no afters.

We kicked off our league campaign with a visit to Firhill, but a 3-2 defeat to Partick Thistle, followed by a home loss to Airdrie confirmed that it would be a long season. It was a case of third time lucky when we beat St Mirren at Love Street to pick up our first points, and I got my first goal. Mind you, I also got my first injury of the season. I remained indoors at the break after getting a knock on the shin, and was sent to hospital for an x-ray. I was out for a month. It was getting beyond a joke. Once again I was sitting kicking my heels in frustration while it seemed everybody else within my profession played football. Some players go through their entire career without as much as breaking a toenail, but me – a fractured ankle, two cartilage ops, two Achilles tendon ops, a knee operation, eight weeks out with a groin injury, etc. I was a walking, talking series of *Casualty* long before the A&E drama was a reality. One serious injury is bad luck, but I must have had five or six. So, what did I think? Was I cursed? I don't think so, I think I was just damned unlucky. But I must've missed three or four years' worth of playing, and that's a serious amount of missed game time for me, and for the clubs paying my wages. But I'm labouring the point. I was out again and would just have to take it on the chin. I never did speak to Bobby Moncur about it but he must've been as pissed off as me.

But at least I did Hearts one good turn. When Bobby left not long after I'd joined (another manager I'd chased away), his assistant Tony Ford took over. Tony was a decent guy, so when he asked me for help I was only too happy to oblige. He told me he needed a good, solid midfielder. Someone who could play a bit, but who also had combative qualities. I knew exactly the man to fill the role: Alex MacDonald. Wee Doddie was coming to the end of his time at Rangers, having spent a dozen years at Ibrox, but I knew he was keen to play on, and I knew he still had mileage left in the old chassis. Doddie looked after himself, hence the reason he would play until he was almost 40. I passed his number to Tony and the deal was done within a couple of days. Doddie was on his way to Tynecastle – minus the Gilbert O'Sullivan songs – and it was a love affair that would last for a decade, both as a player and then as manager.

I returned from the shin injury and made another dozen or so appearances for the Jambos, including a memorable afternoon in Govan when I was introduced as a substitute midway through the second half. I turned to the gaffer and said, 'Cheers boss, here we go.' He just looked at me and said, 'Yeah, good luck Alf!' and out on to the track I went. The jeers rang around the ground, even though it was less than half full, and when I set up our consolation goal for wee Doddie, at least he gave me a hug. As I ran past wee Bud, he slapped me on the back and winked. I was glad to get that one over but there were far bigger problems than my fragile feelings as we lost at home to Partick and found ourselves second-bottom of the table and knee-deep in the brown stuff. We had suffered five straight losses at home (without even scoring a goal) and that, I'm afraid, was relegation form.

We were humbled at Airdrie at the end of November and once again I was on the bench. And all of a sudden a story appeared in one of the newspapers suggesting that I might be on my way back to the United States. The gaffer asked about it and I assured him it was nonsense – and I had cast-iron proof – as I was still banned from playing there. And Hartford was still one of the coldest places in the US!

Anyway, I had recently become involved with a haulage firm and my friend and I, who were partners, were busy overseeing the running of it. I managed to combine it successfully with my playing career.

That said, my time at Tynecastle could hardly be classed as a success, although I'm not sure why. I had come back from the US in a positive frame of mind and determined to make a real go of it. Perhaps it was just one injury too many and it got inside my head. Maybe I was judged against my dad and I let some folk down. But still to this day I have a great relationship with the club and get an invite every year to the Willie Bauld memorial dinner and I think I've only missed one. It's always a fantastic event and it's great to see old faces.

As 1980 turned into '81, it was clear that things weren't working out at Tynecastle and I was on the bench most weeks as the team fought tooth and nail for survival. Completely out of the blue I received a phone call from a guy called Tommy White. Tommy was from Musselburgh and had enjoyed a good career with clubs like Raith Rovers, Aberdeen and Hearts. His brother was the famous Scotland international and

Tottenham midfielder John White, who was an outstanding footballer. Latterly, Tommy had played in England for Crewe and Blackpool, and it was at Bloomfield Road that he became involved in the boardroom. I knew Tommy personally, but it was in his position as a director of Blackpool that he was phoning me. The Tangerines were also battling relegation and he asked if I would come down and help out. I spoke to Hearts and the two clubs agreed a loan deal. I would leave Coatbridge on a Friday morning at 6am and get down to Blackpool in time for training. I would then stay overnight in Tommy's hotel, the Royal Boston, and play on the Saturday. The kids had just started school and there was no way I was uprooting them again. Sue never questioned any of my transfer moves but even I knew this time that moving the family lock, stock and barrel was a no-go.

Allan Brown, the ex-East Fife player, was manager of Blackpool at the time and we got on really well. Three games I played for Blackpool and things were going not too badly, and then it happened. That bloody curse. Injured again. They'd only had eight games left to play and I missed more than half. Blackpool were relegated and I thought that was that, but Allan got me into the office one Saturday morning and offered me a two-year deal. I hadn't seen that coming. I thought it was going to be a 'cheers Alf, and good luck for the future'.

During my brief stay with the Seasiders I had been training all week before joining Blackpool on the Friday, and I thought the agreement was working well, but Allan said the directors were insisting I move down to Blackpool and live there during the season. It was very tempting but I simply couldn't do it. The kids hadn't long started school and nursery and that was my priority. And I couldn't do it to Sue. She had travelled all over with me up to this point and she needed proper foundations. We had found that in Coatbridge so I politely refused the offer and there were no hard feelings, or regrets.

15

On the March With Ally's Army

NEW SEASON, new club. And I was getting closer to home. I contacted Motherwell and asked for training facilities, just to keep myself ticking over in case someone came in for me. The club representative asked the manager, Ally MacLeod, and he said it was no problem at all. I went along and joined in, careful not to overstep the mark and just to appreciate the facility the club had granted me. I completed the whole pre-season training regime and thanked Ally for his help. As I was saying cheerio, he asked to see me in his office and in I went. There and then he offered me a two-year contract and I was glad to accept.

We were in the old Scottish First Division (second tier) along with the likes of Kilmarnock, Hearts (yes, they were relegated), St Johnstone and Dunfermline. We knew it would be tough but we were looking forward to it. Among my team-mates for my first season at Well were Gary McAllister, Brian McClair, Brian McLaughlin and John Gahagan. We had a good squad and the aim was to be in the mix for promotion.

Ally MacLeod was also a terribly positive man and had us believing that we could get promotion to the Premier League. And then …

MacLeod was called into the boardroom and sacked. There and then. The shock we felt was palpable, as no one had seen it coming. I was starting to think that not only was I jinxed, but that the managers I served under were also afflicted. We waited with bated breath to see who the new manager would be. We were all told to be in the dressing room at a certain time on a certain day, and in walked Davie Hay, who had just finished his playing career at Chelsea. From Stamford Bridge to Fir Park. He had enjoyed an excellent career as a player with Celtic, Chelsea and Scotland, and even though he had no previous managerial experience we all completely bought into his philosophy, and his message from the start was loud and clear: let's give this a go! Playing with the handbrake off before it was fashionable.

We had a fantastic season, and I had a fantastic season, and guess what – there are no injuries to report (or at least any that I can remember)! My appearances were a mixture of starts and cameos from the bench, but the team was winning and that was all I cared about. Hay was brilliant to work under and had come in to his first managerial job with his eyes wide open. He set the team up to suit the players at his disposal and it worked. We had the league sewn up with half a dozen games still to play and, boy, did that champagne taste good in the dressing room. I'm also sure that judging by the reaction of the Well fans after we clinched the title, they had also enjoyed not just the success, but the manner in which it had been achieved. We were by far and away the First Division's top scorers that season and fell just shy of the ton. We were ten points clear of our nearest rivals, Kilmarnock, who had been relegated the previous season along with Hearts. This might be overstating it slightly, but I reckon it was one of my most enjoyable seasons in football, and that's probably because I remained injury free and we had a great bunch of lads in the dressing room. And no red handkerchiefs on my locker!

Back in the Premier League and we were all looking forward to see how far we could go. Hay's managerial vision had been simple, effective and to a man we had bought into it. Let's play to our strengths and see where it takes us. There was a lot of experience in our dressing room and expectations weren't unrealistic, especially with a manager who allowed the players to express themselves.

The day after the season ended, we all went our separate ways and Sue and I took the kids on a sunshine holiday. But before leaving for the airport I was told that Davie Hay had quit. Another one I hadn't seen coming. I was so disappointed because I had genuinely believed that he could be a revelation in the Premier League. But he had decided to take a year out and, to be honest, he really hadn't done his CV any harm. Within a year he had replaced Billy McNeill as manager of Celtic, and in his four-year tenure at Parkhead he would win a league title and a Scottish Cup.

Once again, though, we were rudderless, and going into an important season without a manager. When we reported back to Fir Park for pre-season training we were all told to be in the home dressing room at a certain time on a certain day – and in walked a familiar figure: Jock Wallace. I couldn't shake the big man off, although in truth I was delighted to see him. It had been a wee while since our paths had crossed and I was looking forward to working with him, minus the pressure of a club the size of Rangers. I was also more than happy to be hooking up again with Frank Connor, who had been named as Jock's assistant. One of the nicest guys in the game, but also one of the most knowledgeable. The room was full of anticipation. EVERYONE knew Jock Wallace, and his reputation preceded him. As we waited on Jock delivering his opening speech, the wooden benches were crammed full of players and he started to look round the room, scanning the faces, and suddenly this booming voice shouted, 'Some of you might know me, some of you won't, but I can guarantee that by the end of the week you will all f**kin' know me, is that right Alfie?' And he looked straight at me. I laughed and said, 'That's right, gaffer.' Perhaps at that moment a few of the players thought that I would be the teacher's pet because of our time together at Ibrox, but they would soon discover that wasn't how Jock operated. He had NO favourites. He treated everyone equally, and that's the way it should be.

We were all called into his office one by one, and when it was my turn, he smiled at me as I took my seat. 'How are you, son?' he asked. 'I'm good, thanks,' and he said to me, 'So how did you enjoy last season? That was a right good result getting promotion.' I told him the team spirit had been second to none, and that we had played with a certain amount of freedom. Oh, and that I'd enjoyed playing in midfield and creating chances.

'That's great,' he said, 'but you'll be playing up front for me this season.' I asked why, after I'd just told him that it had worked out well for the team with me in midfield. 'Cos you cannae tackle, that's why.' That kind of knocked the wind from my sails.

We didn't have a great season, and I'm not for a moment suggesting it was because I wasn't playing in midfield. Clearly we were in a much stronger league. Dundee United won the title, heading both Celtic and Aberdeen by just a point. Rangers had finished fourth, but quite some distance behind the top three. It was a ten-team league so there was little margin for error, and we escaped relegation by just one spot, but seven points clear of relegated Morton. Kilmarnock went straight back down.

It was a hard season and of course, I suffered another bad injury, to my right knee bone, which was painful, restrictive and damaging to my career. I had gone down to London to have an operation, by the same surgeon who'd performed my Achilles op. The whole middle section of my leg was in plaster, so once again Sue was having to do everything for me. 'Just part of football,' I tried to explain, but getting nowhere. And the best of it was, by this time I didn't even believe it myself. By now, I was starting to believe in curses! We were sitting watching TV one night when there was a policeman's knock at the door. We both jumped and obviously Sue had to go and see who it was. Next minute, Jock Wallace and Frank Connor walk into the living room, 'Awrite, son?' asked the big man. Frank nodded his head.

'I'm good, gaffer,' I said, trying to sit to attention in the presence of such nobility.

Big Jock pointed to the couch and said, 'Right you ya bugger, budge up, geeza seat,' and I tried to bum my way along the small sofa. He planked himself down next to me and said, 'Hey Sue, get the whisky out, hen.'

She replied, 'We don't have any, as Alfie doesn't drink now.'

He let out this almighty harumph and started fumbling around in his pocket. He produced a £20 note, mumbled something along the lines of how he could fair murder a wee goldie, and then handed over the money to Sue and said, 'Right, hen, away doon to the corner shop and get two bottles of whisky.' So away she went and returned a few minutes later with the order.

I don't think wee Frank was drinking but Jock and I had quite a few halves. The whisky certainly didn't make the big man any looser, but the best approach was to take Jock the way you found him. He never changed, regardless of whether he'd had a drink or not. The conversation that night was about anything and everything, although mostly about football. Because he'd come from Wallyford, which was very close to Prestonpans, we never really ran out of conversation. We talked about the teams in that area and all the local personalities. I'm still convinced it was just a wee pep talk to make sure I was OK. Just a social visit, but he was checking up on me at the same time, although in the right way. Wee Frank didn't say a lot. Mind you, no one really said a lot while in Jock's company, but the conversation was never boring.

When I was fit enough to get back into Fir Park, although by no means anywhere near ready to play again, I had a chat with Jock and it was decided I should go to see a respected surgeon to ask when he thought it was safe for me to get the boots back on. What he had to say almost floored me. He told me bluntly that one more knock on the knee and it wouldn't just be career over, but I could expect to spend the rest of my life in a wheelchair. It was the same knee that I'd damaged extensively at Rangers, but this was actually my third operation on it, and the bottom line is that it was a mess. The latest injury had happened at Fir Park and I'd known right away that it was a bad one. The surgeon was effectively telling me that my career was over, and that I now had to concentrate on the second part of my life, the part which came after football. I must admit, he was brilliant with me and described everything in layman's terms. I left the hospital that day surprisingly upbeat. In my mind I had accepted that it was over. My football days were behind me and I had to look forward. I still had my share in the lorry business and that would tide me over.

When I got home, Sue only had to look at my face to know how it had gone. We spoke about it and she seemed surprised at how well I was handling such devastating news. So was I, until the following morning. The moment I woke up, my attitude had performed a complete U-turn. Who was the chancer who had so magnanimously accepted the surgeon's decision the day before? I certainly didn't recognise him. My career wasn't over, and I would show them. Number one on my list was big Jock. I headed into Fir Park and chapped the gaffer's door. 'Can I have a word, Jock?' I asked. 'Of course, son, come in.' Jock knew the prognosis due to a brief call we'd had the previous day – but things had changed, although quite what had changed I had no idea. Of course, I'd had second thoughts, and said to Jock, 'Surely the decision is mine if I want to play on, and not that surgeon's.'

'Of course it is, son,' he appeared to agree. 'But if you tell me you want to play on, and risk ending up in a wheelchair, with someone else having to push you around because you wouldn't listen to a specialist, then it won't be here at my club.'

Jock delivered this message in his usual gruff style, and I sat there looking at him for a few seconds. The message he was sending soon hit home, and it hit home hard. I couldn't put that on Sue; I couldn't take the chance of another tackle condemning me to a life of dependency. Would it be worth it if it happened in the first minute of the first game of the new season? Not a chance. I knew the big man was right and once again my attitude changed completely. I asked what my options were. Off the top of his head he told me that the club could stage a testimonial match on my behalf, or that they could claim the insurance money for me. The decision was mine. I told him I'd probably prefer the latter, although I'd speak to Sue first and confirm it with him the following day. He then had to tell me I was no longer a Motherwell player but that I'd still have to go into training every day, because that was what the rules stated about claiming insurance money. I didn't fully understand it at the time but went along with it. I didn't literally have to train, as it was more of a box-ticking exercise; like clocking in for work.

Anyway, he told me he had set the wheels in motion, and then next thing he's off to Rangers, and I'm left in the lurch. There was no way he was ever going to knock Rangers back, but when I pursued the claim with the office staff at Motherwell they told me they didn't know anything about it. I tried to take it further but hit a brick wall everywhere I turned and it was something that was never sorted out.

Top team: outside the church in Edinburgh

Tearing down the wing in my Spurs shirt …

All together before Steven's christening

Samantha keeping her dad company during another injury

I loved our family gatherings

Proudly representing my country

A family holiday in Corfu

Watching the drama unfold on the big stage

With Bobby Lennox at Celtic

Hugging Jock Stein after the Scottish Cup Final

A skiing holiday in Nice with Sue

Seaside laughs: with Allan Brown, manager of Blackpool

Samantha and her family; husband John, and kids, Laughlan and Iona

Steven and Lorna, with my granddaughter, Emily

Business venture with Wee Willie

Sue and I with Steven, Lorna and Emily

Back at Spurs with Ally Dick and Mousa Dembele

16

Revving Up With the CC

AFTER MY days at Motherwell – and as a footballer – were over, I just got on with my life. I didn't go to watch a lot of games and instead spent time with Sue and the kids. I would also go down to my local for a couple of pints or enjoy an evening at the greyhounds with my pals. One of them was a guy called Willie Cox, who had played a bit of football in his time. After a chance conversation with a mutual friend, Willie had been persuaded to take over a local amateur team called Coatbridge Community Centre, or CC as they were known locally. Once he wrapped his head around the fact that he had agreed to do this, he approached it like everything else – wholeheartedly and with a great determination to succeed.

At the time, CC were in the doldrums. They had slipped way down the pecking order in the amateur ranks and would often struggle for players, even being forced to train under streetlights at one point. Probably not quite rock bottom, but not too far away. We were in the pub one night when Willie had his lightbulb moment. You could almost see the wheels turning inside his head. 'Alfie, my friend,' he started, and I was immediately suspicious. 'How about joining me at the CC as a coach?'

My response was something like, 'Away and raffle yourself,' and we chuckled and kept playing dominoes. But the next morning when I recalled the conversation, I actually gave it some more thought and reckoned it might not be a bad idea. I had been flirting with the possibility of looking for a coaching job and thought it would offer both the impetus and added experience to help with any future job application. Up to that point my experiences as a coach had been limited – very limited. In fact, they stretched to a few sessions at the junior club Thornton Hibs during my early days as a Rangers player. Willie Johnston would go along some nights and help out with training, and he enlisted my services a few times. It was something I enjoyed and we would pass on training hints and tips. Bud and I had really bought into it and enjoyed our visits to Memorial Park.

This was a bit different. It was local, and there were no great distractions: something we could get our teeth into while attempting to restore this club to its former glories. I called Willie and said I'd give it a go, maybe for a month or so. He was delighted and we had a meeting, in the pub of course, and formulated our plans for CC. My intention was to help get Willie up and running, but I ended up staying for three or four years and I loved it. It was tough going at first but within a couple of months we were starting to see the green shoots of recovery.

Some great players came out of Coatbridge and it was our job to know who they were and how to get to them first. Within a few weeks of taking over the club we had a good network of folk in the town who would give us the nod if they heard of any standout players looking for a team.

When we started we were playing up at The Locks, where the new St Ambrose School complex was eventually built. It was called Espeyside Park back then and it was grass, but it wasn't the best, and it was oversubscribed. There were other teams from Coatbridge as well as a few sides from Easterhouse who also played there, and it was often difficult trying to get a park booked.

We grew slowly and built our way up into quite a force and decided to apply to join the Tennent's Caledonian League, which was one of the best in the country at that time. There was a worry that we might be one of the weaker teams in the TCL but everyone knows the only way to improve is to play against better teams each week, and that would hopefully give us the motivation to continue evolving. The league had certain criteria that new clubs had to meet, such as having your own park with floodlights and decent changing facilities. We worked hard and were eventually rewarded with a nice park at Drumpellier. The rugby club had played there but when they moved out, we moved in. We became a well-known and popular amateur club, and probably one of the biggest in the country at one point. And once we became better known we had a load of guys wanting to play for us and would regularly have 22 or 23 at training.

When we eventually won the Scottish Amateur Cup it was an unbelievable moment and a real feather in our caps. Very little is achieved without hard work and we had a good group of coaches at CC. The town was rightly proud of everything we achieved – which also included success in the league and the West of Scotland Cup – and it gave Coatbridge folk a big lift.

Near the end of our involvement it had started to go downhill again and we were lucky if we were getting double figures at training. It was sad to see, but successful clubs enjoy peaks and troughs and we were no different.

I really enjoyed my time with Coatbridge CC and thought at one point that the next logical step would be to try and get a coaching position at a senior side. I phoned Frank Connor as a couple of jobs had just come up, notably at Berwick Rangers and Albion Rovers, and asked if he would put my name forward for them. He said he would, and then asked what coaching badges I had. That threw me. I told him I had just enjoyed a couple of successful years in the amateur game, but told him I didn't have any coaching badges. He was adamant I wouldn't get a job without them, and explained what I would have to go through to get them. The truth is, I wasn't interested in going through that. You go to a coaching course and you have 11 or 12 boys telling you how to do this and do that. It reminded me of when wee Bud took one of these courses. He only lasted a couple of days, but one of his written questions was, 'How do you beat the offside trap?' Wee Bud's answer, 'A long ball over the top!' Two days tops and he was gone.

We had a young lad who came to Coatbridge, Mike Conroy, a centre-forward who played for the likes of Reading, Burnley and Fulham. He came up to train with us for a while and I would give him exercises, tailor-made for a striker. He seemed really taken aback the first time and told me he'd never seen anything like it in his career. But I thought it was normal. It was like midfield players, who I felt had to be trained differently from strikers. They're being asked to do a completely different job, so why put them through the same routines? In my day at Rangers, goalkeepers would do the same training as every other player. Why? That was why I believed that specialised training was the way forward and it was something I introduced at Coatbridge. Was it responsible for our success? I don't know, because there was lots of input from others, but if it contributed to it then job done.

In training, we would practise playing out from the back. The goalkeeper gets the ball and our two full-backs broke wide. In those days you didn't have wing backs. I loved coming up with ideas, or remembering situations that I'd experienced while playing under managers like Waddell, Wallace, Nicholson or Stein. In my mind, the knowledge I'd accrued from these giants of the game was far more valuable than anything I could learn on any coaching course.

After I'd decided not to go through the rigmarole of chasing badges, I found another reason to enjoy the beautiful game. My son was a teenager and had started playing for a team in Coatbridge. He played either right-back, as a right-sided midfielder, or on the wing at times, and had shown a lot of promise. I started to go and watch him, and it was something I enjoyed. He ended up going to Motherwell Boys' Club and appeared to have taken it to the next level. He was also training with Hearts at Springburn Park, just a stone's throw from where he'd been born at Stobhill Hospital. He played a couple of games for the Hearts youth team, and they wanted to put him on an S Form, but I didn't think it was a good idea. He was only 14 and I felt that if he was good enough for that, other clubs would come in for him, so why sign an S Form? Perhaps in hindsight I should've let him, but at the time I genuinely didn't think it was in his best interests. Maybe he became a bit disillusioned with the game after that as he quit football altogether for a while and just went about with his pals.

A couple of years later he decided to make a comeback and he signed for Coatbridge CC, and I would go and watch. He was playing well and his old love for the game seemed to have returned. He'd joined the police and had a good career, so the football was just a hobby, but in one game he suffered a depressed fracture of the cheekbone, and when he came off the park he told me he didn't feel well. I could see the colour draining from his face so I wasted no time in getting him to hospital and he had to undergo an operation there and then. He still has a plate in his cheek to this day.

He eventually got over that injury and made a comeback, but not long after that he suffered a cruciate ligament injury and that was that. His employers were fantastic but he knew the time had come to call it a day, as he had to think about himself and his job. Sometimes there are things more important than football, Mr Shankly!

I was a proud member of the local community in Coatbridge and whenever I was asked to do something I always tried to find the time. One of the things I particularly enjoyed was going along to a local boys' club when they were having a player of the year event. I was often asked to present the medals and trophies and if I had a prior engagement I would try to reschedule.

On one occasion I was invited along to St Bartholomew's Boys' Guild – in the local area – to do the honours at their dance and presentation evening. It was around 1981 and I was playing for Motherwell at the time, and things were going pretty well. Anyway, I went up on stage and handed out the prizes. As each young lad moved along the line I shook his hand and gave him his medal. At the end we had a team photograph and the boys all walked back to their respective tables and families. One of the organisers came over to thank me and said, 'Alfie, you've no idea how happy these kids are now, that a pro footballer has taken the time to come and shake their hands and give out the medals.'

I just looked at him and replied, 'It's no big deal, honestly.' But he told me it certainly was to the kids, and from that night onwards I looked at it from a different perspective. I suppose all I had to do was think back to when John Greig presented my medal to know that the gentleman was spot on. When people talk about 'giving something back', I now know what they mean. It seems such a small thing to do, but it makes a difference. And the good thing is that it gave me just as much pleasure.

Something else which gave me a lot of pleasure was a business venture I entered into with wee Willie Henderson and a pal of mine. There was a vacant pub at the corner of Dundyvan Road and Wallace Street, in Whifflet, Coatbridge, called The Barnyard, and it was up for sale, so we decided to go into business together and see if we could make a go of it. There was soon a new slogan in town, and it became a stick to beat us with, although it was all in good taste.

'Willie Henderson and Alfie Conn invite you to … The New Barnyard'

We worked hard at it and The New Barnyard did quite well. Thursday night was 'Golden Oldie' night – and that referred to the music, not the clientele! Friday night was The Best Disco in Town, which I know was anything but original, but disco music was still massive then and folk loved it. We also had a resident band on a Saturday and they played the type of stuff that we all love, so the recipe was pretty good. Some might say 'standard pub fare' but it worked and we gave the punters what they wanted.

But here's the thing – it was a Celtic pub, and a supporters' bus would leave from there on a Saturday. I had form with both, but I think it made wee Willie a little apprehensive, although he never got any hassle. I was with Motherwell at the time and so I quite enjoyed the different banter it brought. I would go in and take a shot behind the bar and chat to punters and I liked that side of it. I was comfortable in a crowd that size and I soon got to know most of the locals.

Willie used his contacts to get a few star names up for the opening and the place was packed out. We had promised big names, and big names was what we gave them. But we managed to keep it a secret until the opening night, and I'll never forget the moment we announced the star turn – and in walked football god Sir Stanley Matthews. The place went wild. Everyone of a certain vintage knew Sir Stanley and he must've signed a thousand autographs that night, including one for me.

But I kind of felt a bit sorry for our other opening night guest. Anywhere else, Jackie Mudie would've been hailed, quite rightly, as a superstar of the game, but who wouldn't have been overshadowed by one of the world's greatest ever footballers? Jackie was a former team-mate and best friend of Sir Stanley, and both had played a grand part in Blackpool winning the 1953 FA Cup Final against Bolton Wanderers. It was a match in which Stan Mortensen scored a hat-trick, but which became known as the 'Matthews Final'! I remember speaking to Jackie that night and him telling me all about playing and scoring for Scotland in the 1958 World Cup finals in Sweden. What a moment and a great football education.

We had a big, regular clientele, and they never knew the moment another top-line sporting name would pop in. The night Jim Baxter dropped in was another fantastic evening. My idol, and I stood there like a schoolboy lapping up his stories and applauding along with everyone else. Baxter could tell a story as well as he could pass a ball, and he would have everyone on the edge of their seats as he waxed lyrical about his time in the game.

Another guest who enthralled customers with his successful time in Scottish sport was the former boxer Peter Keenan. He was a bantamweight of some repute and at one time held the Scottish, British and European belts. He also challenged for the world bantamweight crown and became a successful publican after his career was over.

The pub was a big success but I called time after five or six years. It was a lot of work, which I didn't mind, but also a huge commitment, and while there were many enjoyable moments, I felt it was the right time to hand back the keys. Wee Willie also had a pub in Chapelhall at the time so he had experience of running bars, and that proved invaluable for us.

I had lived in Coatbridge for many years and we were happy there. I had a load of friends who had little to do with the world of football other than being supporters of different teams, and we would have a laugh. I was in my local one night when a pal of mine asked if I would like to go to Ibrox with him and a few others that coming Saturday. Ibrox, red flag. And it was an Old Firm game. Another red flag. So what did I do? I went of course. To be honest, I quite fancied it and thought, 'Why not?' I should be able to go to a game of football if I want. Alfie!

We were sitting in the Govan Stand and at half-time one of my mates said, 'Alfie, have you ever queued up for a pie here?' I thought about it, and the answer was no. We were having a bit of a laugh and one of the guys said, 'Well, that's what normal fans do.' I told him that today I was a normal fan and that if he wanted a pie I would go and get him one.

It was a freezing cold day and I had my big sheepskin coat on. Not a Malcolm Allison one, something a bit more moderate. I pulled up the collar to cover my cheeks and headed down to the concourse. I'm standing in the queue, minding my own business, and this guy's looking at me. There's always one, isn't there? He gets up close and personal, in my space, just to make sure it's me, and then he opens his mouth. 'Whit team you supportin' the day, then, eh?' I smiled and said, 'Rangers.' He clearly didn't believe me and gave me that 'aye, right' look. And then someone else spots me, and then another, and before you know it I'm getting pelters from all around. The gang mentality. I think we lost that day and that encounter just put the tin lid on it for me. But I toughed it out and got the pie, and said to my mate, 'You better enjoy that!' He told me I was now a bona fide fan.

After the game I was standing in the concourse waiting on my mates, who were in the toilet. I see this big bear coming towards me. He looks seriously pissed and he's staring right at me as he makes his way through the departing crowds, caring not a jot who he bumps into in the process. I'm wondering if he's one of those who were giving me grief in the half-time pie queue. The closer he gets, the more obvious it is that I'm his intended target. 'Alfie Conn,' he growls, and he's just six feet away. Heart in the mouth time. Fight or flight? Neither, but I'm going nowhere. And then he blurted out the words, 'I wish you had been playin' the day, mate!' And he threw his arms around me and gave me this incredible bear hug. And then walks off as quickly as he had appeared. My emotions were all over the place that day, and when my mates came out the toilet they were none the wiser, and thought I was a bit emotional because we'd lost.

It was a while after that before I went to another game, because I decided it simply wasn't worth the hassle of wondering whether someone was going to kiss or kick you. And also because I got fed up being asked the same question over and over – why did you sign for them? I even got it from fans who were too young to have seen me play, but who were clearly being egged on by folk who should've known better.

A few years ago, I was enticed back to Ibrox on a semi-regular basis to work at hospitality. The main attraction for me was getting to work with the likes of wee Bud, Steiny, Doddie and Davie Smith. We had a laugh and when you were working the lounges the comments were playful rather than vindictive. It was good fun and I also enjoyed watching the games with the lads. We would rib one another mercilessly. It was almost like being back in the Ibrox dressing room. I would say, 'Steiny, when Bud left Rangers he went to Birmingham. I left and went to London, so how the hell did you end up in Coventry? Did they have electricity in Coventry when you joined them?' And it used to drive him batty. The three of us still have a fantastic relationship to this day.

On one occasion I was working in Bar 72 and just before the game I had nipped down to the exit to have a quick smoke. It was probably about ten to three and the place was buzzing with fans heading in all different directions, attempting to get inside Ibrox for the start of the game. And then I saw him. He was a big bloke and he was about 50 or 60 yards away, but I knew where he was headed. I could usually spot them a mile off and the way this guy was walking I knew he had something he wanted to get off his chest. Next minute we're face to face and he said, 'What are you doing here?'

'Sorry,' I replied.

'I thought you'd be hiding in the same cave as Osama bin Laden.'

Fair play, but that was quite funny. I told him I was here for the game and said I hoped he enjoyed it too. He smiled and walked away. I always felt the best way to handle aggression was to try and indulge in some banter. If that didn't work then I would try to ignore it and walk away.

But Rangers was still my club and that will never change. What has happened is water under the bridge to me, as I've still to meet someone who can change the past. The vast majority of Rangers supporters I meet these days just want to chat. Sure, they ask 'that' question, but there's no malice, and after 50 years I would probably expect that to be the case.

17

My Friends: the Barça Bears

I'M A firm believer that shared experiences can help deepen the personal connections that allow us to thrive. They not only impact positively on our well-being but strengthen the relationships that are most dear to us. The Covid pandemic proved how important it was to have human connection. The most obvious is with family, but what about work-mates? As a footballer, my work-mates were those I shared a dressing room and a pitch with. When we went abroad on our many trips, whether competitive games or pre-season tours, it meant staying over, sometimes for a week or two, and that's when you really get to know someone. Going deep into European competition also strengthened the many bonds I had at Rangers and made us all want to fight that bit harder for one another. The players who would go all the way and lift the European Cup Winners' Cup in Barcelona became a true band of brothers, and the fortunate 11 who started the final would never forget how lucky they were. We not only won together but that shared experience ensured we would for ever be linked by this success – the one and only time the club has lifted a European trophy. Something so monumental was bound to bring us all closer together, and we became known simply as the Barça Bears. I have never been prouder of a single achievement in my life, and I'm sure it was the same for most of the other guys. Immortality was achieved that night in the Catalan city and, in many ways, it has defined who we are in the ensuing decades. But who were my teammates that night at the Camp Nou, and what kind of people were they both on and off the park? There are so many diverse personalities in a dressing room that it is quite something when everyone gets on and pulls together for the greater good of the team.

Peter McCloy (goalkeeper): Big Peter was not only a safe pair of hands but also a fantastic team member. He was our first-choice keeper for the majority of his 16 years at Rangers for a reason. He was nicknamed the 'Girvan Lighthouse' due to a combination of his height and birthplace. He spent most of his career at Rangers, signing from Motherwell in 1970, after spending four years at Fir Park. After his time at Rangers he did what a lot of our ex-players did in those days and joined Hearts!

I got on very well with Peter even though he was six years older than me. He was a quiet guy off the park but that changed when he donned the goalkeeper's jersey. He would bark instructions at his back four – like all good keepers should – and let his defenders know if he didn't think they were doing their jobs correctly. We had a shared interest in golf, although I was nowhere near his standard. Very few ever got the better of the big man, and if they did, he was clearly having an off day! He really was an unbelievable golfer and when he retired from football he took up a position at the Turnberry golf course, and would invite us down from time to time. He played off scratch and was almost as good with a set of clubs as he was as a keeper.

Peter was a massive part of our success in the 1972 European Cup Winners' Cup and along the way to lifting the trophy he pulled off some remarkable saves. A very good goalkeeper and a thoroughly decent guy.

I remember his wedding to Anne only too well. I told wee Bud I'd take the car down to Girvan and Sue and I picked up him and his wife, Margaret. Off we went and I thought we had loads of time but it was quite a drive and as we were heading down the coast we realised that getting there for the start would be a close run thing. I put the boot down a bit and sure enough, a blue flashing light appeared behind us. Then Bud says, 'Oh, I seen them back there, I should've said, sorry Alfie!' So I pulled over and this young cop tells me to roll down the window. I thought I'd use the old Rangers connection to see if it might help. Usually there was a 50/50 chance. 'Sorry, officer,' I pleaded, 'we're on our way to Girvan for big Peter McCloy's wedding. Do you know him?' 'Yes,' he said, 'I know Peter.' I thought, here we go, I'm getting off with this, so I added, 'We play for Rangers as well, and we were a wee bit late, sorry about that.' 'No problem,' he said, '£50 fine and three points. We don't tolerate speeding in Ayrshire.' Off he went and I was raging.

Talking about speed, big Peter was one of the fastest runners at Ibrox, but he did have the advantage of taking one stride to everyone else's two or three!

Sandy Jardine (right-back): Sandy must be one of the greatest full-backs to play for Rangers. He had the lot: pace, talent, stamina, you name it, and he could score goals. He joined Rangers in 1966 from the youth game in Edinburgh and while he was used as a striker for the first part of his Rangers career, he soon found his true calling and was capped 39 times for Scotland at right-back. Sandy played a huge part in the Cup Winners' Cup run, culminating in a goal against Bayern Munich in that never-to-be-forgotten semi-final at Ibrox under the lights. He left Rangers for Hearts in 1982 and had six successful years at Tynecastle.

Sandy was someone I looked up to when I joined Rangers. He was a few years older than me and had also been at Rangers since he was a youngster. We got on really well and I loved his dry sense of humour. He was an out and out athlete and would always be up front at training. He looked after himself and put his body first. He didn't drink a lot although he was a regular at club functions. But while the rest of us were done by 28, Sandy was still playing at 40 – and that was his reward for taking care of himself during his playing days. When I joined Rangers he stayed near Saughton and we would get the train through to Glasgow for training and games. And then when I moved to Fife, if we weren't driving through, all the boys from Fife would get the train through to Edinburgh and join the local lads for the trip. We would often take up a dozen or so seats for the 45-minute journey to Queen Street. Over the years I got to know Sandy really well and I was distraught when I heard of his passing in 2014.

Willie Mathieson (left-back): One of the real unsung heroes of the Barça side. He joined Rangers from schools football in 1964 but it would be another three years before he made himself a first-team regular. In his first few years there was a trophy drought as Jock Stein's Celtic dominated the Scottish football scene, but Willie worked away at his game and was in the team for the Scottish Cup Final of 1969, and the Fairs Cup semi-final against Newcastle United, both of which would end in disappointment. Believe it or not, Willie's first Rangers medal was secured in Barcelona, but it was well earned as he was one of just five players to start all nine ties. When Willie left Rangers in 1975, injury affected the remainder of his playing career, but he teamed up with good pal Davie Smith in the dugout at Shielfield Park, as the pair tried to bring success to Berwick Rangers.

I got to know Willie well during my time at Rangers, as we travelled together to training and games from our base in Fife for several years. He was a quiet guy but would join in the banter on the many journeys to and from the kingdom. He was a respectful guy, and never in your face. His nickname at Ibrox was 'The Machine', as his running power was phenomenal.

I read somewhere that Jack Russells had the stamina to run from Glasgow to Edinburgh and back – so maybe we had the wrong nickname for Willie. Those were the days when we had two overlapping full-backs of outstanding stamina, long before overlapping full-backs were trendy. We probably had the two fittest full-backs in the league. Willie was a family man, and didn't drink a lot, but we would go to loads of supporters' functions together and that was something he always enjoyed.

John Greig (right-half): There are many reasons why John was voted the Greatest Ever Ranger in 1999. He had served the club in just about every position possible, but it was his great drive and determination on the field that made him such a club legend. On many occasions he would urge his wilting team-mates forward and no cause was ever lost when John was in the side. We could go on and on about the medals and accolades he won during his 17 years as a player, but it's all well documented elsewhere. As a team-mate, John was simply one of the best and the love he had for Rangers knew no bounds. I always got the impression that if John broke his leg during a game he would've refused to come off, and that fighting spirit was also instilled in everyone around him.

Off the park he was also great company. He had a brilliant sense of humour and his jokes were legendary – if not the best! But if there was something going on then John would be in the middle of it. He wasn't just a captain on the park. If any of the players were having a party then John and his wife, Jeanette, would be there to lend their support. He was also a proficient golfer and won his fair share of club competitions.

Derek Johnstone (centre-half): DJ was just 18 when we lined up against Moscow Dynamo, but he had an old head on young shoulders and was one of our star turns in the Camp Nou. He was an outstanding centre-forward, a great header of the ball, and it says everything that he played centre-half for us in a European final. Talk about adaptable. He was just a kid but had already been through so much before his 18th birthday that he almost seemed like a veteran in Barcelona. He was a schoolboy when he joined Rangers in 1968 and signed professional forms almost as soon as he was 16. He had 13 excellent years at Rangers before joining Chelsea. Another travesty was his exclusion from Ally MacLeod's World Cup squad in 1978, just after he had scored more than 40 goals domestically for Rangers that season.

DJ and I got on very well, but because of his age he missed a lot of social events when he first joined Rangers. He was also based in Dundee, which ruled him out as well. But I loved his sense of humour and we had so many great laughs together. There was always a lot of talk about his best position, and I know that he preferred to play centre-half. My take on it? I thought he was the best centre-half in Scotland, bar none. His reading of the game, his timing in the tackle, his ability to head the ball strongly and in the direction he wanted, all combined to make him the best.

When it came to the 1978 World Cup in Argentina, I thought his inclusion was a given. He was arguably at the peak of his powers and would've been a great asset to Scotland. But I was told he didn't go because he wanted to play centre-half in Argentina, and Ally MacLeod wanted him up front. I'm not sure how much truth is in that, but I think his non-inclusion was a huge mistake.

His playing style seemed so effortless, and he seldom panicked while on the ball. I recall Jock Stein saying that DJ was the best footballing centre-half he'd seen. There you go.

Davie Smith (left-half): Probably the closest any Ranger ever got to Baxter, and that's saying something. Davie was a class apart and the day we signed him from Aberdeen was a great day indeed. He joined Rangers the same year as Sandy, after five years with his hometown club. I was able to admire his skills up close and personal and I swear he's one of the best I've ever seen. After eight years at Ibrox his career nosedived a little and he probably never again regained the heights he had reached in that glorious spell in blue. It was quite remarkable that he was even able to star in the Cup Winners' Cup Final as he had suffered back-to-back leg breaks in 1970 and again the following year, yet in 1972 he was simply majestic for us and would go on to be named the Scottish Football Writers' Player of the Year. One of the biggest travesties was that he never played a competitive game for his country. He won two caps, both in friendlies. I could never wrap my head around that one.

I think in all the time I played alongside Davie I never saw him waste a single ball or knock one out of the park. He was the calmest man on the field and although he started out as a midfielder, I think he preferred to play sweeper. His partnership with DJ was simply the best. One of the few guys in the team who didn't play golf!

As a person, Davie was also top-drawer, and despite the near ten-year age gap, we have been friends since the 1960s, and that friendship has never waned. He might live up north in the back of beyond, but we still see each other whenever we can. When I had a charity night to raise funds for motor neurone disease, Davie travelled down from the north-east and wouldn't take a penny in expenses. So many of my old team-mates were there, which was a truly humbling experience.

Tommy McLean (right wing): As wingers go, Tommy was as good as it got. He was a magician with the ball at his feet and the accuracy his right peg produced was simply majestic. Talk about DJ being a centre-forward and you have to include Tommy in the conversation as he could land the ball on a sixpence. He had seven years at Kilmarnock and was there at the same time as both his brothers (Jim was a fellow player, while eldest brother Willie was a coach). He won the league at Killie but would go on to play almost 500 games for Rangers in a fruitful 11-year period. He won 11 major honours in his time at the club and when his playing days were over, he was appointed John Greig's number two, taking over as caretaker boss when John resigned in 1983.

Tommy was another quiet guy, and he didn't play a lot of golf; bowling was his thing, which meant he and Tam Forsyth spent a lot of time together as Tam also loved his bowling. Both were Lanarkshire lads, which was another thing in common, but both were also a massive part of things at Rangers. At that time we were blessed with a truly wonderful team spirit and if I said there were some players who didn't get on with others I would be lying.

Colin Stein (centre-forward): 'The greatest centre-forward the world has ever seen,' sang the Rangers supporters as Steiny scored more than his fair share of goals for the club. His electric start to life as a Ranger in 1968 was characterised by back-to-back hat-tricks and two against Dundalk, in the game where I made my Rangers debut. He was a fantastic goalscorer who answered his critics when Rangers shelled out £100,000 to sign him from Hibs. It was the first six-figure transfer fee between Scottish clubs and Steiny was worth every single penny. He would also score in Barcelona and in his two spells at Rangers – with three years at Coventry City sandwiched in between – he was the darling of the support. He might even be the last Scotland player to have scored four times in a single game, when he did so against Cyprus at Hampden in 1969.

He actually enjoyed playing up front on his own, because he would run all day for the cause. He didn't give defenders a moment's peace and was also fantastic with the ball at his feet, bringing others into play. Jock Wallace loved him, as he was far more than just a goalscorer.

That's Steiny as a player, but as a person I love him to bits. Was he quiet? Aye, so he was! He never shut up, a real talker, but another ex-team-mate with a brilliant sense of humour. He would always come out with the most amazing jokes – but also liked to get the last word in, although not this time, mate! Everyone knows Bud and Steiny as a great double act, but I remember being at a function a couple of years ago when both were on stage, and Steiny was his usual talkative self, and the wee man said, 'That's it Steiny, I want a divorce!' It brought the house down and Steiny had a huge smile etched across his face.

Alex MacDonald (inside-left): Apart from being a fellow Gilbert O'Sullivan fan, Doddie and I were close during my time at Ibrox. He was a good mate and a player I thoroughly enjoyed playing alongside. His never-say-die spirit was probably one of the qualities that enticed Davie White to part with £50,000 of Rangers' cash in 1968. I reckon it was the best 50 grand we spent because Doddie was as valuable an asset as they come. Another of his amazing qualities was his ability to arrive late in the box, at just the right time, and he scored many an important goal because of that. Later on, many supporters would liken Ian Durrant to Doddie, and I must admit there were a great many similarities. Oh, and both were from Kinning Park! Doddie was our engine room – on his own – as everything went through him. He was also a fiery wee guy and would let you know if you'd done something wrong. Any time I made a mistake on the park I would immediately look for Doddie to see if I was getting a row. He was like another captain.

Fancy another travesty? He played just once for Scotland! I mean, how did that happen? When he finished playing he managed both Hearts and Airdrie and did a wonderful job at both, coming within a whisker of winning the title at Tynecastle.

Doddie might have been a fiery, fired-up guy on the pitch, but off it he loved a laugh and a joke, and he was another who was in the thick of things whenever we had a club day out. Doddie and his wife Christine were also very good friends with Sue and I.

Willie Johnston (left wing): Wee Bud remains one of my best friends in football. Again, he is a few years older than me but that didn't affect our friendship because despite achieving what he did in the game, he was never a Billy Big Time and that was a tremendous quality. From the moment he joined Rangers, after being farmed out to Fife junior side Lochore Welfare, Bud played more than 600 times in a sparkling 20-plus-year career. And Bud's greatest quality on the park? He was an entertainer, pure and simple. He was lethal with the ball at his feet, but it wasn't just pace he relied upon to go past players – he had no end of skill in that left peg, as well as some in his right as well. He got kicked up and down the park at times but he was such a brave player and he didn't hide from the thugs masquerading as 1970s defenders. Sure, there were occasions when the red mist descended and he would be sent for an early bath, but he was such a valuable asset to Rangers and Scottish football, as he was the type of player who enticed supporters to grounds.

One of the quietest people I ever met away from a football pitch but put a jersey on him and he turns into the Wild Man of Borneo! I can't explain it, and he couldn't explain it, so we'll leave that one to the scientists. One explanation might be that defenders couldn't get near him, and so they kicked him. He didn't like being kicked and, voila, he took the long walk many a time.

I remember when Willie Waddell sent a few of us through to Edinburgh to train with a professional sprinter. The guy was trying to assess each of us and so he decided he would race us one at a time. He said to Bud, 'OK, it's a 40-yard sprint, you'll get a couple of yards as a start, and we'll ...' And Bud stopped him in his tracks. 'I'd prefer we both start off scratch,' he said. The sprinter shook his head, agreed, and Bud left him standing. The sprint coach was amazed, but we weren't. Over 30 or 40 yards he was the quickest footballer I ever saw. An absolute gem of a man, and one of my best mates in football or otherwise.

Folk of a certain vintage will remember the classic film *Casablanca*. If you haven't seen it, you should. It includes one of the most memorable cinematic lines of all time, when Rick, played by Humphrey Bogart, tells his former love, Ilsa, 'We'll always have Paris,' referring to their brief romance on the eve of the Second World War. I know it's cheesy, but I can say with terrific pride that me and these guys will 'always have Barcelona'! It was a shared experience like no other, and I know it's something that I'll never forget. We lived the dream in May 1972, didn't we guys?

18

Saving the Best to Last

INVERLEITH CHURCH, in Edinburgh, was the venue for the biggest match of my career. It was the day I tied the knot with Susan Bunyan just a long free kick from her home in Granton, and I was the happiest man alive. After I got over the pre-service nerves, of course. I was the guy who could walk on to the pitch at Wembley in a Scotland shirt, or play for Rangers in a European final, and not feel the heat, but stick me in a three-piece suit, tell me to stand at the front of the church with my best man beside me, and I was a wreck. Did I think Sue would leave me standing at the altar on my own? Nope, but there's always that chance, isn't there? And with a guest list including the likes of John Greig, Sandy Jardine, Doddie and Kenny Dalglish ready to slaughter me at a moment's notice, I was a bag of nerves. If I say so myself, I did look rather dapper in my wedding suit and contrasting waistcoat, but the moment I caught sight of Sue walking down the aisle on the arm of her dad, I understood the meaning of true beauty. Sue looked gorgeous and I could add the title of Proudest Man in Edinburgh to the Happiest. It was a lovely ceremony and we emerged on to Ferry Road as Mr and Mrs Conn. What a moment.

And it's moments like this that I'll never forget. It's a well known fact that behind every successful man is a strong woman. Sue and I were a team. We did everything together and when the children came along that team extended to four. Sue, Samantha, Steven and me.

A month or so after Christmas 1972, Sue and I got engaged and about a week later we had a little party to celebrate. It was a nice time and everything was simple. Unlike my cavalier style on the football field, flamboyancy was kept to a minimum at any gatherings we had. We were just regular folk. Before getting married we had decided that we wouldn't be setting up home in Glasgow, even though it would be closer to my place of work. I loved travelling through to the big city for my Ibrox duties, but as a place to live Glasgow simply didn't do it for either of us. I was staying in Kinghorn before the wedding and we had more or less settled on a home in Kirkcaldy, which was just ten minutes up the road.

Kinghorn overlooks the Forth Estuary and was almost directly opposite the Granton district of Edinburgh, and that – and my big mouth – provided me with one of my most embarrassing moments. I remember being interviewed in-house by a reporter from *Rangers News*, and we were sitting having a laugh and I was telling him where Sue lived. I gave him the throwaway line, 'We could probably flash "goodnight" by torchlight if we wanted,' and thought no more of it. There were always copies of the *News* lying around the dressing room and if you had a few minutes you would pick up a copy and browse the pages. Imagine my surprise – and horror – one day when I turned up for training and walked into the dressing room to find a load of my team-mates huddled together reading the *News*. The moment I walked in they all started saying, 'Goodnight, Alfie, love you,' and they were seriously taking the piss. I had forgotten all about the interview but when one of them produced a torch and started flashing Morse code I knew exactly what they were up to. You got away with nothing in that dressing room!

I read the article and had a chuckle to myself, but it was at that point I decided to watch what I was saying whenever in the presence of a journalist. One of the lines said, 'I think getting married will settle me down – and that can only be good for my football. I'm hoping to have a good season and being married will give me extra responsibility which should help. I'll have another mouth to feed and only my best form will ensure I'm in the team and getting the bonuses that go with it.'

And then I was voted Scotland's trendiest footballer by a Scottish newspaper, so you can imagine the ribbing I took for that. We were at a club function and Sue and I were being called Scotland's 'Power Couple'! The banter at Rangers was first-class and that was probably one of the things I missed most when I left to head down south. Don't get me wrong, we always had a good laugh at Spurs, but it was different. I had virtually grown up with these guys at Ibrox and we all knew one another inside out. We were all pals and that brought about something special which just wasn't there at most of the other clubs I played for.

Sue fell pregnant while I was at Spurs and we made a point of keeping the sex of the baby secret. We wanted it to be a surprise. But as the big day drew closer, I started to think, 'What if it's a boy, and he's born in England? He won't be able to play for Scotland.' Sue and I discussed this at great length and we decided that when she got to around four weeks before her due date, she would go back up to her mum and dad's so that the baby could be born in Scotland. When I say we decided, I don't remember Sue being massively happy about it, but she went along with my request and we packed a few things in the car – as well as our old English sheepdog, Blue – and off we went up to the east coast. Sure enough, four weeks later Sue was admitted to the Western General in the capital and Samantha was born. Sadly, Samantha didn't show any interest whatsoever in football and therefore she wouldn't be turning out for the women's international side! She was a girly girl and loved playing with her dolls and when I came in from training she'd be waiting with dolls and outfits and that would be me – designated dresser-in-chief for a couple of hours.

In the days when Samantha was born, players were given one day of paternity leave, which back then wasn't even enough time to get from England to Scotland, so I couldn't be there for the birth, but the moment I had a couple of days off I was up the road in a shot and once Sue was fit to travel we headed back down to London in the car as a wee family. I must admit, when Samantha came into the world I looked at life in a different way. She was born in 1975 and when I went to the hospital to see Sue and the baby the place was crawling with reporters and photographers. It's amazing how your life changes when you become a parent, although the first time I was allowed to pick Samantha up apparently the first thing I did was to count her fingers and toes, just to make sure they were all there. I remember getting halfway through and smiling at Sue, and she was staring at me with this look on her face that said, 'What the hell are you doing?'

As soon as we were back home in London Samantha found her voice, and she really could greet as a kid. We would leave her in the pram and wheel it into our room. She would wake up, get a feed and then we'd try to rock her back to sleep, so we could at least get a couple of hours before morning. I would be shattered every day at training but it was all part of the 'joy' of being a new parent.

There were no such problems when Steven came along three years later. I was playing at Celtic and Steven was born at Stobhill Hospital. I had hoped for a boy and my wishes were granted. But you soon realise that the most important thing is the health of your children, although apparently I managed to refrain from counting Steven's fingers and toes. I was the proudest dad alive and knew there and then that our family was complete. A boy and a girl, the gentlemen's family as they called it. Sue and I were content.

Steven grew up in Coatbridge and most of his pals were either Rangers or Celtic supporters. He would ask me to get him a Rangers top but I refused as I didn't want him to wear either strip in case it caused bother. I tried to keep him clear of that side of things and later in life, when he showed a real interest in football, he would much rather have played than watched.

One of life's most oft-used sayings is that your days pass in a flash, and to make the most of them. I'd like to think that in both my personal and professional lives I did that. There are regrets, obviously, but your whole life is one big learning curve, and for the most part you do what you think is right at a specific time or in any given situation. Maybe I should've worked on a backup plan if the football didn't work out, but to a certain extent the football did work out. Injuries are part and parcel of the game, and while I definitely endured more than my fair share, all you can do is deal with whatever one comes along at any given time. It wasn't just the injuries that were a major source of frustration, but the associated recovery periods, and the reputation you get as they mount up for being made of glass.

The game in the 1970s could be particularly brutal. I think if I was playing in the modern game I would've thrived, under the right managers, of course. We had little protection from referees and retaliation was often treated far more seriously than a deliberate and brutal kick to your legs. That's why situations often boiled over. Nowadays, the protection is there and flair players can operate with a certain freedom, although there aren't too many of them around. But I'm in danger of becoming one of these 'the old days were the best' people. I enjoyed playing when I did, and I didn't mind a bit of rough and tumble. At Rangers we were one of the top teams and that often made us a target for the bully boys, but the benefits of playing for such an incredible club easily outweighed the risks. My six years at Rangers were special, and no one can ever take that from me.

Another highlight is representing my country. As a proud Scot that goes without saying, and is something most kids dream of, especially running out at Wembley in front of 70,000 passionate, tartan-clad supporters. Getting the opportunity to play in the top flight of English football, for one of the best clubs around, and with some fantastic players, is another high point, as was playing under the great Jock Stein. When you put it all together, I fared not too badly, and the memories will never leave me. But if you pushed me for an ultimate high point, I would have to plump for the evening I became a European champion in Barcelona. That trumps everything.

18

I Think I'm Alone Now …

I'VE LONG held an interest in the fate versus coincidence debate. On many occasions when something 'spooky' happens it's clearly just a coincidence, but there are times when I reckon fate plays its part in your life. Take, for instance, one Thursday afternoon when I was 18. Normally, we finished training around lunchtime and were free to do what we wanted for the rest of the day. If it was a nice afternoon we might play golf, or just catch the train home to Edinburgh and have a lazy day. But this particular Thursday was different. For some inexplicable reason we were held back at training and didn't finish until around 3pm. I sensed a mini revolt on the horizon. There were a few of us heading back to Edinburgh so we caught the subway from Copland Road into Glasgow city centre and got the later train from Queen Street to Waverley. Quite early in the journey, I noticed this blonde girl sitting a few seats away from me. I didn't say anything to the other lads. She looked amazing and I was desperate to pluck up the courage to go and speak to her. We were way past Falkirk by the time I had summoned up the necessary bravado and I got up and walked over. I asked her if she minded if I sat down. She smiled, and said, 'Go on.' I sat with her for the rest of the journey to Edinburgh (which wasn't that long) and we chatted about anything and everything. She had been in Glasgow for the day to visit a lot of the shops that we didn't have in Edinburgh at the time. Her main interest was fashion, which she didn't need to mention as I could tell by the amazing way she was dressed.

We chatted for another wee while and I realised the train was getting closer to Edinburgh Haymarket station, which didn't leave much time to ask her out – and I wasn't about to throw away this golden opportunity. We had actually pulled out of Haymarket when I finally found the strength. Massive relief, but now for the answer. More relief as she said yes and we arranged to meet the next night at the Waverley steps, outside Edinburgh's main station. That was probably the most popular place for prospective dates to meet in those days, but it could be extremely humiliating if one of the two didn't show up. I'd heard all about the infamous Boots dizzy corner in Glasgow, where quite often the girl would fail to show and the poor guy would be left standing – and everyone walking past would know that his 'lumber' had 'dizzied' him!

I didn't know this girl's name and she didn't know mine, but that was OK. I had ditched my team-mates and we walked out of the station together and on to Princes Street and went our separate ways. I had that feeling of near elation when I started the final leg of the journey home and was already looking forward to the following night. Of course, I got a bit of ribbing on the train into Glasgow for training the next morning but there was no way of removing the permanent grin from my face – until one of the lads remarked that she probably wouldn't turn up! Cheers, mate.

Later that night, I parked the car and walked down to the Waverley steps, and there she was, this vision of absolute beauty, waiting for me. Hallelujah! On the short walk down I'd imagined a few different scenarios. One was that she didn't turn up, and I would have a quick look around to see if anyone was watching, before making a swift getaway. But no need for the dark glasses, and the first thing I did was introduce myself and we went for something to eat in a nice wee restaurant at the Orange Grove Hotel up Lothian Road way. At the time a lot of the players used it so I thought it might be appropriate. It was a lovely night so it was a pleasant walk from the station to the restaurant. We made some small talk and I felt good being with her. We had a nice meal and Sue had a couple of drinks. I was on the soft drinks as I was driving (and we had a game the next day).

I dropped her home and before she went into the house I asked if she liked football. She kind of hedged her bets by saying it was OK, but that she'd never been to a game. I asked if she would like to go to a game the next day and she said yes. This was getting serious! I arranged to pick her up the following morning at 11 and we drove through to Glasgow. I had only known Sue for a couple of days but we were already comfortable in one another's company and it put me in a relaxed mood ahead of the game.

When we arrived at Ibrox I noticed Sue looking up at the big blue gates and the magnificent red brick façade. 'Nice, isn't it?' I asked.

'I've never seen anything like it before,' she answered.

I stopped the car across the road from the ground and took her into Mrs Cook's, where all the other wives and girlfriends would be. I introduced her to a few of the women and said, 'OK, I'll leave you here and get you after the game.'

She looked at me in a state of confusion, and said, 'What do you mean, you'll leave me here? Am I not coming into the game with you?'

I said, 'You can't, I'm playing.'

The look on her face was priceless, and she said, 'You're playing?'

I smiled, 'Yes, I play for Rangers.'

She smiled back and said, 'OK, I'll see you soon. Oh, and good luck.'

So off I went, played the game and picked her up at Mrs Cook's just before 5pm. She was asking me all about the game on the way home to Edinburgh and we had a laugh about it. She said she'd thought we would be watching together, but wondered why we had been leaving so early in the first place. When we got to Edinburgh we stopped off at a restaurant for something to eat and then I dropped her home. She waved, smiled and in she went.

We had arranged to meet again the following week and when we did, she told me she'd had a huge rammy with her dad when she got in on the Saturday night. I immediately thought, 'Oh, here we go.'

She had said to her dad, 'You'll never guess who I'm going out with?' And he asked who.

'Alfie Conn,' she answered.

'The footballer?' her dad asked, in a slightly concerned tone.

'Yes, that's right,' Sue said, smiling.

That was the moment her dad blew a gasket and shouted, 'He's far too old for you. That's not on,' and she looked at him with a confused look. 'The Hearts player?' asked her dad, who didn't know a lot about football, but who had heard of my dad, just like most others of a certain vintage from Edinburgh.

'No, he plays for Rangers. He was playing today at Ibrox. We're not long back.'

Sue's dad looked at her, and said, sheepishly, 'Oh, I thought you meant his dad!'

We had a good laugh about it, and she told me it was now safe for me to come to her house!

Sue's parents were lovely people and we got on great. Her dad was a carpenter at the Chancellor flour mill at Leith Docks. Her mum had a fashion shop in Leith Walk, hence Sue's love of clothes.

After going out for a couple of years, we decided to get engaged. Well, that's not strictly accurate, but I thought the time was right and decided I would pop the question. Mind you, my timing probably wasn't the best. There was a night organised for the Rangers players and we had arranged to meet in Sammy Dow's pub, just next to Queen Street station. Sue and I had travelled through on the train and as we walked to the pub, in the middle of the street, down I got on one knee (it was before my cartilage operation!). The look on her face was priceless. It was right next to a busy taxi rank and the place was heaving, but I'm a spontaneous guy and, well, when I get the urge ...

Anyway, thankfully Sue said yes and there was mild applause and cheers from those close by. For someone who isn't the most comfortable in crowds I can sure pick the moments. We walked into the pub and told the rest of the guys and wives that we had just got engaged. There followed what I can only describe as a typical 1970s moment. The guys said, 'Right, let's get the beers in,' while all the wives and girlfriends oohed and ahhed as they checked out Sue's engagement ring. Sue was delighted, I was delighted and we were very happy together.

Sue did a bit of modelling and, again, was an absolute natural. She was also quite a confident girl, never cocky, but she was happy to try most things. And then I was asked by a clothing store to model some gents' attire and I thought, 'How hard can this be?' Well, let me tell you, I would rather have been in direct opposition to Greigy for 90 minutes (and extra time) than stand in front of the cameras. You might think, 'As a footballer, he must've been used to cameras flashing in his face.' And, you'd be right, as I probably had my pic taken a million times during my career, but I was only asked a few times. The rest were during games, and I knew little about it. I had an agent back then called Ian Peebles, who worked at *Rangers News*. Without going into too many details, let's just say it wasn't the most successful business venture of my life.

The night before one of my photoshoots, Sue would be trying to teach me how to pose naturally, but we would invariably end up in a heap laughing our heads off. I certainly didn't enjoy the modelling and didn't like the direct attention.

My 21st birthday party was different. It really was a fantastic night. It was in an Edinburgh hotel just after a game at Tynecastle (which we won 1-0 thanks to a Greigy goal) and I was delighted that most of my team-mates could make it. When Sue and I walked into the venue my eyes lit up. Before me sat this unbelievable birthday cake – an exact replica of Ibrox Park. Mum and Dad had commissioned it and I'd never seen anything so utterly amazing. As the evening wore on I just recall all these folk coming up and asking if they could have their photographs taken, but not with me – standing next to the cake! It was a genuine show-stealer, and when it came to cutting it up for everyone, and actually eating it, I did so with a heavy heart.

Midway through the evening the disc jockey invited me to join my team-mates at the front of the stage, where they all started singing 'Happy Birthday'. It was like a cat's choir and most of the other guests either fell about laughing or covered their ears! They then handed me my birthday present and I was thrilled to rip it open and discover a cassette recorder. Believe me, it was a real trendy present at the time and I made good use of it.

The next major event in my life was my wedding day, and I vowed to get through it without pulling a hamstring or tweaking a groin. I crossed my fingers (but not too tightly) and the gods of injury smiled upon me. Although the day wasn't without its issues. First of all, though, it was a beautiful service and the sun was shining as we moved outside for some pics at the front of the church. We then headed to the reception, where the venue had been suitably dressed for the occasion. Sue looked radiant and we were shown to the top table. The hall was a hive of activity as everyone looked for their place name setting. After five or ten minutes it all settled down and we were ready to deliver the speeches. Sue's dad spoke well, and then it was my turn. Cringe. But I got up and did my best and thanked everyone for being there – on behalf of my wife and I, which always gets a laugh. The master of ceremonies then introduced the best man, who was a guy called George Mulholland. I had known George, who was Canadian, for five or six years, and we had met through Willie Henderson. It was only then I noticed that George was missing from the top table. Everyone was looking around the room and I was told that George had taken unwell and was en route to hospital. I couldn't believe it, but thankfully he made a quick recovery and we had a laugh about it afterwards. Enter the skipper. John Greig saved the day by getting up and making a speech off the top of his head, which went down very well indeed, although I think I would much rather have had George doing it as Greigy knew far too much about me!

The years went by and I played for a few different clubs, and we had a few different houses. We had to move with the contracts, but we were a happy family. At first, when it was just Sue and I, it was a bit easier, but then when the kids started to grow up, we would have to think of nurseries and schools, and in the latter stages of my career the priorities had changed and the kids' schooling came first. There were three years between the kids, which seemed like the perfect gap. It also meant that choosing holiday destinations wasn't too much of a problem and we had some lovely family breaks together during the close seasons.

And before you know it, the kids have left school and gone into further education. You watch them grow and you're very proud, but it seems to happen so fast, like a runaway juggernaut that you can't stop. And then one day you're sitting at home and they've left. Moved on to do their own thing and write the next chapter in their lives. Samantha became a nursery nurse, and Steven joined the police, where he is now an inspector. I've loved my kids since the day and hour I set eyes on them, and nothing has ever changed. Well, the only thing that's changed is I now have three beautiful grandchildren. Samantha married John; Steven married Lorna, and we have Emily, Laughlan and Iona. I'm the luckiest grandad alive. Just seeing their wee faces is magical.

I don't want to take anything away from the joy that I get from my grandchildren, but the only thing I wish was different was that Sue was around to enjoy them as much as I do. That breaks my heart, and I don't think that feeling will ever subside.

Sue became really unwell about seven years ago. She was eventually confined to her bed and her speech was limited. Naturally we were all very concerned. But no matter how many hospital appointments or opinions and second opinions we had, there was never a diagnosis. We saw every specialist going in the hope that someone could explain what the hell was going on. Nothing worked. Every blood test came back clear and the medics seemed as baffled as us. Meanwhile, though, Sue's condition was worsening and watching her lie there helpless in bed was the hardest thing imaginable. We were at our wits' end, and this continued for around four years.

One night, I went through to the bedroom to see Sue; just to tell her about my day. She had been really struggling and I was sitting on the edge of the bed, talking away, about nothing of real importance. Swallowing had been an issue for a while, but within a few moments this thick phlegm started coming up, and it wouldn't stop. I was both concerned and frightened but called an ambulance straight away. As soon as we got Sue to hospital, staff ran lots of tests and the nurses were in and out all night. Next morning, a senior doctor came in to see us. We were desperate for answers, but he had that resigned look on his face: something that told us this isn't good. He sat down and the moment he mentioned that Sue had motor neurone disease my heart sank. That was such a hammer blow. We had obviously known that all was far from well, but when he said those words my world collapsed. He continued speaking and I tried my best to take in what he was saying. He told us Sue was dying and asked if she would consider going into a hospice. Our kids were involved every step of the way, and Sue told us that she didn't want to go into a hospice; she wanted to come home. So that's exactly what she did.

We nursed Sue at home for five weeks, and she passed away. It's so hard to put into words how I felt. Of course, it was the worst time of my life but even that seems inadequate. We had been through so much together. We were a brilliant team, the best there was, and now I was on my own. I felt so alone. I still had my kids, but they have their own lives to live, and while I see an awful lot of them, that glamorous girl from Granton – who I'd bonded with instantly the first time we met – was gone. They say time is a great healer, but it feels as raw today as it did when Sue passed in November 2021. I believe there are some things you just don't get over, and that's OK, because it tells me that whatever we had was so worthwhile and definitely the real deal.